Flexibility and Stability in Working Life

Flexibility and Stability in Working Life

Edited by

Bengt Furåker

Kristina Håkansson

and

Jan Ch. Karlsson

First published 2007 by
PALGRAVE MACMILLAN
Houndmills, Basingstoke, Hampshire RG21 6XS and
175 Fifth Avenue, New York, N.Y. 10010
Companies and representatives throughout the world

PALGRAVE MACMILLAN is the global academic imprint of the Palgrave
Macmillan division of St. Martin's Press, LLC and of Palgrave Macmillan Ltd.
Macmillan® is a registered trademark in the United States, United Kingdom
and other countries. Palgrave is a registered trademark in the European
Union and other countries.

ISBN-13: 978–0–230–01364–3 hardback
ISBN-10: 0–230–01364–3 hardback

This book is printed on paper suitable for recycling and made from fully
managed and sustained forest sources. Logging, pulping and manufacturing
processes are expected to conform to the environmental regulations of the
country of origin.

A catalogue record for this book is available from the British Library.

Library of Congress Cataloging-in-Publication Data
Flexibility and stability in working life/edited by Bengt Furåker, Kristina
    Håkansson, and Jan Ch. Karlsson.
        p. cm.
    Papers discussed and revised at several workshops and seminars, the most
    important being the conference 'Labour market flexibility and stability,' held
    in Göteborg in November 2005, and sponsored by the Swedish Council for
    Working Life and Social Research and the Faculty of Social Sciences at
    Göteborg University.
    Includes bibliographical references and index.
    ISBN 0–230–01364–3 (cloth)
    1. Labour market—Great Britain—Congresses.   2. Industrial relations—
    Great Britain—Congresses.   3. Labour market—Sweden—Congresses.
    4. Industrial relations—Sweden—Congresses.   I. Furåker, Bengt, 1943–
    II. Håkansson, Kristina, 1959–   III. Karlsson, Jan, 1948–
    HD5765.A6F59 2007
    331.10941—dc22   2006046894

10   9   8   7   6   5   4   3   2   1
16   15   14   13   12   11   10   09   08   07

Printed and bound in Great Britain by
Antony Rowe Ltd, Chippenham and Eastbourne

Contents

List of Figures

List of Tables

Preface and Acknowledgments

This book has been written by a number of researchers who all have a long-standing interest in flexibility issues, but who are also dissatisfied with the current discussion and the ways in which concepts, as well as empirical facts, are being dealt with. In an attempt to improve the prevailing state of affairs, the authors of the present volume introduce both new theoretical perspectives and new empirical studies. They base their contributions on separate research projects, but, to varying extents, the chapters have been discussed and overhauled in common workshops and seminars. The most important of these was the conference 'Labour Market Flexibility and Stability' that took place in Göteborg in November 2005. It was made possible through funding from the Swedish Council for Working Life and Social Research and from the Faculty of Social Sciences at Göteborg University. We want to express our thanks for this support.

Bengt Furåker, Kristina Håkansson and Jan Ch. Karlsson

Notes on the Contributors

Stephen Ackroyd is Professor of Organisational Analysis at Lancaster University Management School. His current research concerns the activities of the largest British companies. Recent books include *Realist Perspectives on Management and Organisation* (2000, with Steve Fleetwood), *The Organisation of Business* (2002), and *The New Managerialism and the Public Service Professions* (2004, with Ian Kirkpatrick). Ackroyd has also co-edited and co-authored *The Oxford Handbook of Work and Organisations* (2005).

Tomas Berglund received his PhD in sociology in 2001 and is now Assistant Professor at the Department of Sociology, Göteborg University. His thesis was about work attitudes in various Western countries. In recent years, besides teaching he has been involved in several research projects on labour market and working-life issues. Berglund is currently taking part in a project on job mobility and lock-in mechanisms in the labour market.

Åsa-Karin Engstrand is Post-doctoral Fellow at the National Institute for Working Life, Norrköping, Sweden. Her thesis – 'The Road Once Taken. Transformation of Labour Markets, Politics, and Place Promotion in Two Swedish Cities, Karlskrona and Uddevalla 1930–2000' (2003) – deals with local labour market restructuring. Engstrand is presently studying changes in work organization in the Swedish retail industry.

Bengt Furåker is Professor of Sociology at Göteborg University. He has previously held positions at two other universities in Sweden (Lund and Umeå) and he has been Visiting Fellow at Yale University in the United States. His research has for a long time been focused on labour market and working-life issues and the relationship between the labour market and the welfare state. Among Furåker's recent publications are *Post-industrial Labour Markets. Profiles of North America and Scandinavia* (2003, ed. with Thomas P. Boje) and *Sociological Perspectives on Labor Markets* (2005).

Kristina Håkansson is Assistant Professor at the Department of Sociology, Göteborg University. Her main research field is work organization and strategies for flexibility. In particular, she has examined the consequences of flexibility for individuals, work organizations and the labour market. Håkansson is currently involved in research on work environment issues and sustainable work organizations. Moreover, she is Director for the HR programme at the sociology department.

Tommy Isidorsson is Researcher at the Department for Work Science, Göteborg University. His thesis examined the development of working time in Sweden in a broad historical perspective. In addition to research on working time, he has carried out studies on flexibility issues, focusing on strategies for flexibility and their consequences on the individual, workplace and societal levels. Isidorsson is also Director for International Working Life Studies at Göteborg University.

Dan Jonsson is Professor of Sociology at Göteborg University. His research interests include general sociological theory, social psychology, theory and methods of social research, peace research, socio-technical systems analysis and sociology of work. He has published extensively on these topics, besides being a teacher and supervisor at the Department of Sociology. In recent years, Jonsson has been collaborating with researchers at Chalmers University of Technology on workplace design and analysis.

Jan Ch. Karlsson is Professor of Sociology at the Department of Working Life Science, Karlstad University, Sweden. His publications are concerned with the concept of work, modern work organization, class and gender in everyday life, and critical realism and methodology in the social sciences. He is co-author of *Explaining Society: An Introduction to Critical Realism in the Social Sciences* (2002), and *Gender Segregation. Divisions of Work in Post-Industrial Welfare States* (2005).

Anna Pollert is currently Professor of the Sociology of Work at the University of the West of England, Bristol and was previously at the Working Lives Research Institute, London Metropolitan University and the universities of Greenwich and Warwick. Her research deals with gender, class and work, the transformation of European command economies to capitalism and non-unionised, vulnerable workers. Among Pollert's books are *Girls, Wives, Factory Lives* (1981), *Farewell to Flexibility* (ed. 1991) and *Transformation at Work in the New Market Economies of Central Eastern Europe* (1999).

Donald Storrie is Research Manager at the European Foundation for the Improvement of Living and Working Conditions, Dublin. He has previously worked at the Swedish Institute for Social Research and the Ministry of Labour (both in Stockholm), Ostfold University (Norway), and most recently he led the Centre for Labour Market Studies, Göteborg University. His research has been focused on individual consequences of job loss, temporary employment, the evaluation of active labour market policy and geographical mobility.

1
Reclaiming the Concept of Flexibility

Bengt Furåker, Kristina Håkansson and Jan Ch. Karlsson

There is something rotten about the concept of 'flexibility'. It has for a long time been a key concept in the political working-life debate, as well as in research in this area. It has, for example, been stressed by the Organisation for Economic Cooperation and Development (OECD) as an essential part of a regenerated economic development, and it has underlain changes in EU labour law. And research on flexibility is immense. In March 2006, a search on Google Scholar gave 1,080,000 hits for 'flexibility' and 1,400,000 for 'flexible'. But all is not well. The literature is not only abundant – it is also incongruous and confusing. The many meanings of the term make flexibility an excellent basis for forming ideological and value-laden discourses on the new working life. It is not uncommon to play on these paradoxes by formulating oxymorons, such as the title of Dore's (1986) book *Flexible Rigidities*, or the chapter 'Inflexible Flexibility' (Elger and Fairbrother 1992).

In the technical and engineering sciences 'flexibility' has many meanings, as is evidenced in a survey of the literature on manufacturing alone: Sethi and Sethi (1990) found at least 50 terms for different types of flexibility; there were also several terms for the same type. In the social sciences the term has a wide field of application, ranging from an interpretation of a new phase in the development of capitalist societies (Aglietta 1979), through a possible choice of a new system for production and markets (Piore and Sabel 1984), to flexibility in the labour market, flexible firms and flexible employees (Atkinson and Meager 1986). Generally, the word 'flexibility' refers to an ability to react to changes. There are, however, a plethora of meanings, and many researchers have complained about the quantity of denotations – often overlapping and sometimes contradictory (for examples, see Hyman 1991: 280–1). Table 1.1 provides a few examples of typologies of flexibility.

Table 1.1   Types of flexibility

Atkinson and Meager	Functional flexibility Numerical flexibility Financial or pay flexibility Distancing
Boyer	Adaptability of productive organization Propensity of workers to accept a variety of tasks Weak legal constraints on the employment contract Sensitivity of wages to the situation of the firm or the market Elimination of state regulations that restrict freedom of management
Furåker	Employment flexibility Work process flexibility Working time flexibility Workplace or spatial flexibility Wage flexibility
Sayer and Walker	Flexibility in output volume Product flexibility Flexible employment Flexible working practices Flexible machinery Flexibility in restructuring Flexibility in organizational forms
Standing	Organizational flexibility Numerical flexibility Functional flexibility Job structure flexibility Working time flexibility Wage system flexibility Labour force flexibility

Sources: Atkinson and Meager 1986: 3–4; Boyer 1987; Furåker 2005b: 189–202; Sayer and Walker 1992: 199; Standing 2002: 33.

Some of these typologies are in turn built on other typologies and their aims differ. Boyer wants to indicate some broad themes in the flexibility debate; Sayer and Walker aim at showing the variety of meanings of the term, that they are not entirely distinct and that they are often confused; Standing wants to find a context for mechanisms behind social protection and economic security; Furåker's ambition is similar to that of Boyer, that is, to outline some of the most important dimensions along which flexibility issues are debated. Some types of flexibility overlap between them, some are unique and there are also overlaps within most typologies. Some typologies are still at the stage of compilation without any real inner theoretical structure, while others have a stronger theoretical base. Mainly, however, Table 1.1 illustrates the manifold meanings of flexibility.

Further, flexibility is in itself a positively charged term that can be found in many combinations: market flexibility, flexible technology, organizational flexibility, wage flexibility, functional flexibility, time flexibility, and so on. Every combination has positive connotations. Who can be against flexibility? Who can exclaim 'long live rigidity!'? Rigidity, or even stability, is often regarded as the opposite of flexibility – and as such, they constitute something negative.

But we cannot be certain that one type of flexibility entails another type or that flexibility is good for everyone. Some researchers therefore regard the term as ideological; Sayer and Walker (1992:198) write, for example, about its 'double-edged, value-laden character and its tendentious usage in management and political circles: flexibility sounds agreeable in the abstract, but not always when considered in the concrete'. And Standing (1999: 81) remarks: 'When someone calls on workers or on employers to be flexible, it usually means he wants them to make concessions.' In this situation there seem to be two alternatives for serious social science research. One is to give up on the concept of flexibility and leave it to managerial myths, rhetoric and ideologies. The other is to reclaim it for social scientific analysis by conceptual suggestions and empirical analyses. We opt for the second alternative. There is, as we will show in this book, overwhelming empirical knowledge that flexibility has negative traits and that it is reasonable to ask 'flexibility for whom?' But how is it possible, in spite of this knowledge, to continue to use the term in tendentious, ideological and value-laden ways? We can think of at least three reasons. The first one we would like to call the *fun factor* or the *public attention* aspect. It simply means that it is more fun and draws more attention to preach that everything is new and good than – as we do – point a serious finger at the data, shake our heads and say: 'It is a false statement, look at the data.' It is not so much fun – and we will never be gurus.

The second reason is the old *self-fulfilling prophecy*. Anna Pollert (1988: 301) claims that Atkinson's model of the flexible firm could function as a self-fulfilling prophecy, so let us follow this idea for flexibility as such. When Robert Merton (1964: Ch. XI) coined the expression 'self-fulfilling prophecy', he took his point of departure in the so-called Thomas theorem: if people define a situation as real, it becomes real in its consequences. The thought is that if a prophecy becomes an integrated part of a particular social context, it will influence the development of this context. Translated to our framework this would mean that the flexibility rhetoric is presented in order to influence the development of working life towards what can be regarded as a more flexible situation from the perspective of employers. It does not matter that it may be false, as it has the potential to eventually become true. Perhaps this sounds a bit conspiratorial, but for those who think so, Merton (1964: 427) suggests a solution: 'Self-hypnosis through one's own propaganda is a not infrequent phase of the self-fulfilling prophecy.'

The third reason is a logical error, but it has also been called a *dualistic rhetoric* (Sayer and Walker 1992: 193). In analyses of changes in working life there are a number of conceptual pairs that are often used: a development from mass production to flexible specialization, from Taylorism to Post-Taylorism, from 'just-in-case' to 'just-in-time', and so on. A collection of some common terms can be found in Table 1.2. Each of these conceptual pairs is probably fruitful for an analysis of its specific transformation. The problem is that the theoretical point of departure for research – not to mention myths and rhetoric – is not only the horizontal dimension of the table; often the terms and concepts become associated also in the vertical dimension. And thereby a picture of two homogeneous systems is implied – the rubric 'the old (working life)' is placed on top of the left-hand side of the table and 'the new (working life)' above the right-hand side. Thereby a much simplified picture of a

Table 1.2 Common conceptual pairs in research on the 'new working life'

'The Old'		'The New'
Fordism	–	Post-Fordism
Taylorism	–	Post-Taylorism
Mass production	–	Flexible specialization
Large batch production	–	Small batch production
Standardized products	–	Differentiated products
Mass markets	–	Niche markets
Rigidity	–	Flexibility
Large stocks	–	Minimal stocks
Just-in-case production	–	Just-in-time production
Specialized machinery	–	Flexible machinery
Conflicts labour–capital	–	Harmony labour–capital
Alienated workers	–	Engaged co-workers
Deskilling	–	Enskilling

Source: modified from Sayer and Walker 1992: 193.

transformation from an old rigid Taylorist and Fordist mass production of standardized products for stocks and a mass market, performed by alienated workers in an antagonistic social relationship (and so on) to a Post-Taylorist and Post-Fordist flexibly specialized production for niche markets, performed by engaged co-workers in a harmonious social relationship (and so on). We have been in – or perhaps are in the middle of – a process of total change from the old to the new, a change that is good for all concerned and in which the new is in every way the opposite of the old.

Flexibility has become a key concept in discourses on developments in working life. But it is an ambiguous concept in several ways, and theoretical clarity is lacking. Further, large parts of the literature are prescriptive and ideological rather than empirical and analytical. With this book we want to contribute both theoretically and empirically to expounding the importance of clearer concepts in the international debate on changes in economic systems, labour markets and work organizations, and experiences of work. We place 'flexibility' in a new theoretical context as juxtaposed to stability. By relating these concepts to each other it is possible to open up a perspective in which flexibility as well as stability is wanted by someone. Moreover, flexibility for one part may mean instability for another part, while stability for one part may mean inflexibility for another part. Much terminological confusion and ambiguity is cleared up by this suggestion.

Stability is accordingly a conceptual companion of flexibility and we believe that its role has been largely underestimated in the literature on working life developments. Actually, both employers and employees strive for both flexibility and stability, although sometimes with different meanings and consequences for the other side. For example, employers may want to have a flexible workforce in the sense that it can quickly be increased or decreased depending on seasonal variations or business cycle variations. At the same time, however, they also need some stability. It is important for them that there is a core of workers available so that everyday business can be taken care of adequately. The efforts to satisfy these two wishes may have very different consequences for various categories of workers. For employees, there is an obvious parallel. They are certainly interested in having a stable job and a stable income, but they do not want to be tied to their jobs for ever. Employers can be considerably affected if large numbers of employees start to look for another job instead of concentrating on staying with their employer.

Social scientists should be conscious of the level of analysis in their work and those who carry out research on flexibility and stability issues are no exception to this rule. The focus of an analysis of such issues can be individual employees, organizational units (work teams, workplaces, firms), or the labour market as a whole. Although – in a given study – it may be necessary to concentrate on only one of these levels, it is important for researchers to be aware of their interconnections. The individual chapters in this book represent a great variety as regards the character of their units of analysis and they partly extend over more than one level. By this mixture of contributions we hope to offer a deeper analysis of flexibility and stability and their related concepts than would be possible without it. Our next step is to say a little more about the major empirical basis for the chapters to follow: British and Swedish working life.

Empirical studies in Sweden and the United Kingdom

The new theoretical ideas in this anthology are, more or less, put to work in empirical studies. These analyses are in themselves a corrective of the ideological sides of the flexibility debate and they also provide more concrete illustrations of the theoretical arguments. We have chosen to make use of data mainly from Sweden and the United Kingdom. According to existing reports these two countries are roughly opposites when it comes to flexibility and stability in working life. They are regarded as different types of welfare states, of market economies and of institutional arrangements in the labour market. The empirical chapters are in their own right of great interest for the debate, but put in the new theoretical frame they attain an extra sharpness.

Sweden and the UK are both capitalist market economies but differ substantially as regards the institutional settings in which capitalism operates. We find significant dissimilarities between the two countries in the extent to which markets are allowed to function without the interference of the state or of unions. The degree of social protection that workers and citizens enjoy is a crucial aspect, due to its role in working life flexibility. Strong social protection provided by the government or by unions is often taken to be an obstacle to desired workforce adjustments. Sweden and the UK show considerable disparity in this respect; it is thus not surprising that they are usually located in separate categories, when social scientists classify Western nations in terms of their socio-economic system or welfare state regimes. A few examples from the literature can illustrate this.

The UK is commonly treated as a liberal economy, with a rather 'free', unregulated and competitive market and a relatively modest welfare state (see, for example, Hall and Soskice 2001: 17–21; Castles 2004; Korpi and Palme 1998). It is included in the English-speaking family of nations, which have many obvious commonalities concerning, among other things, economic policy and social protection (Castles 1993, 1998). The British system is also usually characterized by a relatively low degree of corporatism – that is, interest organizations, such as trade unions and employers' associations, participate only to a limited extent in societal policy-making (see the overview in Smith 1992: 165–75). Unquestionably, the labour movement has had a substantial impact on British society, but its achievements have been much more modest than those of the labour movement in Sweden. Margaret Thatcher's electoral victory in 1979 and the following long period of Tory rule made the UK a showground for neo-liberal policies and transformation. Also, since Labour's return to power in 1997 the country has remained – compared to other economically advanced Western nations – among the closest to the neo-classical ideal of the 'free' market but has to some extent moved beyond Thatcherism (cf., for example, Driver and Martell 1998, 2002; Heffernan 2001).

Sweden is generally described very differently, as a 'coordinated market economy' with a generous and universalistic welfare state (see, for example, Hall and Soskice 2001: 17–21; Esping-Andersen 1990; Castles 2004). It belongs to the Scandinavian family of nations (Castles 1993, 1998), and it is sometimes even considered the Social Democratic or 'institutionalist' model society (see, for example, van den Berg, Furåker and Johansson 1997: Ch. 4). This does not entail that policies associated with neo-classical economic theory have no significant role, but only that market forces are more regulated than in liberal economies. Moreover, Sweden is usually classified as highly corporatist and thus as more corporatist than the UK (Smith 1992: 165–75), which implies that the influence of organized interests on policy-making is clearly stronger. On this point, however, major changes have taken place since the early 1990s when the employers' association decided to withdraw from such collaboration (see, for example, Kjellberg 1998: 93–4). The development of the Swedish model is commonly attributed to a great extent to strong working class organizations, that is, the trade unions and the Social Democratic Party (Korpi 1983; Cameron 1984; Esping-Andersen 1985, 1990). In contrast to this, it has been pointed out that Swedish governments have been successful in integrating capitalist interests (Swenson 2002).

Social institutions such as the family are important in comparisons of societal models. This aspect is often neglected but taken into account in Duncan Gallie and Serge Paugam's (2000) discussion of how people in different countries are supported in case of unemployment. Countries are then classified according to both unemployment welfare regime and model of family residence. In the first dimension, a distinction is made between sub-protective, liberal/minimal, employment centred and universalistic regimes. The UK is included in the liberal/minimal category and Sweden in the universalistic type, but with respect to model of family residence, both cases are labelled the same (Gallie and Paugam 2000: 17). As to the latter dimension, the two countries come under the heading of 'advanced intergenerational autonomy' in contrast to 'relative intergenerational autonomy' and 'extended dependence'. In other words, Sweden and the UK are not that different on this dimension.

There is no doubt that Sweden and the UK are treated as rather different institutional models in the social science literature. As a background for many of the chapters in this book, we want to provide some empirical information regarding their differences. It will be no more than a few brief examples, concentrating on specific aspects of social protection in working life. The guiding principle is that certain protective arrangements are generally considered very important in relation to flexibility. However, there is no consensus in this respect; some analysts emphasize the possible negative effects of such arrangements on flexibility, whereas others stress their potential positive effects (see, for example, van den Berg, Furåker and Johansson 1987: Ch. 4). Some argue that with strong social protection people can too easily avoid making the needed adjustments to working life changes. Others claim that without some reasonable safety net people do not dare to try anything new but cling to what they already have. In light of this discussion we want to give a summary description of selected characteristics of social protection in Sweden and the UK. Both state intervention and the role of unions are dealt with.

To begin with state intervention, we find it useful to make use of a distinction between three types, suggested by Bengt Furåker and Rafael Lindqvist (2003). The three types are described as legislation, transfers and services. It should be emphasized that given state measures do not necessarily coincide with only one of the categories but can include elements from two or all three of them. For example, labour market training programmes involve not only services to participants but also legislation and transfer of payments (sometimes the same amount as the unemployed receive). The first type of state intervention is legislation. It entails many different kinds, for example dealing with employment protection, work safety and working time. The statutory rules in these respects are indeed important for the relationship between employers and employees. As employment protection legislation is particularly interesting for the themes under scrutiny, we limit ourselves to this dimension. It involves rules for those already employed, as well as rules for the application of temporary employment contracts. The most recent study done by the OECD (2004b: Ch. 2) compares various countries in terms of strictness of employment protection legislation. Two indices are used, both based on the legislation with regard to three dimensions: regular employment temporary employment and collective dismissals. Actually, they are strongly correlated with one another so it does not matter that much which one we choose.

In Table 1.3 we concentrate on Index II and present scores for the late 1990s and 2003. High scores mean restrictive legislation and low scores stand for a liberal scheme. Countries are ranked according to the degree of strictness, with the strictest at the top and the most liberal at the bottom of the table. The highest scores are found for a number of Mediterranean countries and Mexico, whereas the Anglo-Saxon countries – including the UK – are located at the bottom of the table. Sweden has relatively high figures but is still clearly below the top.

Looking at changes over time, we can see whether countries have become more liberal or stricter. If we want to study what has happened in a somewhat longer time span (since the late 1980s), we can use Index I of employment protection legislation (not shown here). It would then turn out that a majority of countries have become more liberal, although some have not changed at all and others have gone in the opposite direction. In the UK, employment protection legislation became slightly stricter between the late 1980s and 2003, whereas Sweden belongs to those countries that unmistakably liberalized their rules during the same period. Comparing the late 1990s and 2003 (Table 1.3), we find that 9 countries had lower scores in 2003, 8 had higher scores (one of them is the UK), and 11 got the same total (one of them is Sweden). Thus, since the late 1980s the gap between the two cases that our interest is focused on has diminished (and this mainly occurred before the late 1990s), but it nevertheless remains substantial.

It needs to be noted that temporary jobs are to some extent functional alternatives to liberal legislation. Given that the possibility of

Table 1.3 Employment protection legislation scores (Index II) in late 1990s and 2003. Rank according to 2003 scores

	Late 1990s	2003
Portugal	3.7	3.5
Turkey	3.4	3.5
Mexico	3.2	3.2
Spain	3.0	3.1
France	2.8	2.9
Greece	3.5	2.9
Norway	2.7	2.6
Sweden	2.6	2.6
Belgium	2.5	2.5
Germany	2.6	2.5
Italy	3.1	2.4
Netherlands	2.3	2.3
Austria	2.4	2.2
Finland	2.2	2.1
Poland	1.9	2.1
Korea	2.0	2.0
Slovak Republic	2.5	2.0
Czech Republic	1.9	1.9
Denmark	1.8	1.8
Japan	1.9	1.8
Hungary	1.5	1.7
Switzerland	1.6	1.6
Australia	1.5	1.5
Ireland	1.2	1.3
New Zealand	0.8	1.3
Canada	1.1	1.1
UK	1.0	1.1
US	.7	.7

Source: OECD 2004b: 117.

establishing temporary employment contracts is not too limited, we can expect it to be used more often in countries where employment protection legislation is generally strict. There is empirical support for this assumption (OECD 2004b: 87; see also Hudson 2002a: 40–2) and the British and Swedish pattern is no exception. At the beginning of the new millennium, the proportion of employees on temporary contracts in Sweden has hovered around 15–16 per cent, whereas the corresponding figure in the UK is 5–6 per cent (McOrmond 2004: 30; European Foundation 2005: 68).

The second type of government social protection is transfers, made possible through redistribution via taxation and income support to various categories (old age cash benefits, early retirement benefits, unemployment benefits, sickness benefits, and so on). Generally, the Swedish welfare state plays a clearly greater role than the British in terms of such transfers. In 1998, social expenditures in Sweden made up 31 per cent of GDP compared to 21.4 per cent in the UK (Castles 2004: 25). We can add that in 1980 the Swedish figure was 29 per cent and the British figure was 18.2 per cent, that is, some increase had occurred in both cases in the period 1980–98.

One principal subtype of social transfers is unemployment insurance. The benefit system is generally more generous in Sweden than in the UK (OECD 2004a: Table 1.2). In the fiscal year 2003/04 the UK spent 0.37 per cent of GDP on unemployment compensation, whereas the corresponding figure for Sweden (in 2003) was 1.22 per cent (OECD 2005: 237, 272–4). This means that for each percentage point of unemployment, 0.22 per cent of GDP was spent on compensation to the unemployed in Sweden, compared to 0.08 per cent in the UK.

Services make up the third category of state protection. Far from all government services can be said to provide social protection for individuals in the labour market, but some of them definitely do so. Among the most important measures in this category we find active labour market policy. It includes measures such as employment services, personal counselling for job seekers, labour market training and direct job creation. Also with respect to active labour market policy, the two countries differ from one another and this unlikeness is reflected in expenditure figures. The UK spent 0.53 per cent of GDP on such programmes during the fiscal year 2003/04 and Sweden spent 1.29 per cent in 2003. Recalculated as proportions per percentage points of unemployment, the British figure is .11 and the Swedish is .23 (OECD 2005: 237, 272–4).

Unions represent another type of social protection in working life. They are basically organizations to defend and promote employee interests. As regards the strength and power of these organizations we again find obvious dissimilarities between Sweden and the UK, with Sweden ahead in terms of unionization rate, collective agreement coverage and general impact of trade unionism in society (see, for example, Bamber, Lansbury and Wailes 2004; Visser 2004). After the British 'winter of discontent' 1978–9 and the subsequent long Conservative reign, the trade unions were pushed back significantly, but they have had no great comeback since Labour's return to power in 1997 (for example, Blyton and Turnbull 2004: Ch.5; McIlroy 1995, 1998). Also the Swedish trade unions appear to have lost some of their influence over recent decades, but this setback has been less far-reaching (cf. Kjellberg 2002).

Despite some decline after the mid-1990s, the union density rate in Sweden still remained the highest among Western countries in 2002, with 78 per cent of all employees being unionized (Visser 2004: 19). In 1990 it was 80 per cent and five years later it was 83.1 per cent. One crucial reason behind the high figures in Sweden is that unemployment insurance is union-based. This is not the case in the UK and the proportion of organized workers is also much lower. For quite some time, union density has been decreasing in Britain and more so than in Sweden. In 1990 approximately 4 out of 10 British employees were union members and by 2002 this proportion had fallen to about 3 out of 10 (Visser 2004: 17, 19). The two countries also diverge from one another in respect of coverage of collective agreements. In Sweden collective agreements covered more than 90 per cent of all employees in 2001 and this figure exceeds that of 1990 (Visser 2004: 30–1). For the UK, we find the opposite trend during the 1990s. The bargaining coverage rate went down considerably and was just a little more than one third in 2001.

Moreover, there are important dissimilarities between the two countries with respect to how much influence trade unions have at the workplace (Visser 2004: 20–4). In Sweden unions have the legal right to information, consultation and negotiations, whereas this is not the case in the UK, although there may be sector/company agreements. This 'representation' and 'participation gap' at the workplace level in the UK can be expected to lead to an absence of discussions and negotiations concerning flexibility issues (cf. McIlroy, Marginson and Regalia 2004).

The differences between British and Swedish trade unions are not only a matter of bargaining power and bargaining coverage, but also of their focus on issues of work organization. At both the local and national levels, the Swedish LO (Trade Union Confederation) has been engaged in several 'change' programmes aimed at organizational development. Active participation by both employees' and employers' organizations in these programmes, together with public funding, distinguishes Sweden from most other countries (Gustavsen 1996). This interest in work organization issues goes back to the idea of socio-technical systems with autonomous (self-governing) workgroups, an idea that has had much stronger impact in Sweden than in the UK (Rubery and Grimshaw 2003).

To sum up, both Sweden and the UK belong to the developed capitalist world, but they are usually treated as rather different concerning ways in which market mechanisms are allowed to operate. They differ along several dimensions that must be considered important in relation to flexibility issues. In broad comparison with the British case, the Swedish economy is more regulated and the Swedish welfare state is more generous, which can be illustrated by, for example, employment protection legislation, unemployment insurance and active labour market policy. Moreover, there are significant differences in terms of unionization levels and general trade union impact. In Sweden, employees are unionized to a much greater extent and their unions have a stronger influence at the workplace and in society as a whole. Regarding all these institutional arrangements, the employees' position is generally more advantageous in Sweden than in the UK. At the same time, we should keep in mind that the two countries are not all that contrasting in every respect. For example, as mentioned above, Gallie and Paugam (2000) classify them as belonging to the same model of family residence. Nevertheless, Sweden and the UK are different enough along relevant dimensions so as to make them useful as illustrative cases in our empirical analyses. Let us now turn to a brief presentation of each of the chapters to follow.

The contributions to this book

In Chapter 2, Jan Ch. Karlsson reviews the rather comprehensive literature on flexibility and in doing this he is guided by the following question: For whom is flexibility said to be good and bad – employers and/or workers? There are four possible answers: (i) It is good for employers as well as for workers, it is thus simply good; (ii) it is good for employers, but bad for workers; (iii) it is bad for both parties, that is, simply bad; and (iv) it is bad for employers, but good for workers. The chapter is organized according to these answers and the main conclusion of the overview is that 'flexibility' is a double-edged concept and that there is a strong need for terminological development.

Chapter 3 is written by Dan Jonsson who argues that some of the confusion and controversy in the flexibility debate stems from the fact that different authors mean different things by flexibility. In many cases, this concept is treated as an inherent property rather than one which is relative to a particular point of view, disregarding the fact that we always deal with 'flexibility for somebody'. Jonsson suggests that flexibility should be defined as desirable variability. However, although flexibility is desirable for one part it may mean undesirable variability for another. As a consequence we need to employ another concept, namely that of instability. Moreover, invariability can also be desirable; thus, the concept of stability is introduced as juxtaposed to flexibility. And, to spell out the whole conceptual chain, stability for one part may mean inflexibility for another. This chapter contributes to a terminological clarification of flexibility and stability and provides a conceptual framework for the remaining chapters in the book.

Anna Pollert is the author of Chapter 4, called 'Britain's flexible workforce: new barriers to individual employment rights'. Although Britain's New Labour government has enacted a range of laws enhancing individual employment rights, this is in the context of an overarching neoliberal policy, which espouses the virtues of a 'flexible' labour market. Statutory regulation, already weaker than in other European countries, is becoming neither more accessible nor easier to enforce. In a situation where the majority of workers lack collective representation, individual advice and support services are expensive or depend on an underfunded voluntary sector. There is no free legal aid for Employment Tribunal representation; yet employment law is becoming increasingly complex, and new legislation has added severe obstacles to enforcing statutory rights. Pollert discusses the recent changes, the underlying political processes and the possibilities for change.

The subsequent contribution (Chapter 5) is provided by Åsa-Karin Engstrand. It is called 'Flexibility's new clothes. A historical perspective on the public discussion in Sweden'. Recently, the European Commission has emphasized the concept of 'flexicurity' as a way of combining competitiveness and a social model. Interestingly, the notions of flexibility and security echo the discussions that took place in Sweden during the 1950s, 1960s and 1970s. This chapter gives an account of how the flexibility concept has been transformed in Sweden over the years, from the economic restructuring perspective in the so-called Rehn-Meidner model during the 1950s and 1960s, to an individual employee focus in the 1970s, and to an employer perspective in the 1990s. According to the author, since, historically, different actors have appropriated the concept of flexibility for their own agendas, it ought to be possible for employees to reclaim it today.

Stephen Ackroyd in Chapter 6 – 'Large corporations and the emergence of a flexible economic system: some recent developments in the UK' – focuses on change toward a more flexible organization at the industry or economic system level. In the UK, major corporations, called capital extensive firms (CEFs), have been involved in developing new flexible patterns of operation and cooperation. Such organizations undertake diverse activities in many markets, and while they are effectively decentralizing for various operational activities, they are also highly centralized for key strategic decision-making. CEFs can be considered distinctive types of network in themselves, as they often constitute much of their own business environment. The flexibility generated in such arrangements is actually quite limited but is often exaggerated. It is accomplished by a new and powerful combination of market processes and retained elements of hierarchy.

Chapter 7 brings up one dimension of labour market flexibility that has become increasingly relevant, namely the use of temporary work agencies. Donald Storrie starts with an outline of the most recent developments in temporary agency work in Europe as regards both legal developments and employment levels. He continues with an economic analysis of the potential efficiency of agency work. The main focus of the chapter is an analysis of the pending EU Directive on Agency Work, which will require equal treatment of agency workers compared to in-house workers. The author identifies three main means of trying to realize the objectives of the directive, namely, by statutory regulation, the market and collective agreements. These three means broadly correspond to the current Continental, Anglo-Saxon and Scandinavian national modes of regulation of agency work. They are analysed with respect to obtaining the twin goals of economic efficiency and equal treatment.

Temporary work agencies are relatively more often used at British than Swedish workplaces. This is demonstrated in Chapter 8, co-authored by Kristina Håkansson and Tommy Isidorsson. It is a common argument that employers' striving for flexibility can explain why this usage has increased. With the help of survey data, the authors show that another explanation is likely to be more important. The survey focuses on user firms and their motives in relying on agency work. It turns out that the most common motive for using agency workers both in Sweden and in the UK is to cover for staff absence. Replacement of absent personnel reflects a need for stability and not for flexibility. Still, the need for numerical flexibility is the second most common motive in both countries. Even though this kind of flexibility is a more frequent motive in the private sector than in the public sector, the most often reported motive in both sectors is numerical stability.

The relationship between flexible work situations and employees' thoughts of leaving the organization is the topic of Chapter 9, written by Tomas Berglund. A distinction is made between core and peripheral workers. In the first case, employees are allowed a high level of discretion and a high degree of cooperation with workmates. In the second case, they work on temporary contracts or part-time. The assumption guiding the chapter is that the internal striving for flexibility in organizations affects employees' preferences for staying with or leaving the employer. In his analysis, Berglund uses data collected in 2003 from more than 3000 employees in Sweden. Among core workers, characterized by functional flexibility, withdrawal cognitions are less common due to high job satisfaction and high organizational commitment. Among peripheral workers, characterized by numerical flexibility, withdrawal cognitions are more frequent because of feelings of job insecurity and low commitment to the organisation.

Bengt Furåker investigates the role of temporary and open-ended employment contracts respectively for employees' attitudes toward certain forms of flexibility. In Chapter 10, it is asked whether type of employment contract has an impact on people's readiness to change place of residence in the event of unemployment and to accept a wage reduction if that is the only way to keep a job. Data from three different surveys among employees in Sweden are used. Only one survey provides empirical support for the hypothesis that temporary contracts make people more inclined, if unemployed, to move geographically. Other factors such as age and family situation are more robustly linked to such a preference. With respect to wage cuts to save one's job, those on permanent contracts more often tend to agree, although again only in one survey. It appears that people with permanent positions have more to lose by being laid off and are therefore more apt to accept other changes to defend their job. This indicates that there might be functional alternatives; when demands for adjustment are put forward, adjustment can take different forms.

In the last chapter of the book, Dan Jonsson makes use of the concepts developed in Chapter 3 to analyse the meaning of 'flexibilization'. Increasing demands on employees from their employers with regard to working time flexibility and other forms of flexibility are often justified by increasing demands for flexible supply of goods and services from customers. It can be argued, however, that employer-assessed employee flexibility can be a means of attaining other goals than customer-assessed vendor flexibility. In particular, employer-driven working time flexibility can be used to reduce slack and thereby increase labour productivity. To investigate the connection between flexibility, stability and labour productivity, data have been collected from a representative sample of

Swedish employees. Empirical findings reported in this chapter concern variability-related aspects, including variation in working times, working time flexibility for employees, time flexibility during work for employees and working time instability for employees and also productivity-related aspects such as work intensity and temporary slack.

2
For Whom Is Flexibility Good and Bad? An Overview

Jan Ch. Karlsson

When reviewing the flexibility literature, one observes that in much of the management literature three parties are said to benefit from flexibility: customers, employers and workers – flexibility is good for everyone. Another observation is that it is very hard to find any claims at all that flexibility is bad for employers, and even harder that it at the same time is beneficial to workers.

The question that has guided me through the flexibility literature is this: 'For whom is flexibility said to be good and bad – employers and/or workers?'. Thereby I limit the survey to employers and workers, leaving customers out of the picture. I do not propose objective definitions of 'good' and 'bad'; I only note what is regarded as good and bad for each party by different authors. There are four possible answers to the question: (i) flexibility is good for employers as well as for workers, it is simply good; (ii) it is good for employers, but bad for workers; (iii) it is bad for both parties, it is simply bad; and (iv) it is bad for employers, but good for workers. The chapter is organized according to these answers.

Flexibility is good

There are no difficulties finding literature in which flexibility is held to be good for employers as well as for workers – and there are mainly

Note: This chapter was written as part of the research project 'Flexible workplaces and conditions of work – replication of an empirical study', and I want to thank the Swedish Council for Working Life and Social Research for its support for the project.

two sources of inspiration for this view: Piore and Sabel's (1984) plea for flexible specialization, in which networks of firms use new technology to cater for rapidly changing market niches, which requires cooperation with, rather than control of workers, who operate in a social relation of trust and are constantly being enskilled. Examples are also abundant in the management literature, notably in Boston three-letter acronyms such as HRM (Human Relations Management), TQM (Total Quality Management) and BPR (Business Process Reengineering). They all promise flexible organizations that are more effective, easier to run and provide higher profits, at the same time as workers will be empowered by teamwork and multiskilling, having feelings of trust and work satisfaction.

Two features of Piore and Sabel's analysis are not often noted, but I see them as important here: the status of the concept of flexible specialization and the fate of some of their empirical examples. But before going into these questions, I will (briefly, as it is taken to be well-known) outline their basic argument; at the same time I am aware that such brevity cannot do justice to the complexity and sophistication of their analysis.

The first part of the title of the book is 'The second industrial divide'. An industrial divide is an historical moment when a – more or less conscious – choice of technological path is made. The first industrial divide occurred in the nineteenth century when mass production technology replaced craft technology. Stable mass markets were established through the activities of large corporations, and on this basis mass production technology with Fordism won the battle against the earlier craft production. The associated work organization developed an extreme division of labour, applying Taylorist principles of task fragmentation. Employment relations were characterized by low trust, material incentives to work and a low degree of worker autonomy.

This description goes for the United States; many other countries, especially in Europe, showed other patterns, in which the craft economy survived to a larger degree. In a study of France, Germany, Italy and Japan, Piore and Sabel (1984: Ch. 6) find that they all followed the trajectory of mass production and strove to stabilize mass markets, but that the state had a much more active role in these processes compared to the United States. At the same time, the four countries diverged in the organization of work (Piore and Sabel 1984: 164):

In Germany and Japan, the idea of the plant as community structured shop-floor relations even in the mass-production firms. In France, management imposed a bureaucratic organization on the shop floor, creating a system in many ways as rigid as the New Deal resolution of industrial relations. In Italy, no compromise held; the mutability of shop-floor control that is seen only in the early industrial history of more stable countries has there been a fact of daily experience.

Starting in the late 1960s however, the mass production economy entered a state of extended crises of saturated markets, lack of innovation power, high unemployment and economic decline. Piore and Sabel's ambition is to suggest a way out of this precarious situation for the United States. And that is where the subtitle of the book, 'Possibilities for prosperity', comes in. The crisis opens the possibility of a second industrial divide, in which flexible specialization – a revival of the old craft technology – can become an option again. In certain countries residual craft elements slowly began paving the way out of the crisis, while this option was very weak in others (Piore and Sabel 1984: 223):

> Where historical experience lit a way – as in Italy, Germany, and Japan – fumbling hunches were rewarded with success. This success, in turn, encouraged further exploration of the same route – now accelerated by an increasingly clear view of it. Conversely, where historical experience led to a dead end – as in the United States and France – attempts at reorganization stalled.

Markets in which flexible specialization systems operate are quickly changing niche markets. It should be noted, though, that these markets are no more 'natural' than mass markets; they are created by artisan production, which in its turn has to adapt to them. This market specialization requires flexible production, for example, through 'just-in-time' techniques. In consequence, worker responsibilities and skills must be upgraded and jobs redesigned, resulting in a high degree of autonomy. Employment and wage security for workers is necessary to build the trust without which these systems cannot function.

In flexible specialization there is a constant drive to innovation in cooperation with others, who are also competitors. Competition is encouraged, but also limited by a community; the community can be a firm such as IBM, but also a district or a region such as 'the Third Italy' and Baden-Württemberg in Germany, to mention a couple of the most common empirical examples.

Features of Piore and Sabel's analysis can be found in other works before them, but the basic distinctions have been extremely influential: mass markets and niche markets, mass production and flexible production, task fragmentation and job redesign, low trust and high trust relations – and several more. The distinctions, regarded as two eras in working life, have also been widely adopted. But they have also been subjected to massive criticism; a catalogue (from Thompson and McHugh 2002: 167–9, where more detailed references can be found) may look like this: mass production is still alive and well and even growing in some sectors at the expense of niche markets. Mass markets are far from saturated and companies often have trouble creating niche markets. The use of programmable technology does not seem to be as common as it should be according to Piore and Sabel, especially among small firms. Multi-skilling among workers, product range and system versatility in the Third Italy and Japan leans more heavily on Taylorist and Fordist than on flexible specialization conceptualizations. Empirically, large firms are more innovative than small ones; the profitability of the latter is to a larger degree than the former based on long hours and low wages. And so on.

Although the empirical evidence against the flexible specialization thesis seems quite strong, I want to point out an oversight that both followers and critics of Piore and Sabel share: they take flexible specialization as an empirical description of the new working life. But Piore and Sabel (1984: 258) intend it only as 'an exercise in imagination'; it is 'speculative' and 'abstract'. Its future realization is also, as we have seen, dependent on a choice of going along this path. And: 'it is hard to see (. . .) any reason to think one of these two outcomes any more probable than the other' (1984: 252). 'Flexible specialization' is an abstract model, used by Piore and Sabel in a politically prescriptive rather than an empirically descriptive way. But in much of flexibility literature it has been regarded as an already existing turning point in working life.

On the other hand, there are empirical descriptions of cases to illustrate the argument. Judging from what has happened to some of these cases since the book was written (if I might add something to the critical catalogue above), the possibilities of prosperity through flexible specialization are cast into doubt. A simple example: the authors claim that IBM executives are 'never laid off' (1984: 269), as that would be detrimental to the company community. But only a few years later they were, on a large scale. And a more comprehensive example: two countries that have entered the flexible specialization road to prosperity are said to be

Japan and Germany. That was in 1984; as I write in early summer 2006, the Japanese economy has been in crisis for more than a decade; and Germany is one of the most crisis stricken economies in the EU.

In the management literature the descriptions of the background of the need for change and the ways in which the changes benefit workers and management are very close to those in Piore and Sabel's analysis – although with less analytical depth and much clearer normativity. Let us take 'Business Process Reengineering', BPR, as an example. In the basic texts of BPR (Hammer 1990; Hammer and Champy 1993), most American corporations are said to be in a state of crisis, a crisis that will not be overcome until the old ways of organizing work and doing business are totally abandoned. Those that do not reengineer are doomed.

The roots of the crisis are threefold: customers have taken charge of markets, turning them into small niches; competition has been intensified and diversified, partly through globalization; and change has become the normal state of affairs. This makes it necessary for American business to break with the past and apply the revolutionary BPR; discontinuous thinking is necessary; the principles of the Industrial Revolution must be inverted. But at the same time there is a link to traditional American culture (Hammer and Champy 1993: 3; for 'them' in the quotation, read 'the Japanese'):

> Reengineering capitalizes on the same characteristics that have traditionally made Americans such great business innovators: individualism, self-reliance, a willingness to accept risk, and a propensity for change. Business reengineering, unlike management philosophies that would have 'us' become more like 'them,' doesn't try to change the behavior of American workers and managers. Instead, it takes advantage of American talents and unleashes American ingenuity.

Basically BPR means that processes – starting with what is of value to the customer and going backwards – and not tasks, are the principle for organizing work. Advanced information technology plays a crucial role as it is the tool that enables employers to destroy the old rigid structures and create new and flexible ones. BPR is good for employers, indeed it is necessary – the only road to survival for American companies, and for others as well.

But it is also beneficial for workers, especially as compared with the working conditions of the task based organizations. Those are characterised by a functional division of labour, in which workers perform simple and alienating tasks, constantly controlled and directed by management. In 'the new world of work' (Hammer and Champy 1993: Ch. 4) of the reengineered organizations, people do multi-dimensional work in teams with a collective responsibility for a whole process. Workers are like entrepreneurs in that they are focused on the satisfaction of customers, rather than bosses or bureaucrats. They continuously learn new things – they are not trained anymore, they educate themselves. The responsibility for a process also means that workers are empowered with the authority to make their own decisions on any problems arising in the work process, sometimes coached by a leader; they are inevitably autonomous and self-directing.

From the point of view of employers this means that recruiting policy becomes more complex as compared with the old working life (Hammer and Champy 1993: 70): 'If the old model was simple tasks for simple people, the new one is complex jobs for smart people, which raises the bar for entry into the work force.' What the authors call the 'character' of the workers becomes important; employees must be self-starting, self-disciplined and motivated to please customers in any way required.

An important point is a change in values, so that every employee feels that he or she really works for the customers, not the bosses. It is not entirely clear how this culture is to come about, mostly it seems to be expected to emerge automatically, but at least two mechanisms are pointed out. First, the management system, that is, wage criteria and evaluation measures, shape the employees' values and beliefs; second, management must set good examples by living up to the values, not only in words but also in deeds.

BPR is widespread, although seldom implemented in its revolutionary form, as the old organization is usually left intact to some extent (Gunge 2000; Knights and Willmott 2000); a combination with principles of 'total quality management' (TQM) has, for example, been empirically shown to be possible (Kelemen et al. 2000); but the most common empirical picture is that it simply fails (Knights and Willmott 2000). The same type of criticism concerning lack of accuracy in the picture of the development of mass and niche markets and the use of advanced technology that has been launched at Piore and Sabel, has been directed at Hammer. What has been called the 'paradox of BPR' has also been pointed out: the flexible, flat organization with its autonomous and empowered workers is to be created in an authoritarian, top-down way by a strong hierarchy of managers. One of the conclusions from this is the following (Gall 2000: 137): 'Empowerment is thus akin to responsibility without power, and that responsibility is to work harder and work better within set parameters.'

One thing to note in the literature claiming that flexibility is good for both management and workers is that there are not many empirical studies. Piore and Sabel provide an abstract model of flexible specialization with some – according to the critics, dubious – empirical illustrations. (There is, though, a rather rich later literature on industrial districts, but it does not contribute much to the present theme: flexibility as good for both employers and workers; see, for example, Pyke and Sengenberger 1992; Sabel and Zeitlin 1997.) And management literature often lacks even systematic empirical illustrations; it is an 'evidence-free zone' (Thompson and McHugh 2002: 149).

Flexibility is good for employers, but bad for workers

In a large number of, mainly empirical, studies it is argued that although flexibility is good for employers, it is bad for workers. Usually, though, it is taken for granted that it is beneficial to employers – it is the *raison d'être* of flexibility – while what is investigated are its effects on workers.

In an analysis of empirical knowledge about changes at work in the USA, Cappelli et al. (1997) paint a more complex picture than we have met before of the pressures that force restructuring. They discuss harder competition, mainly through globalization and changing markets; but to the usual catalogue they add an ambition on the part of employers to neutralize and counteract labour laws that protect workers, a stronger power position of stockholders against management resulting in a much more pronounced insistence on profit maximizing, and an abundance of new management ideas such as TQM, BPR and lean production.

When it comes to effects of flexibility, the conclusion is that it is mainly positive for employers through, for example, better product and service quality, higher productivity and higher profits. They warn, however, of a number of contradictions inherent in flexibility and the most important one for employers is that employee attachment to a specific employer and employee morale declines. This creates new problems when employers push more of the market risks onto employees in work systems that require more autonomy of workers.

Although the authors stress that there is no single model of flexibility, they find that 'the central principle is increased employee power and responsibility. However, the extent to which this occurs is not uniform across all employers that introduce elements of the new systems' (Cappelli et al. 1997: 91). One such element is work teams, in which employees have a lot of responsibility, are broadly skilled and there is some job rotation. Workers are also empowered by being involved in problem-solving groups and in questions of the quality of the product and customer satisfaction. This requires more training at the same time as new wage systems provide opportunities to enhance income.

But this rosy picture in the flexibility models is modified by empirical evidence on the consequences of flexible work organization for employees. Downsizing has hit employees hard and given rise to looser connections between employers and employees. A consequence thereof is that employers are actually less inclined to invest in worker training. Another consequence is, of course, a sharp decline in job security. Teams often result in moving pressures from management into the teams themselves. And most of the responsibility and autonomy comes in the form of more work intensity. In sum, the authors find that there are some possible positive developments, such as a potential for more autonomy, but most effects of flexibility are negative for workers (Cappelli et al. 1997: 206):

> Current trends suggest that employees are increasingly confronted with greater risk, often longer hours, increased work loads, and stress and are offered less by employers in return. (. . .) Employees seem to have borne a very large share of the costs of restructuring companies, and they are suffering for it.

Although there are modifications, the general thrust of the analysis of empirical material results in flexibility being good for employers, but bad for employees.

In a British study, combining quantitative and qualitative methods, of a number of firms the conclusions are similar (Burchell et al. 2002). Among background factors of a drive towards flexibility (Lapido and Wilkinson 2002) we find some that we are familiar with, such as changes in markets and technology, globalization and stockholders' stronger pressure for profits. But the authors further discuss the commercialization of the public sector as one of the causes; privatization and the creation of internal markets require flexibilization. They also identify a number of factors that have facilitated firms' introduction of restructuring and flexibility. Among them are high rates of unemployment and a decline in the influence of trade unions, but also the weakening of worker protection by labour laws and social benefits, as well as the general political strength of neo-liberalism.

It seems clear from the study that almost all employers report that they gain from flexibility – they increase productivity and raise profitability, and in some cases the restructuring is regarded as the reason that they are still in business (Mankelow 2002: 138). But like Cappelli et al. the researchers also warn against possible long-term negative consequences for organizations due to flexibility being bad for employees (Lapido and Wilkinson 2002; Mankelow 2002). And according to this study, as well as a great number of European and American large-scale investigations referred to, the effects of flexibility *are* mainly bad for workers: layoffs, job insecurity and work intensification (Burchell 2002; Hudson 2002a and b). In their turn these consequences lead to weakened health and well-being of workers at all levels, including managers (Wichert 2002), and to family problems (Nolan 2002).

It is of course generally difficult to make sharp distinctions between good and bad (at least outside management literature), and it is especially noticeable when it comes to good and bad for workers. Often some aspects of flexibility are found to be beneficial, while others are detrimental – especially in empirical studies. Still, a rather clear picture emerges from this part of the reviewed literature: flexibility is good for employers and bad for employees.

Flexibility is bad

We have seen that both Burchell et al. and Cappelli et al. warn against the possibility that flexibility can become bad for both employers and employees. Usually this type of argument says that the insecurity for workers that flexibility involves is bad also for employers, as it reduces worker motivation and incentives to contribute to the results of the organization (for example, Brown 1997; Treu 1992). But as a rule, flexibility is judged to be bad for employers only to the extent that workers are not handled right.

The possible conflict is also expressed in the term 'flexicurity' – a combination, of course, of 'flexibility' and 'security'. EU labour market policy (European Commission 1997) and especially that in the Netherlands (van Oorschot 2004) and Denmark (EU 2006) are the main sources of inspiration, and the basic idea is a need to balance flexibility and security. In the social science literature there are several definitions of flexicurity, but the combination of flexibility and security is always present. In the most cited definition (Wilthagen and Tros 2004: 169–70) it concerns, on the one hand, security for workers in jobs, employment, income and combinations of these, and, on the other hand, numerical, functional and wage flexibility to make it possible for labour markets and firms to adjust to changes. This state of affairs can only be reached through welfare state policies that enhance this combination.

In this formulation flexicurity, of course, belongs to 'good flexibility'. My reason for placing it under the present heading is that the mechanism behind the flexicurity 'pursuit of win–win outcomes' (Wilthagen and Rogowski 2000: 250) is fear of the lose–lose outcome of bad flexibility. What flexicurity can result in, it is argued (Wilthagen and Tros 2004: 179), is 'an increase in the acceptance of flexibilisation among employees', or even in a more general social acceptance (Keller and Seifert 2000: 294).

There are as yet few empirical studies of flexicurity and the existing ones mainly deal with labour law and/or social security systems. This underlines my judgement that the flexicurity field is about avoiding or balancing negative consequences of flexibility: security tends to be regarded as a dependent variable – dependent on the forms and scope of flexibility. Warnings against too much flexibility are therefore much scarcer in the flexicurity literature than cautions against problems that can arise if workers have too much security (for example, Klammer and Tillmann 2001: 16–17). One of the very few studies of the current labour market situation in Europe finds that the development has mainly meant more flexibility and less security on the part of employees (Seifert and Tangian 2006).

Flexibility is good for workers, but bad for employers

In the literature a whole catalogue of reasons for employers to avoid rigidity and target flexibility can be found. The idea that flexibility is bad for the organization seems hard to maintain, and in combination with flexibility being good for workers it is almost non-existent in the literature – at least as far as I have been able to find. I say 'almost' as there are findings indicating that front line managers do not always regard flexible and 'family friendly' working time arrangements in a positive light, although they are beneficial to workers (Powell and Mainiero 1999; Yeandle et al. 2003).

Conclusion and a first terminological suggestion

The main conclusion of the overview is that 'flexibility' is a double-edged concept. Three observations lie behind the conclusion. The first concerns the variation in those for whom flexibility is said to be good and bad; the second the mechanisms behind trying to obtain flexibility;

and the third is the variation in what is regarded as the opposite of flexibility.

The overview indicates that flexibility can comprise different phenomena for employers and workers, especially as what is studied is usually flexibility from the organization's perspective. There are also some empirical findings pointing in that direction. Bruhnes (1989: 12) found in a study of companies in four countries that workers are interested in the type of flexibility that gives them 'the possibility of taking time off from work for family reasons, and the possibility of accumulating leave so as to be able to take long weekends or long holidays'; they were not interested in flexibility in the meaning given by management. And in a case study a union representative said: 'We're looking for counter-flexibility, flexibility that suits the employees and not just the employers' (Davidson 1990: 702). This is one way in which flexibility is double-edged.

The second way concerns the driving forces behind seeking flexibility. A catalogue from the literature mentioned above may look like this: an intensification of competition, mainly due to globalization; technological changes; development of niche markets with fickle and strong customers; growing demand from stockholders for profit maximization; an abundance of new models for work organization, propagated by successful management consultants; commercialization and privatization of parts of the public sector. This flexibilization has been facilitated by a weakened position of trade unions and the dismantling of the welfare state.

It is worth noting that the catalogue does not include any mechanism on the part of employees. All analyses of why flexibility is desirable or even necessary concern employer interests – flexibility is, again, regarded as a management concept. The argumentation about good flexibility takes its point of departure in possibilities of finding solutions to a rigidity crisis in companies, and better working conditions are part of this. The reasoning about bad flexibility tends to take organizational flexibility as given, at the same time as it emphasizes the need to balance this with worker security. Also, the more critical and empirical studies of working conditions and work environment presuppose, more or less explicitly, that flexibility is good for employers. And the difficulties of finding any literature at all under the heading 'good for workers, but bad for employers' underline the observation.

Thirdly, when employers and work organizations are analysed, flexibility is the answer to the rigidities of mass markets and mass production, old forms of work organization, labour laws, and so on. Here the antonym of flexibility is *rigidity*. But when employees are analysed, the threats of flexibility must be met with security – hence, for example, the term 'flexicurity'. The antonym of flexibility in these contexts is not rigidity, but *security*. A variation in the antonym indicates that there is variation in the basic concept, in this case making it double-edged.

The conclusion calls for terminological development, taking account of 'flexibility' as a double-edged concept. A first terminological step can be, I suggest, to make a distinction between *having flexibility* and *being flexible* (Karlsson and Eriksson 2000): if employers are to have flexibility, workers must be flexible; for example, if the organization is to have functional flexibility, workers must be flexible in accepting constant reskilling and changing work tasks whenever required to do so. If, on the other hand, workers are to have flexibility, employers must be flexible; for example, if workers are to have flexibility in accumulating leave, management must be flexible in working time arrangements.

But this is only a first step. In the next chapter a more elaborate terminological proposal will be presented.

3
Flexibility, Stability and Related Concepts

Dan Jonsson

What is flexibility?

Flexibility in working life has been an extensively debated issue for many years. In spite of this, it cannot be said that flexibility is a concept with a well-defined, shared meaning. Indeed, some of the confusion and controversy in the flexibility debate probably stems from the fact that different authors mean different things by flexibility. It is thus difficult to know whether an apparent disagreement – for example a disagreement about whether flexibility is desirable or undesirable in a particular case – is also a real disagreement, or if it is due mainly to the fact that one term is given multiple meanings.

Furthermore, in many cases flexibility is treated as an inherent property rather than one which is relative to a particular point of view, disregarding the fact that flexibility is always 'flexibility for somebody', as explained below. For the purpose of scientific analysis it is also a problem that terms such as 'flexible' and 'flexibility' are not value-neutral. These terms have strong positive connotations; it is difficult to be against 'flexibility', whatever that means.

The fact that flexibility language as described above tends to be vague, incomplete and value-imbued makes it well suited as a rhetorical tool. For analytic purposes, however, we need well-defined, more value-neutral terms, and, to be fair, attempts to provide such definitions can also be found in the literature on flexibility.

The most common approach seems to be to define flexibility as essentially capacity of adaptation. For example, Mandelbaum (1978) defines flexibility as 'the ability to respond effectively to changing circumstances'. According to this definition, flexibility is related to two kinds of change. First, there are 'changing circumstances'; second, there is a 'response' to these changing circumstances which involves a change in some state or activity. Furthermore, the requirement that this latter change constitutes an 'effective' response implies that it is desirable in relation to the changing circumstances. In view of these observations, it is possible to state the following more elaborated definition of flexibility: *Flexibility is the propensity of an actor or a system to exhibit variation in activities or states which is correlated with some other variation and desirable in view of this variation.*

For example, working time flexibility may mean that the length of working time per day, per week or per year changes in response to changes in production volume, or that although the length of working time is the same for each period of time, the location of working time within each period of time varies between periods according to changing circumstances. To gain a deeper understanding of the concept of flexibility as defined here, let us consider some key words in the definition above.

The first two important words are 'actors' and 'systems'. In Mandelbaum's (1978) definition of flexibility, cited above, it is not clear what kind of entity can be characterized by flexibility. In the definition above, flexibility is a property which can be attributed to actors or systems. Actors include individuals as well as business enterprises and other organizations, while systems include production systems, labour markets and corporate networks such as those discussed in Chapter 6.

Actors and systems are complex and interrelated concepts. For example, labour markets may be seen as systems that include actors such as employees and potential employees. Flexibility from a labour market perspective and flexibility from the perspectives of individual labour market participants are clearly empirically related, but they do not necessarily coincide, and the two perspectives represent different ways of thinking about flexibility. In this chapter, flexibility is mainly seen from the actor's point of view.

Another important word in the definition of flexibility is 'variation'. Let me introduce a distinction between two types of variation by means of an analogy. Although it may be a myth, chameleons are said to be able to change their colour to match that of the background. For example, after moving from a brown background to a green one, they are supposed to change colour from brown to green. This exemplifies one type of variation: *variation over time*, or simply *change*. However, it would also be useful for chameleons to have adaptive multi-colour capacity. For example, if a chameleon's head was close to a brown trunk, while its tail was surrounded by green leaves, it would be useful if its head was brown while its tail was green. This exemplifies another type of variation: *variation in a mix*, or *diversity*.

Working hours that change according to changes in demand for goods and services or according to changes in employees' preferences exemplify variation over time. On the other hand, a situation where working hours vary between employees but not over time for each employee exemplifies variation in a mix. Similarly, so-called mix flexibility, which refers to the capacity of a production system to simultaneously produce different kinds of products, exemplifies variation in a mix.

The definition of flexibility given above is thus more general than Mandelbaum's in the sense that the present definition refers to variation in general, whereas Mandelbaum's definition deals only with change, variation over time. While flexibility based on variation over time may be the most important type, it is convenient for some purposes to extend the definition of flexibility so as to include also variation in a mix.

Yet another key word is 'propensity'. The 'propensity of an actor or a system to exhibit variation' may be referred to as *variability*. It should be noted that variability and by implication flexibility are so-called disposition concepts (see, for example, Hempel 1965). These concepts refer not to a manifest property but to a disposition to perform certain activities or assume certain states in certain, specified situations.[1]

There is a difference to be noted, then, between the propensity to exhibit variation – variability – and the actual variation, which serves as an *indicator* of variability in the sense that variation indicates underlying variability, although variability does not always manifest itself as variation. There is also a distinction to be made between variability and *preconditions* of variability. With regard to individuals and similar actors, preconditions of variability include capability factors as well as motivational factors. Both capability and motivation are needed to create a propensity for variation. For example, ability to change will not lead to a propensity to change when there is no willingness to change, and willingness to change will not lead to a propensity to change if there is no ability to change.

---

[1] This conceptualization agrees with the etymology of the word 'flexible'. The stem 'flex-' derives from the Latin word 'flectere', to bend, while the suffix '-ible' expresses ability, capacity, and so on. Thus, that something is flexible literally means that it can be bent; metaphorically, something is flexible if it can take different forms so as to adapt to varying circumstances. The word 'can' indicates that we are dealing with a disposition concept.

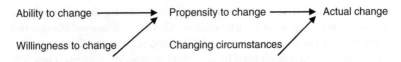

Figure 3.1 Causal model relating propensity to change to other factors

According to this analysis, actual adaptive change of activities occurs as a result of (a) ability to change, (b) willingness to change and (c) changing circumstances in view of which change of activities becomes desirable. The underlying causal model is shown in Figure 3.1.

Finally, 'desirable' is also an important word in the definition of flexibility. Perhaps the most notable feature of the present definition of flexibility is that it takes care of the problem of how to handle the value bias of terms such as 'flexible' and 'flexibility', albeit with an Alexandrian cut. Flexibility is desirable variability; thus flexibility is, by definition, desirable. Variability that is not desirable is not flexibility. While this way of defining flexibility may be surprising, it is in line with common usage, as the comparison with Mandelbaum's definition showed, and it provides a solid foundation for an analysis of related concepts.

Note, however, that desirable variability is not necessarily desirable for all actors involved. It makes sense to ask 'flexibility for whom', because variability which is desirable for one actor may be undesirable for another one. Thus, as discussed below, the same variability may be regarded as flexibility by one actor but as instability by another actor.

It should also be emphasized that the fact that flexibility is desirable *per se* does not rule out the possibility that it may have undesirable consequences or side-effects. For example, as noted in Chapter 2 increased flexibility for an employer may involve increased instability for his employees, provoking negative reactions such as increased labour turnover and decreased work motivation, so that in the end the employer may lose more than he gains from increased flexibility. But although flexibility may be 'bad' in this sense, it is nevertheless always desirable if its consequences or side-effects are disregarded.

Flexibility and stability

It should not be forgotten that variability is not always desirable. For example, it is not desirable that manufacturers make products that deviate from the product specification; indeed, the fabrication and assembly of standardized and therefore exchangeable parts is at the core of modern industrial production. Similarly, working times should be 'standardized' or at least predictable; employment relations should not be too volatile, and so on. Such examples suggest that attention to flexibility should be complemented by attention to *stability*. The two concepts are in fact closely related; they are symmetrical in the sense that flexibility is desirable variability, whereas stability is desirable *invariability*.

A definition of stability can be given which is analogous to that of flexibility: *Stability is the propensity of an actor or a system not to exhibit variation in activities or states which would be undesirable in view of the non-existence of some other variation.*

Thus, both stability and flexibility are desirable; on the other hand, instability (too much undesirable variability) and inflexibility (too little desirable variability) are both undesirable. The interrelations between the four concepts are summarized in Table 3.1.

Alternatively, the relationships among the concepts in Table 3.1 may be illustrated as shown in Table 3.2. Each table indicates that both flexibility and stability are desirable, while both inflexibility and instability are undesirable. From another point of view, variability can be both (desirable) flexibility and (undesirable) instability, and invariability can be both (desirable) stability and (undesirable) inflexibility.

Flexibility, stability and their opposites, as defined above, are very general concepts and may be seen to include or be closely related to many other concepts. For example, labour market rigidity and

Table 3.1   Interrelations among the concepts of flexibility, stability, inflexibility and instability

	Variability is desirable	Variability is undesirable
Situation with variability	Flexibility	Instability
Situation without variability	Inflexibility	Stability

Table 3.2   Alternative representation of interrelations among the concepts of flexibility, stability, inflexibility and instability

	Desirable situation	Undesirable situation
Situation with variability	Flexibility	Instability
Situation without variability	Stability	Inflexibility

wage rigidity, as discussed by economists, can be regarded as forms of inflexibility, while security and predictability are closely related to stability. As another example, so-called flexicurity may be seen as flexibility for employers combined with stability for employees. As hinted at in the Introduction, 'more flexibility' has become a frequently heard prescription for work–life reform. By contrast, 'more stability' has been a less frequently used battle-cry. This may partly be due to stability concerns having been discussed under other headings such as employment security. It may also reflect the fact that in many cases sufficient stability has already been achieved, since it is a *sine qua non* for efficient production, whereas flexibility is a relatively new concern still awaiting fulfilment. However, none of these explanations of why flexibility has been given more attention than stability imply that stability concerns are less important than flexibility concerns.

An exchange-relation perspective on flexibility and stability in working life

This section is devoted to an analysis of the flexibility and stability of employees and employers, using an exchange-relation perspective. In this perspective, employment relations between employees and employers are seen as exchange relations where each actor makes a contribution desired by the other actor. By making these contributions, each actor incurs a cost, but for each actor this cost is smaller than the reward gained from the contribution received from the other actor.[2]

In an employment relation, the employee contributes work, while the employer contributes compensation or remuneration for this work. In an exchange relation perspective, flexibility and stability are based on the variability of these contributions, and the desirability of this variability. Specifically, the variability of (a) the employee's contributions, (b) the employer's contributions and (c) the very exchange of these contributions – the relation itself – may be seen as desirable or undesirable. Furthermore, the variability of these phenomena may be seen as

---

[2] There is thus a conceptual symmetry between employers and employees in this perspective, but this does not imply that there is also a substantial symmetry. The conceptualization of employment relations as exchange relations does not involve *a priori* assumptions that employers and employees gain equally from the exchanges taking place, that they are equally dependent on each other, and so on.

desirable or undesirable by each actor in the employment relation – the employee as well as the employer.

This means, for example, that the employee's contributions – and by extension the employee himself or herself – can be regarded as flexible, inflexible, stable or unstable from (at least) two points of view: the employee's and the employer's. The same applies to the employer's contributions. Furthermore, there is no guarantee that the two actors will view variability of the employee's contributions, say, in the same way with regard to desirability. It is not unlikely, for example, that one actor will regard such variability as flexibility and the other one as instability. Thus, if we combine the two dimensions *whose contribution is variable* and *which actor evaluates variability as desirable or undesirable* we obtain four combinations, as illustrated in Tables 3.3 and 3.4.

In cases (1) and (2), the employee is flexible – that is, the employee's contributions to the employer may vary according to varying circumstances in a desirable way. For example, length of working time may vary between different days or different weeks. However, in case (1) working time changes in response to changes in the employee's environment and preferences, whereas in case (2) working time changes in response to changes in the employer's environment and preferences.

Table 3.3 Examples of flexibility characterized with regard to 'who is flexible for whom'

Actor with variable contribution	Actor assessing variability as flexibility	
	Employee	Employer
Employee	(1)	(2)
Employer	(3)	(4)

Table 3.4 Examples of stability characterized with regard to 'who is stable for whom'

Actor with non-variable contribution	Actor assessing non-variability as stability	
	Employee	Employer
Employee	(i)	(ii)
Employer	(iii)	(iv)

In cases (3) and (4), the flexible actor is the employer, whose contributions to the employee may vary according to varying circumstances. For example, the salary paid to employees may vary over time. There is, however, a big difference between a situation where the employer temporarily pays a higher salary because of economic problems for the employee, as in case (3), and a situation where the employer temporarily pays a lower salary because of economic problems for the employer, as in case (4).

In cases (i) and (ii), the employee's contributions to the employer are in some regards not variable, which is in these cases seen as desirable. Case (i) could be exemplified by stability in the sense that unscheduled overtime does not occur, which would be desirable for the employee, while an example of case (ii) could be that the employee always begins work on time, which is desirable for the employer.

In cases (iii) and (iv), there is some kind of desirable invariability in the contributions from the employer to the employee. Case (iii) could be exemplified by stability in the sense that the employee has a fixed monthly wage rather than a wage based on a piece-rate, which would probably be desirable for the employee. Finally, a situation when there is a long-term agreement on wages, which employers seem to favour, can be seen as exemplifying case (iv) stability.

It should be noted that the same type of analysis can be applied to exchange relations between a company and its suppliers or customers. For example, demands on suppliers for 'just-in-time' deliveries or 'zero defects' are essentially demands for stability achieved by suppliers and assessed by their customers. Similarly, end customers' demands for product differentiation or unusual delivery times are demands for flexibility achieved by producers and assessed by their customers.

A typology of flexibility and stability

Many types of flexibility have been defined in the flexibility literature, but there may still be room for a systematic typology based on the analysis above. The typology proposed here is based on the interpretation of an employment relation as an exchange relation between employer and employee. Specifically, it concerns if, when, where and how exchanges between employees and employers occur. In addition, this typology is not a typology of flexibility alone, but a typology of both flexibility and stability, taking into account the close relation between these concepts as discussed above.

The employment relation

On the most fundamental level we look at the flexibility and stability of the employment relation itself: *employment flexibility and employment stability*. These concepts concern whether or not a person is employed by a particular employer. Employment flexibility and employment stability thus concern situations where a person begins an employment, terminates an employment, or goes from one employment to another.

For example, from the point of view of what is desirable for the employer, employment flexibility could exist when the employer is able to get rid of employees quickly and cheaply, when, due to decreasing production volume or increasing productivity, they are not needed anymore. For the employees affected, however, this could mean employment instability. Conversely, if labour laws make it difficult for employers to terminate employment relations, employees may see this as contributing to employment stability, whereas employers may see these laws as causing employment inflexibility.

Employment status may of course also be changed by initiative of the employee, and the concepts of employment flexibility and employment stability can be used also in this case. For example, a key employee who terminates employment at short notice might look upon this as employment flexibility, whereas the employer may regard it as employment instability.

Working time

During the period of employment, the employee makes contributions to the employer during working time. *Working time flexibility and working time stability* concern the length of working time, as when an employee works overtime some days but not others, as well as the location of working time, as when an employee works three days every week but on different days during different weeks.

From the point of view of what is desirable for the employer, working time flexibility could mean that employees extend their working time when demand is above average. From the point of view of what is desirable for employees, on the other hand, flexible working times could mean working hours that vary with regard to length or location according to varying life situations. Of course, working times that vary according to employees' needs could be seen as unstable by employers, whereas working times that vary according to employers' needs could be seen as unstable by employees.

Workplace

We may ask not only when the work occurs but also where. Accordingly, we may speak about *workplace flexibility* and *workplace stability*. A change of workplace may or may not be a consequence of a change of employer. A change of workplace is probably in most cases a manifestation of workplace instability for the employee affected, but for the employer involved it may represent workplace flexibility. Conversely, situations where the workplace does not change would often represent workplace stability for employees but workplace inflexibility for employers.

Work

Yet another aspect concerns the actual work performed by the employee during working time, corresponding to *work flexibility* and *work stability*. This applies to work content as well as work intensity.

We are reminded, in connection with this type of flexibility and stability, that while there is no guarantee that employers and employees will evaluate some specific variability in the same way, there is also no guarantee that they will evaluate it in opposite ways. In the examples considered above, flexibility for one actor has frequently been instability for the other actor in the exchange relation, but it is also possible that both actors will regard some specific variability as desirable, so that it represents flexibility for both. For example, variability of work content may be seen as desirable by employees, since it tends to make their work more interesting, and also by employers, since it may increase productivity. It probably makes a difference, however, if changes in work content are initiated by the employer or by the employee.

Remuneration

The final aspect concerns remuneration, the contribution made by the employer to the employee during the employment, corresponding to *remunerative flexibility and remunerative stability*. For example, an employer may wish to reduce wages to compensate for changes in business conditions that reduce profitability. From the point of view of the employer, this would be remunerative flexibility, but from the point of view of the employee it would most likely be regarded as remunerative instability.

To summarize the definitions above, employment flexibility, working time flexibility, workplace flexibility and the corresponding types of stability concern *if*, *when* and *where* exchanges between employees and employers occur. Work flexibility and remunerative flexibility, as well as the corresponding types of stability, on the other hand, concern *how* these exchanges play out. Specifically, work flexibility and work stability as defined here focus on the employee's contribution to the employer, the work, while remunerative flexibility and stability focus on the employer's contribution to the employee, the remuneration.

The typology presented in this section is of course very similar to that proposed by Furåker (2005b). As described in Chapter 1, Furåker's typology comprises employment flexibility, work process flexibility, working time flexibility, workplace or spatial flexibility and wage flexibility. There are also parallels with other flexibility concepts discussed in Chapter 1 and used in other chapters of this book. For example, what I call employment flexibility is similar to what has been called numerical flexibility, and work flexibility is similar to functional flexibility. The present typology differs somewhat from other typologies, however, because it includes both flexibility and stability and also because all concepts are explicitly based on an exchange-relation perspective.

Conclusions

According to the conceptual analysis above, flexibility and stability are concepts related to variation and variability. Flexibility may be defined as desirable variability, whereas stability may be defined as desirable non-variability. When variability is seen as flexibility, some variation made possible by variability is regarded as desirable in relation to the existence of some other variation; when non-variability is seen as stability, some non-variation ensured by non-variability is regarded as desirable in relation to the non-existence of some other variation.

In addition, desirability is not an inherent, objective property of some given variation or variability. In other words, desirability, flexibility and stability are always desirability, flexibility and stability *for* somebody.

Flexibility and stability are thus contextually defined or relational concepts in two senses. First, some particular variability or invariability is regarded as flexibility or stability (respectively) only in relation to some actor's definition of the situation. Second, this actor's definition of the situation is related to the existence or non-existence of some independent variation. Specifically, variability is desirable if it facilitates adaptation to a changing or heterogeneous environment, but undesirable if it tends to disrupt an existing adaptation to a non-changing or homogeneous environment.

Finally, the analysis in this chapter has been guided by a quest for symmetry. It has been pointed out that there is a conceptual symmetry between flexibility and stability, and that both concepts are needed. Similarly, the relation between employer and employee is seen, conceptually, as a symmetric exchange relation, with contributions from each actor to the other. This conceptualization approach helps to unveil biases where either the employer's or the employee's perspective is taken for granted.

Thus, defining flexibility, stability and related concepts as has been done above – looking for contexts and symmetries – should help to move flexibility discourse from the level of partisan rhetoric to that of scientific analysis.

4

Britain's Flexible Labour Force: New Barriers to Individual Employment Rights

Anna Pollert

This chapter focuses on Britain, and the continuing quest to free employers from laws which might 'impose' burdens and costs on business. 'Flexibility' is conceptualized in the neo-liberal sense, that is, on employers' terms, entailing instability and precariousness for employees – a British interpretation discussed elsewhere at greater length (Pollert 1991). The New Labour government, elected in 1997, has pursued the free-market policies entrenched by its Conservative predecessor. Asserting Britain's neo-liberal position in Europe, in 2000 Prime Minister Tony Blair opposed the legal enforcement of the Charter of Fundamental Rights while in draft and in 2004 reiterated this during discussions of the proposed European Constitution: 'We are not prepared to have anything that takes away the ability to make sure our industrial laws in this country remain as flexible as they are now' (*Guardian*, 16 June 2004).

Although Britain's New Labour government has enacted a range of laws enhancing individual employment rights, this is in the context of an overarching neo-liberal policy which espouses the virtues of a 'flexible' labour market. Appeal to statutory regulation, already weaker than in other European countries, is becoming more inaccessible. In a context where the majority of workers lack collective representation, professional legal support is prohibitively expensive for the lower paid, leaving

Note: This chapter is based on the article 'Britain and individual employment rights: paper tigers, fierce in appearance but missing tooth and claw,' *Economic and Industrial Democracy*, 28 (1) (forthcoming February 2007). It is part of the ESRC project 'The unorganized worker: routes to support and views on representation'. Thanks to the Citizens Advice Bureau and to Paul Smith, Gary Morton and Sonia McKay for helpful comments.

most to depend on an underfunded voluntary sector. There has never been publicly funded legal aid for employment tribunal representation, in spite of the fact that employment law is becoming more complex and requires expert advice. New legislation, in operation since October 2004, has added severe obstacles to enforcing statutory rights. This chapter addresses this process in the context of Britain's decollectivized workforce, the legacy of the free-market tradition, its voluntarist industrial relations tradition and the manner in which New Labour pursues a neo-liberal strategy in a discourse of modernization and reform. It concludes by suggesting that searching questions need to be asked to defend democratic rights at work.

Employment policy for a 'flexible' workforce

The decline of collectivism in British industrial relations has remained a key trend over the past 20 years. From a union membership density of over 55 per cent in 1979, it stood at just 29.3 per cent in 2003, a 0.1 per cent increase over the previous year due to an increase in the proportion of UK employees in the public sector, not an increase in union membership. Among young workers (16–24 years) it is only 11 per cent, and in small workplaces (under 50 workers) it is 19 per cent. In the private sector non-unionism is the norm (Dundon and Rollinson 2004), with density unchanged since 2002 at 18.2 per cent and as low as 12 per cent in retail and 5 per cent in hotels and catering (DTI 2004a: 7). Collective bargaining coverage dipped from 70 per cent of employees in 1984 to 41 per cent in 1998 (Cully and Woodland 1999: 242) and 35.9 per cent by 2003 (DTI 2004a: 35). Its scope has narrowed and its impact on management discretion has diminished (Brown et al. 1999; Brown 2004) in the context of a 'hardening of employer attitudes to unions since the mid-1980s' (Gallie et al. 1998: 107; Bryson and Wilkinson 2001: 1). Individual statutory rights are now the key form of employment regulation for the majority of workers, and are the main emphasis of New Labour's employment relations strategy. However, the government's priority is to foster a free market and a 'flexible' (in the British sense of lightly regulated) labour force, and its legislation has been minimalist, enacted in a two-pronged process of new individual rights accompanied by laws which impede their legal enforcement.

This dynamic emanates from New Labour's hybrid policy of dominant neo-liberalism and subordinate social democracy (Hall 2003), with weak concessions to the unions through limited reforms to collective rights and the introduction of individual rights, most of which are obligatory under EU Directives. New Labour has reorientated its strategy towards the unions from the Conservatives' overt hostility to the encouragement of a cooperative 'partnership' role, without altering the erosion of workers' collective power. The union recognition legislation in the 1999 Employment Relations Act (ERA) leaves intact Conservative laws preventing unofficial action, solidarity (secondary) action, mass picketing and the closed shop; compulsory strike ballots remain and the earlier role of the Advisory, Conciliation and Arbitration Service (ACAS) of encouraging collective bargaining has not been restored (Smith and Morton 2001: 121, 123). The 2004 Employment Relations Act retains the exemption of small firms (below 21 employees) from the union recognition rights of the ERA 1999, and reforms on freedom of association and collective bargaining are minimalist and individualist, rather than collectivist in nature (Bogg 2005). The new individual rights have been enacted in a minimalist manner. These include the 1998 National Minimum Wage Act, the level of which has given rise to recurrent battles between the government and the unions, as well as the Low Pay Commission recommendations and a range of laws implementing European Council Directives, including the Working Time Regulations (1998), the Part-Time Workers (prevention of Less Favourable Treatment) Regulations 2000 and the Maternity and Parental Leave Regulations 2000. In Labour's second term from 2001, the 2002 Employment Act provided further rights for maternity and paternity leave, rights for fixed-term workers and rights for workers to request changes in working hours. In all cases, implementation has been limited and accompanied by blocks, delays and loopholes. For example the government attempted to confine part-time workers' rights to *employees*, and only extended this to all *workers* under duress and Britain maintains its 'opt out' from the 1998 Working Time Regulations (Smith and Morton 2001: 123).[1]

Apart from the Minimum Wage, which can be enforced by the Inland Revenue, the other individual rights require individual enforcement through the Employment Tribunal (ET) system. Recent government legislation has aimed at reducing the number of ET applications, which rose from 40,000 in 1980 to a peak of 130,000 in 2001, in a period when individual workplace disputes increased, while collective disputes in the form of strikes dropped from around 1400 to 200 per annum (Burkitt 2001: 14).

---

[1] On the EU Information and Consultation Directive, see Terry (2003: 276); on the Working Time Directive, see Barnard et al. (2003); see also (more widely) *The Guardian* (27 September 2004).

The rise in tribunal applications, the government contended, was due to a new climate of litigiousness (DTI 2001a: 4). This ignored the logic that increasing individual rights would entail more opportunities to enforce them, and failed to analyse the real reasons for the increase. The trend was complex: the 130,000 claims in 2000–1 were atypical because of several large multiple claims[2] and by 2002 the number had fallen to 98,617 (ETS 2003: 2). Although this rose again to 114,042 in 2003–4, 40 per cent of cases still being dealt with from 1997 were due to the part-time worker regulations in part-time worker pension cases (ETS 2004: 2). More widely, the government claim ignored the overwhelming evidence of *lack* of recourse to the law. The government's own consultation paper in preparation for reducing access to tribunals, *Routes to Resolution*, registered the low level of litigation, noting that only 15 to 25 per cent of disputes involving a breach of legal rights went to tribunal (DTI 2001a: 3). The 1998 Workplace Employee Relations Survey (WERS) found only one in ten employee dismissals went to an ET (Cully et al. 1999: 129). Genn (1999) calculated that between 1992 and 1997, only 18 per cent of employment problems with potential legal redress reached tribunal application and the Citizens Advice Bureau (CAB) reports large numbers of aggrieved workers who, even when advised of their rights, fail to take them further (Citizens Advice 2001a, 2001b). This is despite the fact that individual problems at work appear to be increasing, or at least, that there is a growing need for advice about them. In 2003–4, the 3000 Citizens Advice Bureaux (CABs) outlets dealt with 510,000 employment problems (Citizens Advice 2004f: 13) and the number of calls to the ACAS helpline increased from 755,449 in 2001–2 to 796,649 in 2003–4, the proportion of calls from employees or workers rising from 34 to 55 per cent of the total over this period (ACAS 2004:52).

None of this evidence deterred the government from new legislation preventing ET application until all 'internal procedures' were exhausted (DTI 2001a: 21). Alongside its insistence on preliminary internal workplace resolution was an appeal to 'soft law', backed by *The Better Regulation Task Force* (a Cabinet-appointed private sector body), whose brief is to press for alternatives to state regulation and exhort companies to improve 'best practice' and establish voluntary standards (Cabinet Office 2002). Yet British statutory employment rights are already weak in two senses. They are weak substantively, in terms of

---

[2] This peak was partly due to 12,000 part-time worker pension cases under the Sex Discrimination jurisdiction in 2000–1.

minimalist interpretation, and weak procedurally in terms of monitoring, access to support and enforcement. Employers' adherence to proper procedure and knowledge of employment legislation is poor, especially among small firms (Earnshaw et al. 1998; Neathey and Arrowsmith 2001; Blackburn and Hart 2002; Edwards et al. 2003), but there is no Ministry of Labour or Labour Inspectorate in Britain, as in most other European countries (Citizens Advice 2001b; Burkitt and Dunstan 2001; Burkitt 2001:18; Ewing 2003: 141). The process of redress in ETs is individualized and requires the applicant's knowledge of a changing and increasingly complex legal system in order to register an employment rights 'problem' in the first place (Dickens et al. 1985). The low level of knowledge has been well documented (West Midlands Low Pay Unit 2001; Meager et al. 2002). Information and advice are uncoordinated and spread across informal help, libraries, the Internet, the non-profit sector (CABs, Law Centres, Low Pay Units and other advice centres), telephone helplines, equality bodies, ACAS, solicitors and other legal advisors. Finally, the ET system itself has no powers of enforcement in England and Wales, unlike Scotland. Failure by an employer to comply with a tribunal compensation ruling can only be challenged through a protracted and often unaffordable process of registration with the County Courts (Citizens Advice 2001b: 11; Citizens Advice 2004d) and ETs cannot enforce re-instatement or re-engagement following successful unfair dismissal cases, but can only increase compensation awards.[3]

British collective and individual employment rights in context

Weak regulation and preference for alternatives to statutory instruments in Britain flow with a global movement away from 'hard' to 'soft law'. This entails a decline in the rate of ratification of recently adopted ILO conventions and a shift at the EU level from Directives to voluntary Codes, with an 'explosion' of charters, codes and new individual employment rights based on ineffective enforcement and sanctions procedures – 'paper tigers, fierce in appearance but missing in tooth and claw' (Hepple 2003: 238). The shift to 'soft law' is part of the strengthening of neo-liberalism, both at EU level (van Apeldoorn 2000; Pochet 2005), and at national level, with weakening of employment

---

[3] Employment Rights Act 1996: para. 117.

law in many countries since the 1990s. Italy, France, Spain, Germany and Holland have an agenda to limit employment rights, particularly in terms of relaxing regulations on dismissals, fixed-term and temporary work (Hepple and Morris 2002: 246; Waddington 2005).

However, in most of Continental Europe, collective regulation remains significant and neo-corporatist traditions of 'general political exchange' between the state, labour and capital (Crouch 1993) still challenge the neo-liberal project.[4] Britain, however, has a different legacy and the 1979–97 Conservative government's erosion of employment protection and collective rights bore on one of the most lightly regulated employment systems in Europe. The deficit of state regulation in this area, which left Britain its distinctively voluntarist labour relations traditions, can be traced to the championing of and appeal to the *common law* by the ascendant capitalist class in pre-industrial conflict in its struggle for *individual market freedom* against the legal constraints imposed by the state – then the Church and Crown (Fox 1985: 11–29). Wedderburn (1989) relates this institutional inheritance to the ease with which Hayek's (1960, 1984) neo-liberal creed became the orthodoxy of the post-1979 Conservative programme. Collective rights, upheld since 1871 by *negative immunities from the common law*, were eroded both by legislation and by case law pursued by 'living judges', who pressed an ideological attack on union 'immunities' as unfair 'privileges' (Wedderburn 1989: 12).

While the rest of Western Europe developed state legislated positive rights for workers and systems 'of publicly accountable enforcement', such as labour courts (Hepple 2003: 246), Britain, apart from in the area of health and safety, confined regulation to women, young people and 'vulnerable' workers in poorly organized sectors (Ewing 2003: 144).[5] Otherwise, common law remained the sole basis for individual employment rights until the 1963 Contracts of Employment Act and the 1965 Redundancy Payment Act, which established statutory individual employment rights, with an Industrial Tribunal system to enforce them

---

[4] See Visser (1999) and Regini (2003) on the survival of tripartism. On opposition to proposals to relax unfair dismissal protection in Italy in 2002, see EIROnline (2002). On opposition in Austria to attempts to remove tripartite consultation on social security in 2003, see EIROline (2003).

[5] Chiefly through the Wages Councils, set up in 1909, weakened by Thatcher in 1986 and abolished in 1993 (apart from for agricultural workers). But see McCarthy (1992: 10) on the debate on whether this legislation was just 'marginal' to *collective laissez faire* or fundamental to those left out of the system.

(Dickens et al. 1985; DTI 2002: viii). These were extended to unfair dismissal and other areas by the 1971 Industrial Relations Act, after the 1968 Donovan Report acknowledged the lack of collective protection of non-unionized workers. Other key provisions for individual rights were also enacted during the 1970s, especially on gender and race equality, but these too required the ET system for enforcement.

While ETs are broadly tripartite judicial bodies, overseen by a legally qualified Chairman (sic), the common law tradition persists in that ultimate enforcement powers remain with the County Courts.[6] At an ideological level, the single confrontation of employee and employer in the tribunal conceals the asymmetry of power in the employment contract, while the fact that the worker bears the responsibility for asserting legal rights makes it much easier to label the worker as the 'problem', if recourse to the law appears 'excessive'.

The problems of access and low success rates for employees pursuing their rights through tribunals has long been noted (Dickens et al. 1985) and in the context of de-collectivization, new and more complicated employment legislation, the need for greater accessibility and simplicity has been emphasized by reviews of the system (Leggatt 2001). Instead, however, New Labour, responding to business demands (chiefly voiced by the Confederation of British Industry, the CBI) has legislated to make individual employment regulation still less accessible to workers.

New Labour's neo-liberalism in a 'modernization' discourse

The distinctive manner in which new employment rights have been enacted, then minimized, then turned into problems of litigiousness, is symptomatic of what Hall (2003) has characterized as New Labour's policy of 'double shuffle' – the hybrid regime of forging a strong neo-liberal project, which dominates a weak social-democratic programme. These social-democratic concessions, aimed at the traditional working-class and public sector middle-class electorate, are presented within the discourse of 'active government', 'reform' and 'modernization', with the neo-liberal agenda couched in 'opportunity', 'choice' and 'better value'. The process is a dynamic, whereby a social-democratic agenda 'is *constantly being "transformed"* into the former, dominant one' (Hall

---

[6] This applies to England and Wales. In Scotland, the tribunals have powers of enforcement.

2003: 19; emphasis in original), with language – 'Third Way waffle, double-talk, evasions and "spin" ' – playing a key role in creating 'the new common sense' and altering meanings to a neo-liberal programme (Hall 2003: 12, 18).

The absorption into the neo-liberal trajectory of new individual employment rights follows this discourse of modernization and double-talk. In recent years, two areas of access to justice illustrate this. First, the Access to Justice Act (1999) illustrates the subordination of affordable and publicly funded access to justice, including legal advice, to a neo-liberal agenda of funding cuts and rationing, couched in a 'modernizing' rhetoric which appears to be about broadening the delivery and availability of legal help. The Law Society (2002) dubbed it 'Access Denied'. Secondly, the introduction of new individual employment rights was accompanied by instruments to restrict their take-up, including 'privatization' of enforcement through channelling conflict into Alternative Disputes Resolution (Hepple 2003; Colling 2004), and legislation in the 2002 Employment Act which sets complex procedural hurdles before an ET application can be made.

'Modernizing' justice: access to justice or access denied?

The Access to Justice Act (1999) was directed at the legal-aid budget. Its impact on employment advice occurred both through the depletion of publicly funded solicitors and on the services of the voluntary sector, with the CABs, for example, the single largest source of advice for employment problems – 48 per cent in one study (Genn 1999: 91) and 32 per cent in another (Meager et al. 2002: 185). Under the Act, the Legal Aid Board was replaced by the Legal Services Commission (LSC) and the Community Legal Service (CLS) now oversaw legal aid. The White Paper, *Modernising Justice*, which preceded the Act (Lord Chancellor's Department 1998) proclaimed *broadening access* to legal aid. However, this referred to the broadening of legal aid provision to the not-for-profit sector, which could now contract with the CLS with a quality 'kitemark'. The real agenda was to cut spending: the budget was cut and remained capped.

Rationing took place through the CLS 'funding assessment' rules, which, in addition to means testing, evaluate the legal strength of the case and prospects of a successful outcome, the importance and potential benefit to the assisted person, likely cost, the availability and likely demands on resources and the wider 'public interest' (Lord Chancellor's Department 1998: 34). The effect was to reduce the eligibility of cases for legal aid, and hence, of legal aid solicitors – as was predicted (Genn 1999: 103; Consumers' Association 2000). The Law Society found a 12 per cent decline in the number of solicitors' firms providing legal aid in the two years since the new contracting arrangements (Law Society 2002: 4) and the LSC found 50 per cent of solicitors' firms 'seriously considering stopping or significantly reducing publicly funded work . . . overwhelmingly because of remuneration and profitability' (LSC 2002: 8). Both the Law Society and the LSC studies found the largest decline in CLS work *was in employment law*, where legal aid is confined to Legal Help or advice and preparation work (a drop of 15 per cent in the LSC Report and 12 per cent in the Law Society report). A major reason for this is the restrictive criteria which place the low-paid in a 'Catch-22' dilemma: legal aid is available to those on income support (therefore excluding the employed), or for those on very low pay, with disposable income below £600 per month.[7] The minimum wage plus tax credits would, for example, put a worker above the permissible legal aid limit. The 'sufficient benefit test' (to the client and the 'community') could also exclude client advice, if CLS outlay were considered too great in relation to likely compensation, which might be as little as £200 for a low-paid worker, effectively discriminating against the low-paid (interview with CAB advisor 2004). The limited criteria for workers thus narrow the constituency for solicitors' legal aid work, as well as the ability of CABs and others to use their CLS contracts, instigating a vicious circle, as solicitors leave the employment law area, which increases the pressure on those who remain to give advice. Meanwhile, the government's policy of privatising legal enforcement is expanding the no-win, no-fee sector (Lord Chancellor's Department 1998: 24).

The effect of the funding cuts has been to deplete the solicitor referral base for CABs so severely that 39 per cent of bureaux judged their office was in 'an advice desert', with no recourse to legal aid lawyers or other services, 27 per cent reporting difficulties in finding one in employment (Citizens Advice 2004b: 12). The CLS funding regime also impedes the service provision of CABs and other not-for-profit advisors, which held 416 CLS franchises in 2004. This financial precariousness of the voluntary sector is exacerbated by rules which allow funds to be retrospectively disallowed, if CLS outlay is regarded as incommensurate with likely ET compensation. More broadly, the CLS funding regime is based

---

[7] The exact figure is calculated on a website (http://www.legalservices.gov.uk/civil/calc/whatis_calculator.asp).

on the business model of the solicitor's firm, with no allowance for an under-resourced sector's ability to deal with its new administrative burdens. CLS budgets are tied to specified CLS hours (which cannot always be met if clients do not fulfil all the CLS funding-assessment rules). Paid time does not cover dealing with clients' correspondence, and since 2003 the contracts have demanded even more paper-work, with no additional funding. The net effect of CLS contracts is to eat into advice and tribunal representation time, which is already compromised by time spent on seeking funding. It has been concluded (Citizens Advice 2004b: 15):

> There is a real fear that contracts will become unviable and many bureaux will have to withdraw from publicly funded legal services, leaving many people without access to appropriate services.

Evaluating the impact of the 1999 Access to Justice Act five years on, the Select Committee on Constitutional Affairs (2004: para. 105) judged that: 'At present, the legal aid system is increasingly being restricted to those with no means at all'. It emphasized the unfair continuing exclusion of tribunal representation from legal aid in the employment field, citing Lord Irvine of Lairg, the architect of Modernizing Justice, before he was appointed Lord Chancellor by the incoming New Labour government, in May 1997. This was a:

> gap which cannot be rationally justified . . . there is no greater unfairness than the legally unrepresented applicant against the legally represented employer in industrial tribunals. (Lairg 1996: 5)

The Select Committee on Constitutional Affairs (2004: para. 111; emphasis in original) concluded that

> It is not acceptable that in employment cases employees can be forced to represent themselves in circumstances where private employers are able to employ lawyers to represent them. If proceedings are to be fair, there needs to be equality of arms. Legal aid should not automatically be excluded from such tribunal hearings.

The poor success rate of ET hearings (about 13 per cent; ETS 2004: 24) must be related to the fact that 40 per cent of applicants have no legal representation compared with 15 per cent of employers (Colling 2004: 562), and reinforced the submissions to the Leggatt review of

tribunals, urging the government to introduce legal aid to ET representation (Leggatt 2001: 285).

The Access to Justice Act 1999 was thus part of an Orwellian world
in which words turn out to mean their opposite. Access to justice
was restricted, while the 'modernizing' programme failed to address
deficiencies in the historical legacy. It strikingly failed to address the
anomaly that free support and advice in an increasingly sophisticated
legal framework is overwhelmingly provided by a struggling voluntary
sector. The CABs, established in 1939 to assist civic life in war-time
Britain, have been left as a key institutional support for legal advice and
representation (Richard 1989; Citron 1989). They have been chronic-
ally underfunded, with mounting pressures to find short-term grants as
the contribution by local authorities declines proportionately (Citizens
Advice Annual Report 2002/03: 17). While legal training and updating
is continuous, and CABs attempt to refer difficult cases to 'second tier'
specialist support, the service is struggling to cope and most legal professionals consider it is unable to deal with complex issues. In 2003/04,
79 per cent of a total staff of 26,500 were volunteers, just 60 per cent
of whom were trained advisers, while only 5600 were paid staff (correspondence with CAB Social Policy Officer, August 2004). Respondents in
Paths to Justice experienced difficulty in accessing bureaux because of
limited opening times, waiting times for an appointment and difficulty
in making telephone contact (Genn 1999: 76, 89). Most use the voluntary sector because they cannot afford anything else. In 2003, 43 per cent
of ET applicants desired additional advice from a solicitor, barrister or
other type of lawyer, and 24 per cent did not use their preferred choice
because they 'could not afford it' (DTI 2004b: 108).

'Modernization' has made cosmetic changes, such as creating a CLS
website. This was hailed as making 'help accessible for everyone, but
especially people living in remote locations, or confined to home by
disability' (Lord Chancellor's Department 1998: 17). These declarations
ignored the fact that, in spite of the rapid overall increase in home
Internet access from 9 to 47 per cent of households between 1998 and
2003, this masks the sensitivity of this figure to income inequality. Only
12, 14 and 22 per cent, respectively, of the lowest three gross household
income deciles had home Internet access in 2003, compared with 71,
77 and 86 per cent in the top three deciles (National Statistics 2003). In
fact, the website proved to be a further cost-saving strategy. In summer
2004, the government stopped producing DTI booklets and leaflets on
employment rights and left text available only via the Internet (Citizens

Advice 2004c; Citizens Advice 2004d: 3), thus shifting the costs of paper and printing onto the vulnerable, low paid worker.

In sum, the growing crisis of unmet legal advice and redress was exacerbated under the rhetoric of 'a listening government', 'efficiency', 'best value', 'streamlining', 'simplifying', 'reform' and 'modernization' (Lord Chancellor's Department 1998).

New barriers to accessing individual employment rights

Rather than making the legal process more accessible, the government's strategy is to draw individual workplace disputes away from legal enforcement. One way has been by a new Alternative Dispute Resolution (ADR), the other by directing them to internal workplace resolution, as obligatory under the EA 2002. Both are forms of privatisation in their avoidance of state regulation, the resort to 'soft law' weakening protection by avoiding public example, where justice is *seen to be done*, shames bad employers and can set precedents as case law (Hepple 2003: 252; Colling 2004: 573). A significant shift in this direction was the Employment Rights (Dispute Resolution) Act 1998, which gave ACAS an additional role as arbitrator in cases of unfair dismissal in England and Wales in 2001.[8] The system requires a waiver of statutory rights 'to a public hearing, the cross-examination of witnesses... Most important of all rights to have the dispute resolved in accordance with the law' (Hepple 2003: 249). There is limited right of appeal and the system fails to address the inequalities of the parties in terms of their ability to secure professional advice and representation, which is demonstrated by the fact that only 42 per cent of applicants are represented at a tribunal, compared with 72 per cent of employers (DTI 2004b: 105). However, the system has so far had little impact. ACAS dealt with just 23 cases in the first full year of the operation of the Scheme and only 10 per cent of unions surveyed by the TUC in 2004 expressed themselves in favour of the arbitration alternative. Only four had any experience of taking claims through binding arbitration, one fewer than in the 2002–3 survey (TUC 2002: 4). It remains to be seen whether private companies, such as the Centre for Effective Dispute Resolution, build business here (Colling 2004: 570).

---

[8] This was extended to requests for 'flexible working' in 2003. The system was extended to Scotland in April 2004 for unfair dismissal and October 2004 for flexible working.

The 2002 Employment Act and 'reform' of the employment tribunal system

'Not so much a curate's egg; it is more a manky meat sandwich. Parts 1 and 4 are first class, but Parts 2 and 3 leave a great deal to be desired' (Lord McCarthy 2002: col. 1369, referring to the passage of the Employment Bill 2002).

The 2002 Employment Act presents progressive reforms implementing new rights for child-care leave, union learning-representatives and the EU Fixed Term Work Directive, but at its core is legislation which dilutes the very process of implementing any rights at all. This centres on new restrictions on ET applications. The government estimated that the new rules on access to the statutory process would reduce applications by 23 to 31 per cent, or 30,000–40,000 applications, saving £14–19 million to the taxpayer and £65–90 million to the employer (DTI 2001b: 7). The government, obsessed with the rise in ET applications, argued that restriction was justified because of a rise in litigious, vexatious claims (DTI 2001a: 4). This was despite its own commissioned research, which explained the rise largely in economic and labour market terms (the rise in female labour force participation and hence in discrimination cases, growing employment in small enterprises, the decline in manufacturing and the growth in redundancy claims and the decline in union member-ship associated with a more adversarial climate precipitating a rise in unlawful deduction cases) (Burgess et al. 2001). Its most widely orches-trated claim was that 'sixty four per cent of applications to employment tribunals come from employees who have not attempted to resolve the problem directly with their employer in the first instance' (DTI 2001a: 8).

This government's selective misrepresentation of evidence to build its case has been widely noted (Hepple and Morris 2002: 251; Lord McCarthy 2002: col. 1371; Lord Wedderburn 2002: col. 247; TUC 2001; Citizens Advice 2001a; IDS 2002: 2). The 1998 Survey of ET Applications (SETA 98), which stated that '65 per cent of employers and 60 per of applicants said there was no meeting to try to resolve the dispute', emphasized that 'these findings have to be interpreted with some care'. Including 'other attempts' to resolve the dispute internally, it concluded that '37 per cent . . . is probably the most comprehensive indicator of (lack of) dialogue available from this data' (DTI 2002: 24). But it also omitted SETA 98's major other findings that workers rarely use, and are generally ignorant of, the law: 95 per cent of applicants had never made a previous ET application, 54 per cent said they knew 'nothing at all' about the ET system, and a further 35 per cent knew only 'a little'

(DTI 2002: 13). Its policy of deterrence from legal redress also left out what its own research acknowledged is the major *raison d'être* of the tribunal system in Britain, to serve the most vulnerable workers: the mean annual pay of applicants was '£15,000 per annum, not far below average earnings at the time' and '78 per cent of applicants were not members of trade unions or staff associations' (DTI 2002: viii).

The July 2001 consultation paper, prior to the 'reform' of ETs and dispute resolution in the EA 2002, was stated to sit alongside the Leggatt report on the entire tribunal system (Leggatt 2001; DTI 2001a: 5). Yet it ignored the report's findings and recommendations. Published in March 2001, the review of tribunals had expressed concern about the accessibility of the ET system, the quality of advice and the fact that 'cases were becoming progressively more difficult for the unrepresented user' (Leggatt 2001: 282–4). However, the government engaged with none of these issues, emphasizing that its own proposals were 'concerned with good practice, conciliation and a faster and more efficient service for employment tribunal users' and stating merely that there would be 'Government consultation on the Leggatt Review report' (DTI 2001c: 10).

Research on advice and dispute resolution was also disregarded. Genn (1999: 43, 112) had found that over half of workers with workplace problems took advice and communicated with the 'other side' about them, and three-fifths had made contact with 'the other side' *before* obtaining advice compared with three per cent of employers who tried to make contact in order to resolve the problem. The CAB's response to *Routes to Resolution* cited at least 400,000 of 640,000 employment advice enquires in 2000–1 who had been denied one or more of their statutory rights, were largely unaware of them and even when advised on them 'were particularly reluctant to take enforcement action through the employment tribunal system, for fear of losing their job or otherwise being unfairly treated by their employer as a result' (Citizens Advice 2001b: 1). Respondents with employment problems expressed 'a *very low degree of satisfaction* with the advice received from their first point of contact' (Genn 1999: 113; emphasis in original) and once action had been attempted, over half (52 per cent) found no agreement was reached and no formal resolution to the problem was achieved. Similarly, just under half of the respondents to a survey of users of a West Midlands employment advice line resolved their problem (Russell and Eyers 2002: 2).

Despite all the evidence that there was a need to improve advice and simplify access and procedure in the ET system, the government proceeded in the opposite direction. This began with financial deterrence in 2001, and extended to procedural restrictions to submitting ET applications after the EA 2002.

New costs ruling

Initial financial deterrence was enforced with the Employment Tribunal Regulations, 2001. These increased the cost of a pre-hearing review (held if the application is considered weak or might be struck out) from £150 to £500; extended the scope for costs against either party from behaving 'vexatiously, abusively, disruptively or otherwise unreasonably' to 'the bringing or conducting of the proceedings by a party (being) *misconceived*' (Employment Tribunals 2001, Schedule 1, rule 14 (1); emphasis added). The latter is a perilously vague term under which an applicant is now liable to costs. Added to this threat is the enormous increase in the maximum cost which can be levied against either party from £500 to £10,000. These changes were in direct opposition to the Leggatt (2001: 291) report's counsel:

> We would not recommend the introduction of a general costs regime. That would create across the board a powerful disincentive to go to a tribunal.

The TUC, individual unions, the CABs and the Legal Action Group censured the lack of research or consultation prior to the Regulations and underlined the absence of legal aid to cover costs, lack of specialist employment law advice for many applicants, fear that costs could deter well deserving cases and the fact that ETs already had powers to deal with weak cases. Criticism delayed the legislation from April until July 2001, but it was passed under 'negative resolution' procedure, which meant there was no debate or vote in either Houses of Parliament.

The Leggatt review's warning that the costs regime might deter applicants has proved accurate. Among those who made an ET application in 2002–3, the costs regime made 41 per cent of those who withdrew 'more likely' to do so, while it affected 18 per cent of those who privately settled and 24 per cent of ACAS settlements (DTI 2004b: 67). The CAB reports 'an explosive increase in the making of costs threats to applicants – and even to CABs representing them – by employers' lawyers' (Citizens Advice 2004a: 3). The Legal Action Group refers to similar experiences among workers advised by Law Centres, the Free Representation Unit and the Equal Opportunities Commission (LAG 2001: 9, 12–16).

New workplace dispute resolution procedures: simple rules for employers, new hurdles for employees

Following the EA 2002, new Dispute Regulations came into force in October 2004. These apply to all employers, including those employing fewer than 20 employees, and to employees, but not 'workers'. Failure by an employee to comply with the statutory grievance procedure (GP) bars an ET application and mistakes oblige a tribunal to decrease an employee's award by 10 per cent and up to 50 per cent. Conversely, failure by an employer to comply with the dismissal and disciplinary procedures (DDP) obliges an increase in award by 10 per cent and up to 50 per cent – unless there are 'exceptional circumstances'.

The DDPs require either a three-stage 'standard' procedure, or a two-stage 'modified' procedure. The standard DDP requires, first, a statement of grounds for contemplating dismissal or taking disciplinary action and an invitation to attend a meeting; second, a meeting; and third, an appeal stage triggered by employee request, which must be followed by the employer's invitation to a further meeting. The modified DDP, applying only if the employee has already been dismissed for gross misconduct, requires a written statement explaining the grounds, and an appeal stage with an invitation to a meeting. Failure to comply with the statutory procedures by the employer introduces a new form of automatically unfair dismissal. However, the DDPs require only *minimal* procedural standards and a potential downgrading of best-practice (Hepple and Morris 2002: 260). Failure to apply other 'fair procedure' (for example, a company procedure and/or one following the ACAS Code of best practice) will no longer be considered automatically unfair. This is a reversal of case law, which ruled that procedural impropriety meant automatic unfair dismissal. Proving procedural automatic unfair dismissal under the minimal DDPs might be difficult, since the 'meeting' required of it is so vague as to be hard to question by an employee challenging procedural fairness. A likelihood of poorly developed procedure is indicated by WERS 1998, which found that 91 per cent of workplaces had formal grievance procedures but only 30 per cent of these had been activated (Cully et al. 1999: 77). Employers also have a higher estimation of their procedural compliance than workers. In 2003, 84 per cent of employers claimed to have a written disciplinary and grievance procedure compared with 41 per cent of employees who thought this was the case, and 54 per cent of employers thought these had been fully followed compared with 22 per cent of employees (DTI 2004b: xviii).

The new GPs likewise require either a three-stage 'standard' procedure, or a two-stage 'modified' procedure. For the standard one, tribunal claims are barred unless the employee sets out the grievance in writing, sends it to the employer and then waits for 28 days. If Step 1 is completed, the employer must then invite the employee to a meeting, after which there is a possibility of an appeal and a further meeting as the last step in the process. The modified GP applies only when employment has ended, which is likely for most unfair dismissal claims (39 per cent of main jurisdictions in ET applications in 2002–3; ETS 2003) and entails a written statement of the grievance and its basis as Step 1, and a written employer's response in Step 2. However, *both* parties must agree to this procedure, and an employer can refuse, insisting on the standard GP with a meeting, thus deterring employees who regard such a meeting as both distressing and futile. This tactic might be used by employers to prevent ET applications (IDS 2004: 52).

The inequality between the new statutory demands on employers and on employees have been elaborated in academic and parliamentary debate (Hepple and Morris 2002; Lord McCarthy 2002; Lord Wedderburn 2002). Whereas the statutory DDPs are looser than the ACAS Code of Practice, the GPs add new burdens on employees. There is nothing in the legislation to say that the formal procedures have to be *agreed* with workplace representatives (McKay 2001: 332). The TUC pointed out that it is unjustifiable to deny workers their statutory rights or reduce their compensation, for example on equal pay or discrimination, because of procedural flaws, particularly since unrepresented applicants find it hard to judge at what stage they can proceed with a claim (TUC 2001: para. 1.22, 1.31). The former President of the Employment Tribunals (England and Wales), Judge Prophet, remarked on the degradation of being debarred from a tribunal following 'a blatant disregard of his [sic] legal entitlement. Not only is this degrading for the employee, it could well be a denial of his [sic] human rights under Article 6 of the Convention. Incidentally, how does an internal grievance procedure apply to a person who is no longer an employee?' (Joint Committee of Human Rights 2002a, Memorandum: para. 7.) There is the further problem of how a worker is to be protected from a continuation of a grievance during the 28-day wait before a tribunal application is allowed (Lord Wedderburn 2002: cols. 244, 248).

The Disputes Resolution legislation was matched by further Employment Tribunals Regulations, which also came into force on 1 October 2004, and debarred applications unless a new, eight-page ET application form is completed, indicating that the grievance procedures had been followed.[9] They also introduce a 'fixed period of conciliation', altering ACAS's former duty to conciliate for as long as both parties want to continue, to fixed periods during which it is not permissible to start ET hearings. The exceptions are discrimination jurisdictions. Otherwise a 'short conciliation period' of seven weeks covers breach of contract, unlawful deduction of wages, rights to time off and Transfer of Undertakings Regulations and a 'standard conciliation period' of 13 weeks covers other jurisdictions. This introduces a further delay to proceedings. The 2004 ET Regulations also implement the sections of the EA 2002 that broaden the costs regime to a party's representative for reasons of 'conduct' and may include payment in respect of the other party's preparation time, thus further broadening the criteria for costs heightening the adversarial climate.

The government's assertion that this legislation will raise 'the standard of dispute management in the workplace' by 'developing appropriate procedures which both sides can use when problems arise' (DTI 2001a: 14) obscures its chief purpose of introducing barriers to legal enforcement. Those without legal representation are likely to flounder along the way. They are unlikely to be cost-saving, since the procedures are predicted to increase the number and length of disputes, as tribunals deal with procedural verification problems (Hepple and Morris 2002: 257; Colling 2004: 574; Chapman 2004: 9). Chief among these are whether or not the correct grievance and/or dispute procedures have been adhered to before lodging a tribunal claim, making compensation adjustments and disagreements over costs.

The future of employment rights

The hurdles impeding employees' access to a tribunal came under widespread criticism regarding possible contravention of the European Convention on Human Rights (Article 6.1).[10] Despite this potential violation of human rights, the legislation passed the Joint Committee on

---

[9] However, the Employment Appeals Tribunals were already challenging the government's requirements in 2005, overruling tribunal rejections because of inexact completion of the forms as 'unfair' (Barnett 2005a, 2005b).

[10] The memorandum from Judge Prophet (Joint Committee for Human Rights 2002a) argued that the Employment Bill would fetter judicial discretion, and the requirement to fulfil workplace procedures which could lead to exclusion from access to a tribunal in Clause 33 of the EA 2002 could be a denial of

Human Rights' 12th Report in March 2002 as 'legitimate', although it was forced under further scrutiny in the 18th Report the following June, following a submission by Lord Wedderburn and others that the government had provided misleading evidence to justify its policy (Joint Committee of Human Rights 2002a: para. 15, 2002b: para. 23). While it was again just passed, on each occasion, the Joint Committee expressed concerns and reservations, and requested further debate by both Houses of Parliament. Nevertheless, the EA 2002 was rushed through just one month later and received royal assent in July 2002.

It is too soon to assess the consequences of the 2002 Employment Act. It is likely to further disadvantage the unorganized worker and 'put the heaviest burden on the weakest, unsupported applicant' (McCarthy 2002: col. 1370). However, in September 2005, after one year's operation of the legislation, the CBI was still not satisfied with its deterrence effect and demanded an even more stringent costs regime against workers, with more costs awards against 'unsuccessful claimants to send the message that there are adverse consequences to bringing weak claims' and proposing a charge to bring a claim to an ET. At the same time, it called for more leniency towards employers, exhorting ETs to take 'a common-sense approach in applying the new rules to employers' (CBI 2005: 29).

Its imposition of further barriers to workers' access to employment rights in a climate of de-collectivization should sharpen debate about the future regulation of the employment relationship. For some time, organizations such as the CABs, which address individual workers' problems, support the centralization and strengthening of government inspection, information and enforcement institutions, with a 'pro-active Fair Employment Commission' (Burkitt 2001; Citizens Advice 2001b: 3, 2004e). However, the trade union movement has not been sympathetic to this strategy, regarding it as undermining its strategy of collective organization, and remaining wary of state interference in independent trade unionism. Established scholars in the British industrial relations tradition, who have consistently supported collectivism, may be beginning to accommodate these apparent polarizations in suggesting a convergence with continental European practice, with 'Britain [following] the example of most other industrialised countries

---

human rights under Article 6 of the Convention. See also Lord Wedderburn (2002: col. 246).

in developing a comprehensive Labour Inspectorate, monitoring the enforcement of *all* individual employment rights... In short, British trade unions should see a Labour Inspectorate not as a potential rival, but as an essential complement (Brown 2004: 201).

At the same time, I suggest that organizations which support individual workers, such as the CAB and law centres, should be able to supply workers with information on their collective as well as individual rights, such as their rights to pursue union recognition in the ERA 1999 and ERA 2004.

Conclusion

In its first two terms of office, New Labour brought Britain into line with EU Directives with a range of individual employment rights. However, European social policy was forced upon even the reluctant previous Conservative government, and interpretation and implementation by New Labour has been minimalist. Britain remains a strongly neo-liberal state committed to 'competitiveness' through 'flexible' labour laws and a 'flexible' labour force.

Soft law is New Labour's preferred alternative to statutory rights in a period when legal redress has become the key defence for workers in a period of de-collectivization. Contrary to easing access to legal employment rights, as advocated by major reviews of the tribunals system and access to justice (Leggatt 2001; Select Committee on Constitutional Affairs 2004), the government has imposed restrictions. It has ignored research on the ignorance, vulnerability and passivity of workers, criticism of its weak and misleading policy justification, and advice to scrutinize further the human rights compliance of its legal programme. Dismissing the real concerns expressed in its 'consultation' exercises prior to legislation, it introduced severe impediments to an already weak enforcement process. It achieved this through a distinctive, dualist programme – a 'double shuffle' (Hall 2003) – in which a 'modernizing' rhetoric of 'active government' subordinates weak social-democratic concessions to a relentless neo-liberal programme. 'Double-speak' created policies meaning the opposite of what they say. Thus 'Access to Justice' in 1999 meant restrictions to justice, through rationing legal aid and burdening with bureaucratic requirements a precariously funded support infrastructure for vulnerable workers. The 2002 Employment Act sandwiched legislation which obstructs access to ETs between new rights for workers. There has been no serious attempt to revitalize collectivism in the 2004 Employment Relations Act, nor any response to those calling for a Labour Inspectorate and providing a unified enforcement system.

The government's arguments for legal reform have been based on efficiency, fairness and economics. However, new dispute resolution and tribunal regulations are likely to increase the length, complexity, workload and hence costs of the ET system. In the longer term, the impact of raising barriers to social and employment rights increases employment instability and crisis in civil law (Pleasence et al. 2004: 3), contributing to social exclusion and raising welfare and health budgets. There are thus strong arguments that the restrictions to the statutory process are part of an ideological dogma of neo-liberalism. They are likely to exacerbate 'labour markets which are pervaded by insecurity, a restructured workforce and a profoundly hostile legal framework' inherited from the previous administration (Hyman 1997: 314). There are major challenges to the defence of a European 'social dimension'.

5
Flexibility's New Clothes: A Historical Perspective on the Public Discussion in Sweden

Åsa-Karin Engstrand

The European Commission recently introduced the concept of 'flexicurity' as a way of combining European competitiveness with the European social model. In this context, Denmark appears as the role model for flexible labour market policy. This model seems to solve the problem that certain types of employment, such as part-time and fixed-term jobs, considered important for the flexibility of labour markets, also harbour risks of permanent market segmentation. Interestingly, current ideas about flexibility echo discussions in Sweden 50 years ago. Historically, Sweden's public discussion of flexibility has changed, from the 1950s' focus on labour market flexibility and general, rational labour market functioning, through the 1970s' employee flexibility regarding working hours, to the 1990s' flexibility in favour of employers. This shift may have occurred because a managerial perspective took over the flexibility concept from labour and the labour unions. Therefore in Sweden, the concept of freedom of choice has become increasingly attached to the neo-liberal agenda, although it was previously used in trade union rhetoric.

This chapter discusses the history of the flexibility debate in Sweden and its transformation over the years. It questions current assumptions of radical breaks with the past, which often occur in discussions on post-Fordism, the service economy, and so on. As Pollert (1991: xviii) has argued, there is (still) a polarization between 'change' and 'nothing much is happening'. This polarization in the discussion must be overcome because the history of flexibility is one of continuity and change.

Note: The author wishes to thank the National Institute for Working Life for financing this research.

It is also striking how the flexibility concept came to be used as a panacea for all types of labour-related changes – from employment contracts to labour legislation – while discussion of economic policy strategy focused on stability. And the stability policy assumed a flexible labour force from an employer's perspective. The chapter also illustrates cracks in the current managerial discourse. One example of this is the sabbatical year scheme, a discussion that goes back to the 1980s. The chapter ends with a brief discussion on how the flexibility concept might be reclaimed in terms of *recognition*.

Labour market flexibility: the Rehn–Meidner model in the 1950s and 1960s

As early as 1944, LO (Swedish Trade Union Confederation) economist Gösta Rehn (1944) argued for increased working-life flexibility to combat unemployment. To this end, he advocated a three-month holiday for employees, besides the standard length of vacation.[1] This extra vacation would be introduced when employment opportunities were scarce, instead of having firms laying off workers. Moreover, an added benefit could be conferred on society as workers might spend this time in further education rather than on the dole (Rehn 1944: 127). Rehn's proposal essentially criticized the labour market policy of the time and the employment service, which in times of high unemployment did not have work to offer but rather served as a control institution, that is, it just kept track of the unemployed.

At the beginning of the 1950s, Rehn contributed to a report by the LO. It emphasized that 'an important task for the union movement is to create conditions for a flexible, dynamic labour market, which in turn promotes sensible measures of rationalization. This facilitates transfer of labour from areas of unemployment to areas with a labour shortage. So the individual gains a greater amount of freedom' (LO 1951: 72–3).[2]

In the report, raising the standard of living was an important vision. Productivity growth constituted the main foundation for a general rise. Labour mobility, in turn, was a precondition of productivity (LO 1951: 103). The policy in the report became known as the Rehn–Meidner model, named after Rehn and his colleague Rudolf

---

[1] Annual vacation was 14 days at the time.
[2] All translations by the author.

Meidner; Rehn was responsible for financial policy and Meidner for policies with respect to wages and the labour market. The model rested on three pillars: financial policy, wage policy and labour market policy. It was suggested that indirect taxes should be used as an instrument for a tight financial policy. The main elements of wage policy, it was suggested, should be coordinated negotiations and solidaristic wages. This meant a rejection of a wage structure based on the financial strength of different industries; instead, wage policy would subject industries with low productivity to rapid restructuring that could lead to unemployment. An active labour market policy was advocated to handle this problem (cf. Holmlund 2003: 57–8).[3]

It is important to note that the Rehn–Meidner model was not easily implemented in terms of government policies. The ruling Social Democrats assumed a negative attitude to these 'daring' methods; Prime Minister Tage Erlander was sceptical of the LO analysis unit and asked in 1950, 'What is wrong with the boys at the LO?' (Ekdahl 2003: 16). Rehn was labelled as 'stubborn and doctrinaire', while the Rehn–Meidner team was characterized as 'pure wreckers'. But a decade later the Rehn–Meidner model was accepted.

Flexibility, understood as mobility in the labour market, became a key part of (or the very basis for) the Rehn–Meidner model. Mobility, as a goal, turned out to be a cornerstone of active labour market policy in the ensuing years. Because rationalization in the agricultural sector, as well as in trade and industry, demanded a flexible labour force, active labour market policy became directed toward retraining and geographic mobility. The employment principle continued to be more important than the cash allowance principle (Wadensjö 1979: 103).

As indicated elsewhere (Engstrand 2003), some politicians questioned the mobility policy, but it took a while before this alternative discourse had an impact in the political arena and was turned into policies for regional development. This new agenda emphasized the importance of jobs moving to people, instead of moving people to jobs. Awareness of the individual employee and his/her opinions was growing and the mobility policy was regarded as causing negative social consequences. Accordingly, the flexibility discussion of the 1970s, which was focused

---

[3] The model is predominantly known as the Rehn-Meidner model. But Meidner emphasized that this name is misleading. He argued that the name gives the impression that he and Rehn worked as a team, which, he claimed, was not the case. Meidner stated that they, in fact, disagreed on several issues (Meidner 2003: 218). Economist Holmlund (2003: 57) prefers to call the model a *programme*.

on reduced working time, should be seen in the light of the previous mobility policy and its perceived effects. There was a shift toward flexibility on employees' terms and conditions, such as reduced working hours.

Flexibility for the individual employee in the 1970s

In 1962, Rehn became director of the OECD labour market division in Paris. From there, he could propagate active labour market policy and his ideas of increased working-life flexibility, which were linked to freedom for the individual. Flexibility continued to be discussed in the OECD in the early 1970s in terms of more flexible work schedules, with a clear emphasis on social considerations (see, for example, OECD 1970). Evans (1973: 11) has put it as follows:

> Preoccupation with [new and more flexible forms of working time] fits well into the general trend of the work of OECD, which is increasingly concerned with stimulating policies designed to improve the quality of life as opposed to purely quantitative economic growth.

The individual employee perspective was exemplified in the 1968 official investigation on working-time reduction, which accounted for employees' wishes: 'The committee concluded that employees are prepared to choose longer leisure at the expense of a stronger wage increase' (SOU 1968: 109). Fewer work hours, which had previously been a safety issue, had now become an option for the individual; improvement in the standard of living could mean either higher income or more leisure time (SOU 1968: 184).

Rehn (1975, 1985) continued to develop his ideas on the individual's need for flexibility in the mid-1970s. He stated that it was important to start by asking what the people wanted: how did they want to divide their time between work and leisure and what preferences did they have in terms of leisure and increased income? The premise was that *life working time* was a better concept than *annual working time*. But even if a policy could be based on individuals' average needs concerning life working time, this would not satisfy each individual's needs. Rehn saw only one solution to this problem: the individual himself/herself should decide, because the old patriarchal system (in which society or employers decided for employees) was over. The time had come for the individual citizen 'to come of age' (Rehn 1975: 73).

To support this notion, Rehn proposed general income insurance with individual drawing rights. The idea was to develop a comprehensive system for financing all periods of voluntary or age-related non-work, including study, holidays, childcare, sabbaticals, temporary retirement and old-age retirement. It was suggested that the system should be financed by employers (by fees) and the individual employee (by taxes). The proposal would have labour market implications by increasing the individual's ability to escape from an unsatisfactory job situation. In essence, the general income insurance system should be used for education or for changing jobs without the need for permission (Rehn 1975: 76):

> I think that we must counter the tendency toward an over-stable society in which the individual does not dare to move, because so much of his security and safety hinges on his immobility. While we build security, we must give people opportunities to break free from the security attachment to a particular workplace.

Rehn went on to say that, luckily enough, there were tendencies toward freedom and flexibility. The pity was that this freedom was distributed unevenly. The author also discussed a tendency in post-industrial society toward freer and more 'undisciplined behaviour' from certain groups. Therefore society had two choices: restore order or accommodate this tendency by organizing society and companies in such a way that freedom of variation and flexibility became natural elements. Rehn argued that it was quite peculiar that industrial democracy, as a notion, had come to comprise everything except any thought of co-determination of working hours' duration and placement.

Besides proposing a more comprehensive system of drawing rights, Rehn also discussed flexible working hours, or flexitime. These ideas emanated from his time at the OECD where the notion of flexibility had been discussed. Rehn referred to more advanced countries in this respect than Sweden, for example, Germany, Switzerland and France, which had found that increased flexibility in all areas was advantageous for the individual and for the company; in industry as well as in office work-places. To maintain the balance in the labour market, it was important to stimulate employees to vary the labour supply freely so that the market could match labour demand in time and place. If this worked, 'the less mobile workforce would be spared the tough demands of adjustment, which is currently the case' (Rehn 1975: 79).

The part-time issue: employer or employee flexibility?

Rehn was not the only one discussing flexibility in the 1970s. During this period, two diverging opinions existed in discussions on part-time work; one emphasized the right to part-time work and the other the right to full-time work. Here we see flexibility diverge: individuals' right to flexibility on the one hand and employers' demand for flexibility on the other.

The 1976 public investigation into family support emphasized the individual's needs and preferences during various life phases, in that work and leisure time needed to be flexible. This investigation prompted a new type of wage compensation for parents who reduced their working hours to six hours per day (SOU 1975: 12, 62). On a similar note, it is important to bear in mind that parental leave was then much shorter than it is today. In 1974, parental leave was six months, with benefits corresponding to 90 per cent of regular income (up to a ceiling); today it is 13 months with benefits a maximum 80 per cent of the regular income.[4]

Another public investigation examined part-time work as a whole and was highly critical of its large quantity. The investigation concluded that women working part-time actually wished to work full-time, although the women surveyed had indicated that they wished to work less than full-time (SOU 1976: 65).

At that time, the Commercial Employees' Union identified a conundrum: women needed part-time work but at the same time wished that employers would offer them full-time work. In the union's eyes, the problems were on the demand side and came down to business opening hours. Women's interests were in conflict: on the one hand, a growing number of women needed to do their shopping after work; on the other hand, women in the retail industry did not want long working days (Jonsson 2004: 15–16).

One researcher, who argued that several institutional changes had promoted the development of part-time work, provided a contrary interpretation. These changes included the introduction of individual taxation in 1971, the partial pension reform of 1976 and the 1979 legislation

---

[4] An important factor is that many employers pay their employees additional benefit to compensate for the loss of wages because the sickness benefit is limited to a fixed amount. This means that employees may receive 90 per cent of their regular income if they work for the right employer.

that shortened working hours for parents with children under the age of eight (Pettersson 1981).

In other words, the part-time issue could be viewed from two sides: as flexibility for the employees, or flexibility for the employers. Håkansson and Isidorsson (1999: 25) differentiate between employee-determined part-time work and employer-determined part-time work. This perspective signifies the importance of not categorizing women or flexibility as homogeneous entities. Women may use flexibility or be used flexibly in the labour market, depending on where they work.

A 1979 public investigation emphasized that the concept of flexible working time had obtained a wider meaning during the past few years. Flexible working time no longer concerned only certain days of a given week, but work and leisure time could be mixed in many different ways over longer periods. The transition toward a more flexible working life demanded recurring education, childcare periods and so forth. The Swedish Employers' Association (SAF) proposed that the labour market parties should agree on adjusting the length of working time in tune with economic cycles. But the LO and the Federation of Salaried Employees in Industry and Services (PTK) rejected this proposal; both contended that an active business policy should drive business cycle changes. The public investigation also indicated that current research aimed to find models for greater flexibility in working life throughout the life cycle, and furthermore, referred to a discussion on working-life flexibility in the United States (SOU 1979: 46).

Hence, an employee perspective concerning flexibility came into focus during the 1970s. This was reflected not only in the views on reduced working time but in a general anti-authoritarian atmosphere. Workers' positions were strengthened with respect to, for example, work environment and employment protection. There was also a change of perspective regarding labour market policy because it was perceived to have negative implications. Consequently, subsidies to firms to preserve or increase employment expanded during the 1970s. Job security in the local labour market or in the company replaced security in the labour market as a whole. The Rehn–Meidner model ceased to be the guiding star for labour market policy and general economic policy (Erixon 1994: 87).

Interestingly, Rehn played a part in the early discussion on mobility in the labour market *and* in the more employee-oriented discussion during the 1970s. Also Meidner continued to discuss flexibility in the 1980s, to which we now turn.

Labour market flexibility and rigidity in the 1980s

In 1984, Anna Hedborg at LO, and Meidner, then at the Centre for Working Life, argued that the trend in the Swedish labour market was toward greater rigidity and increased segmentation. They saw this as an 'erosion of flexibility' (Hedborg and Meidner 1984: 88–9).

In 1986, the OECD argued that the traditional mechanisms for achieving the economic and social goals of the labour market appeared to have been functioning less well over the last decade or so than in the 1950s and 1960s. Wage adjustment was one important means of adapting to structural change and providing signals and incentives for the reallocation of labour. Manpower and social programmes needed to be 'substantially reviewed and stepped up' if they were to play effectively 'their traditional role of providing not only social protection, but also of helping to construct a framework within which individuals will accept rather than resist change' (OECD 1986: 7–8).

A sabbatical year to promote flexibility

In 1986, mobility was once again discussed when Hedborg and Meidner proposed a sabbatical year to which everyone would be entitled. The idea was that the social insurance system would fund it. The two authors argued:

> If mobility and adaptation ability should continue to be typical characteristics in the Swedish economy, increasing demands are arising on changes combined with security. Mobility must be positive and voluntary. (Hedborg and Meidner 1986: 41)

They stressed that a general work schedule reduction would cause a blanket decrease in demand. Consequently, a decline in production would be forced at a stage where it could be higher. Crucially, a boom might be prevented where it might occur. From another standpoint, a more flexible form of reduced working time might well mitigate any decline in production (Hedborg and Meidner 1986: 39). The sabbatical year would be organized through a distributive system, which meant that one year's fees would be used to cover another year's expenses, similar to the pension system. Or, one could fund others' leave and vice versa (Hedborg and Meidner 1986: 46–7). There were only three necessary limitations: (i) the period of leave had to be longer than six months; (ii) the sabbatical year should not be a prolongation of parental leave; if so gender equality would be jeopardized (and therefore parents with young children were not eligible); and (iii) the employee must have worked for at least ten years (Hedborg and Meidner 1986: 41–2). However, according to Standing (1988: 134), Meidner considered his proposal to be closely related to the parental leave scheme of the time, claiming 'the next priority is a six-hour day at full pay for one parent for the first seven years of his or her child's life'.

Hedborg and Meidner referred to sabbatical year proposals in Germany, which resembled those in Sweden. In their proposal for Sweden, however, quality of life and free choice for the individual were primary, followed by the secondary issues of unemployment and job-sharing. In the United States as well, a few proponents had criticized the linear life plan and proposed forms of long-term leave (Hedborg and Meidner 1986: 33–4).

In 1988, Standing (1988: 93) discussed wage flexibility and labour market flexibility in Sweden and concluded that 'employment is extensively regulated in Sweden'. But functional flexibility within companies had grown with rationalization, automation and experimental methods of work reorganization. Standing also contended that the employment principle had been abandoned in favour of the cash allowance principle. He argued that a growing proportion of the adult population had to rely on cash support from the state rather than on regular, temporary or even relief work (Standing 1988: 122). However, he also drew the conclusion that despite the abandonment of the employment principle, the Swedish labour market had proven to be relatively flexible. The most impressive indication of this was that, since the early 1970s, Sweden had achieved a remarkable structural adjustment without a period of mass unemployment (Standing 1988: 146–7). Swedish economist Erixon (1994: 89) argued that the low unemployment of the 1980s was due to an undervalued krona and an expansive financial policy, not a comprehensive labour market policy.

Meanwhile, in the UK...

In the early 1980s, the flexibility discussion in the UK focused on employers' needs for flexibility. In 1984, organization researcher Charles Handy wrote about the 'organisation revolution' and John Atkinson (1984) developed Handy's ideas, arguing that firms looked for three types of flexibility: functional, numerical and financial. The reasons for this strategy were the financial situation and the lack of competitiveness in the UK, at the same time as high unemployment and a weakened union movement made it easier to achieve a flexible labour market

(Atkinson 1984: 28). Handy later developed his ideas of a flexible labour force in his book *The Age of Unreason* (Handy 1989).

Whiteside (2000: 120–1) argues that flexibility in the UK has been positioned as a diametric opposite to 'old Labour', the collective expression of working class resistance to capitalist exploitation. Official promotion of labour market flexibilities has encountered little opposition, except from academics addressing the darker side in terms of job insecurity, poverty and social consequences.

Concurrently, a Swedish business magazine maintained that there was a clear dividing line between countries such as the US and the UK – both of which advocated increasing labour market flexibility such as greater wage differences – and Sweden, which instead was said to call for an active government labour market policy (*Veckans Affärer*, 17 May 1984). In 1988, another Swedish business newspaper commented on the strikes in the UK, which it claimed to be due to 'man's natural reluctance to and fear of change' (*Dagens Industri*, 12 February 1988). The workers also rejected companies' demands for flexibility, which were defined as 'the employer's natural instinct to use their resources in an optimal way'.

Thus the notion of flexibility for the employer was well under way in the UK discussion before its appearance in Sweden. But the discussion on the importance of a stable economic policy came first.

Economic theory: focusing on stability

As briefly mentioned earlier, it is probably safe to say that the Rehn–Meidner model was gradually abandoned during the 1970s in terms of financial policy and mobility. Thus, the 1970s and the early 1980s saw a mixture of Keynesian policy and classic austerity policy during the recessions of that time. In 1981, the non-socialist government devalued the krona; the Social Democratic government also chose this strategy after its election in 1982. The monetary devaluations in the early 1980s, combined with a strong dollar and an international boom, led to a profit boom for Swedish export industry. The overheated economy was further fuelled when the credit market was deregulated during the latter half of the 1980s, causing a rise in inflation (Erixon 2003: 120–1).

In this climate, the Centre for Business and Policy Studies (SNS) published a book called *Sweden: the Road to Stability*. The economists discussed interventionism (Keynesianism) and non-interventionism and came to the conclusion that 'the interventionist view is well provided for in the Swedish economic-political discussion' (Söderström 1985: 10–11). Accordingly, the economists chose a 'critical examination of the economic policy with non-interventionist features'.

The conclusion was that a global approach was needed to bridge the political and economic conditions, which would build on the concept of stabilization. Here the economists referred to a research tradition that had lain dormant since the Keynesian revolution of the 1930s (Söderström 1985: 45). Tax-financed expenditure was considered important and the proposal included reductions in government spending; restricted transfers; loans instead of allowances; changes in the pension system; lower pensions; and increased financing of public activities through contributions rather than taxes (Söderström 1985: 65–6). Deregulation of currency control and the credit market were two other vital components (Söderström 1985: 125–7).

The economists were convinced that a norm-based policy, aimed at price stability, was more likely to secure full employment in the long run than an interventionist accommodation policy. The state's primary task should be to create a stable framework for the activities of households, companies and organizations (Söderström 1985: 123).

In the early 1990s, the economic theory advocated by SNS economists gained ground. Erixon (2001: 35) has contended that the Keynesian policy of full employment was finally abandoned in Sweden during the early 1990s when the Social Democratic government bowed to criticism of its accommodating economic policy. The new policy was intended to please international capital markets and to reduce inflationary expectations in labour markets. The ruling Social Democrats could no longer devalue the krona, and the government considered using incomes policy to control prices and wages.

The non-socialist government's *only-way* policy in 1991–4 was a continuation of the Social Democrats' economic policy. Sweden was entering the EEC and politicians wanted to adapt economic policy to the rules of convergence stipulated in the Maastricht Treaty of 1991. But a growing budget deficit brought on a severe currency crisis. The defence of the krona failed, and Sweden abandoned its system of fixed exchange rates in November 1992. According to Erixon (2003: 126–7), the non-socialistic government's only-way policy resembled the Rehn–Meidner model through its prioritization of labour market policy and reluctance toward income policy. After the Social Democrats regained power in 1994, they pursued a financial austerity programme that Erixon has described as 'unmatched' among OECD countries. In a situation with mass unemployment, the party previously advocating Keynesianism

now implemented a very restrictive financial policy and simply abandoned the Keynesian model and the Rehn–Meidner model (Erixon
2001: 38). With this economic policy picture in mind, the next section
examines how the flexibility discussion developed during the 1990s
and 2000s.

Flexibility for the employer: a new agenda in the 1990s

In the early 1990s, SAF initiated a project aimed at addressing firms'
needs for flexibility as regards forms of employment and working hours.
A business economist was consulted to write about flexibility inside
firms. SAF's managing director stated that effective organizations must
be characterized by flexibility. A flexible workforce was essential, and the
labour market had to be allowed to function as a market in which agreements on forms of employment and working hours could be reached to
match the needs of firms and individuals (SAF 1992: Foreword).

The SAF book concluded that flexibility was already a feature char-
acterizing efficient organizations. Charles Handy was cited and it was
concluded that fast, flexible action was needed on the part of firms
and organizations in this turbulent world (SAF 1992: 8). Modern firms
strove to organize their businesses in networks and 'post-hierarchical
cluster organizations', which contributed to the firms' increased flexibility. Important expressions in this discourse were 'adaptation to the
situation', 'smoothness', 'mobility', 'diversity' and 'ability to change'
(SAF 1992: 25–6). The text was normative, stating how it was and how
it must be. The book concluded with a commentary that, since firms
must be able to adjust quickly to market demands for efficiency and
productivity, the ability to grow and to downsize was a prerequisite
for their survival. In addition, the labour market must be allowed to
function as 'a market that strives for mobility' (SAF 1992: 29).

The European Commission as well as the OECD propagated flexibility at this time. In 1993, the Commission's Economic and Social
Committee presented a white paper on growth, competitiveness and
employment, which stated that the labour market's inflexibility was
largely responsible for Europe's structural unemployment. Discussions
on external flexibility led to proposals concerning geographic mobility,
access to vocational training and adjustment of labour market and taxation rules (European Commission 1993). Almost simultaneously, the
OECD (1994) argued that lack of flexibility and adaptability led to
growing structural unemployment.

The Swedish 1996 public investigation on working hours argued that issues concerning working time were to be regulated in agreements between the social partners. However, at the same time the investigation concluded that 'the employee's possibilities of influencing the determination of his or her working time should be considered' (SOU 1996: 30). The investigation emphasized that their assignment had not been 'to propose a general reduction of working hours'. The investigation had come to the conclusion that, on the basis of theoretical research, it was not possible to advocate a general reduction of working hours with the aim of reducing unemployment (SOU 1996: 32). Thus, the individual employees were dependent on unions successfully negotiating with employers in respect of this kind of flexibility. Since unemployment was high at the time and the strength of employees relative to employers had thus been weakened, the individual employee's wishes could not easily be fulfilled.

At this point, the flexibility discussion in the Swedish media referred increasingly to international best practices. Swedish economists linked flexibility in the labour market to the problem of locked minimum wages, which were assumed to lead to unemployment. The demand for adaptability focused primarily on manual labourers with little education and relatively low wages. The United States now appeared as the economists' role model (*Dagens Nyheter*, 18 February 1994). The Employers' Association publication *SAF-tidningen* (22 August 1997) referred to flexibility and adaptation as lodestars for the economic policies in Ireland and the UK. Labour market deregulation was taken as an illustrative example. A business magazine described the UK as a 'role model in a Europe of stagnation'. The choice was said to be between the UK model with its existing social tensions and growth and the continental model with its increasing social tensions and stagnation. The concept of flexibility was, in this respect, discussed in relation to Thatcher's deregulations and low taxes (*Affärsvärlden*, 12 February 1997).

Flexible employment contracts and temporary work agencies

The discussion in the Swedish media also focused on a dramatic shift from permanent employment toward contingent contract work and the importance of temporary work agencies in promoting flexibility. Swedish research on the topic has generally treated the trend as regards employment contracts in terms of the distinction between core and periphery, predominantly using Atkinson's core/periphery model as the starting point (Engstrand 2006).

In the media, above all two kinds of temporary employment were discussed: project employment and on-call employment. Project employment was primarily discussed in the business media, while the LO called attention to the problems of on-call employment. The business press and the Employers' Association were the most eager proponents of radical changes. The Swedish labour market was characterized as rigid and regulated. Permanent employment was not regarded as a matter of course in the future. On the contrary, short-term jobs, part-time, project employment and flexible working time were becoming increasingly common (Engstrand 2006).

The discussion on temporary work agencies promoting flexibility may be seen in a larger context, where bureaucracy represents rigidity and the market (that is, private employment agencies) stands for flexibility. In 1993, Sweden decided to terminate ILO convention number 96, which regulates private employment agencies. Several years before this, the Employers' Association tried to abolish the employment agencies' monopoly (SOU 1992: 79).

A public investigation in 1997 of temporary work agencies concluded that the previous standardized mass production seemed to be developing toward increasing variation in product design and even toward tailor-made solutions to individual customers' demands. In other words, new employment forms developed out of a need for increased labour market flexibility. The investigation concluded that the required flexibility should not be opposed, but rather be focused on new methods for organizing work, such as varying working hours during the year and shifting between periods of paid work and education (SOU 1997: 25).

The business press regarded temporary work agencies as 'a response to their customers' or the market's demand for flexibility' (*Finanstidningen*, 15 October 1996; *Veckans Affärer*, 26 October 1998). Companies demanded flexibility and achieved competitiveness by retaining a small core of strategic people and hiring staff as needed (*Finanstidningen*, 5 February 1999). According to the business press, the temporary work agencies' rapid expansion was due to requests by large firms to hire non-strategic personnel rather than employing them, which in turn led to increased flexibility for these organizations (*Dagens Industri*, 29 September 1999). According to an economist, flexibility in the labour market increased after the deregulation of the employment service monopoly (*Nyhetsbyrån Direkt*, 19 December 2000; 15 February 2002). The vice-president of one of the temporary work agencies expressed another point of view, explaining that flexibility in the labour market was the very reason for the success of these agencies, as many people preferred not to work at one place but instead wanted greater personal freedom to influence their own work situation (*Affärsvärlden,* 25 September 2002).

The downside of flexibility

In Sweden, the LO's ambivalent attitude to the concept was reflected in the union magazine, *LO-Tidningen*, which called for an 'unprejudiced attitude to a flexible labour market' and explained that the 'employers' view of the flexible labour market was inherently false'. Still, in 1996, a few union representatives admitted that flexibility did have positive effects. They wanted to reclaim some of the positive features of flexibility connected to the concept of 'good work'. But at this point in time flexibility had increasingly negative connotations. *LO-Tidningen* had headlines such as 'Few choices in the flexible labour market' and 'Flexible times harder for women'. LO economist Dan Andersson concluded in 2001 that flexibility for the individual was freedom of choice coupled to trust in the social welfare system. This was no new insight for the labour movement, but it had been forgotten during the crisis of the 1990s (Winlund and Sturesson, forthcoming).

Swedish working life researchers now began to pay attention to the negative consequences of flexible working lives, such as the right of the employer to dictate workplace flexibility, while the individual had to adapt to the employer's directives. People wore themselves out because flexibility had become an issue of creating advantages for production rather than for the individual (Winlund and Sturesson, forthcoming).

Several researchers have identified health problems caused by companies' flexibility policies and they have questioned the common perception that labour law regulation caused rigidity (Aronsson 1999). Grönlund (2004) has argued that labour legislation is not a hindrance for flexibility because it can be bypassed – to mutual satisfaction – through local agreements. Her study does not verify the argument that flexible firms tend to increase temporary employment, because firms attempt to achieve flexibility in other ways as well, such as work rotation and overtime. Another problematic issue is the direct connection between flexibility and mobility. Isidorsson (2001: 300–1) has emphasized that flexibility strategies can in effect increase employment security because employees need to be multi-skilled and thus require in-house training. This investment in employees makes employers reluctant to dismiss personnel and as a consequence mobility will decrease. Flexibility in terms of mobility is thus only intended for specific groups in the firm.

Reclaiming flexibility for the individual employee

The sabbatical year revisited

During the 1990s, the sabbatical-year discussion resumed, this time as a way of decreasing unemployment. The Green Party proposed a sabbatical year, referring to the Danish model. In 1996, Margareta Winberg, the labour minister, presented a proposal for a sabbatical year. She rejected the Danish model and instead wanted to connect it with the old Hedborg–Meidner proposal. Therefore the government introduced a trial sabbatical year in the municipality of Trelleborg. In this model, employees could take leave with full unemployment insurance cover, on condition that long-term unemployed individuals filled the vacant positions.

The sabbatical year proposition was met with scepticism, with TCO (the Swedish Confederation of Professional Employees) and LO contending that a sabbatical year as in the Danish model would be too expensive for many citizens (*T T Nyhetsbanken*, 17 September 1996). The government also faced internal criticism of the idea, among others from the minister of finance who argued that a reform with state-financed reduced working hours was 'dangerous' (*T T Nyhetsbanken*, 26 September 1996). A spokesperson for the working-time committee also rejected the Danish variant (*Nyhetsbyrån Direkt*, 30 September 1996). A business magazine stated that 'to reduce work schedules and thus decrease the labour supply was against government policy' (*Affärsvärlden*, 2 October 1996).

The Green Party accused the government of delaying the sabbatical year (Miljöpartiet 1999), but in 2000 it reached an agreement with the government to investigate the advantages and disadvantages of a comprehensive reform. This was in effect a concession from the minority Social Democratic government that relied on the Green Party to pass its budget (*T T Nyhetsbanken*, 13 December 2000). After much discussion, the sabbatical year was introduced throughout Sweden in 2005 (Government Bill 2004/05).

Despite the fact that the final form became rather watered down (for example, the payment was reduced to 85 per cent of the daily allowance from the unemployment insurance fund, only limited numbers of sabbaticals were granted and these were at the employer's discretion), the discussion was quite heated. It evolved around the theme that individuals should work more, not less, and that the former employment strategy had been abandoned (*Dagens Nyheter*, 25 August 2004). The European Commission 'warned' Sweden that inauguration of the sabbatical year and shorter working hours risked reducing labour supply. A business magazine exclaimed 'Protect us from the sabbatical year!' (*Dagens Industri*, 16 January 2004).

Many union representatives were critical of the concept and a manager at the Swedish Academics' Central Organisation (SACO) called it 'political foolishness', as the decision was 'sending the wrong signals' and 'work was the primary act of love in modern society' (*Svenska Dagbladet* and *Dagens Nyheter*, 4 March 2004). SACO's chairman argued that the sabbatical year was an 'immoral system' (*Dagens Nyheter*, 10 April 2005). Economists called it 'populism' (*TT Nyhetsbanken*, 21 September 2004). The opposition parties claimed that through the sabbatical year the government had introduced 'a right for the healthy to live on allowances'. At the same time, however, the Liberal Party regarded increased flexibility and empowerment as answers to a demanding working-life situation (*Dagens Nyheter*, 25 August 2004).

Despite what we might think of the sabbatical year, it is interesting to note that the discussion during the 1990s and 2000s focused on the employment principle and a disciplinary perspective, both of which have a long history. The focus was on the individual, but from a moral rather than a distributive perspective, which has its roots in the late nineteenth and early twentieth century. During the 1990s, scarcity and unemployment became more of an individual problem, whereby individuals should be activated and rehabilitated to adjust to the system rather than the other way around. The morals and work ethics of the unemployed and the generous welfare system were increasingly questioned (Junestav 2004: 248). Thus, despite the talk about new times for companies and about the need for flexibility, old views on work and wage earners began to surface.[5]

Flexicurity: closing the circle?

In 2001, the European Commission (EU 2006) launched the concept of *flexicurity*. The rapid growth of global trade and of a global workforce, increasing shifts in the traditional division of labour, the growing importance of human capital, and the trend toward the knowledge society had raised awareness of the need for a common 'European social model'. Flexicurity was considered a way of addressing the question of 'how European competitiveness and the European social model' could

---

[5] This, as is often the case, is an international tendency with popular slogans such as 'welfare to work', 'active line' and 'work, work, work' (van Oorschot 2004).

'be maintained'. The approach was seen as a comprehensive political strategy of coordinated measures to promote (i) flexibility in the labour market and modernization of work organization and labour relations; and (ii) job security and social protection, taking account of vulnerable, disadvantaged groups in the labour market.

The Danish approach was used as a reference, based on the three pillars of low protection from dismissal, wide access to relatively generous unemployment benefits and an active labour market policy. A strong focus was also put on 'activation' and 're-integration' (EU 2006). The Netherlands was also given as an example, in particular the Flexibility and Security Act of 1999, which facilitated the conclusion of fixed-term contracts. According to van Oorschot (2004), Dutch flexicurity policies addressed the three policy areas of part-time work, social security and labour legislation. An increase in part-time work and flex-work was an indication of job insecurity. Accordingly, policies aimed at improving social protection of flex-workers, that is, those holding flex-jobs with no permanent contract (van Oorschot 2004: 16).

The Swedish media did not focus on the Dutch flexicurity model, but instead followed the Danish variant. It could be mentioned that, in connection with this, a business newspaper article discussed the Rehn–Meidner model and its emphasis on mobility. In fact, the first lines in the article resemble Rehn's ideas in the mid-1970s: 'Mobility in the Swedish labour market is too low. Too many people stay in jobs that they do not like, rather than moving on to workplaces where they could showcase their skills' (*Dagens Industri*, 4 March 2006).

After this brief look at the flexicurity concept, it seems reasonable to conclude that some of the ideas of the Rehn–Meidner model linger on. But for the present the concept of flexicurity is discussed in another economic-political environment.

So far in the 2000s, a norm policy (aimed primarily at stability) has characterized financial policy. Consequently, inflation must not exceed two per cent, while the state has a ceiling on its expenditure. In the middle of the renewed flexibility discussion, stability has come to replace full employment as a goal for financial policy (*LO-tidningen*, 28 January 2005). The concept of flexicurity appears as a way of mitigating two seemingly opposing interests, flexibility and security, within a framework of economic stability. One might get the impression that flexibility is solely an issue for employers and that employees are mainly interested in security rather than flexibility.

Conclusion: toward recognition of the individual employee

This historical perspective illustrates that the meaning of flexibility has changed over the years, depending on the balance of power of employer and employees. During the 1950s and the 1960s, much emphasis was placed on individuals' geographic and occupational mobility for the labour market to function rationally during rapid economic restructuring. In line with the Rehn–Meidner model, mobility was to be backed by active labour market policies. As these policies were associated with certain problems, they came into question during the late 1960s and the 1970s. In the following years, an employee perspective came to the forefront with respect to the flexibility discussion. Several legislative acts were passed to support flexibility for the benefit of the individual employee, such as the reduced working time scheme in 1971 and 1973, the parental benefit programme of 1974 (and its extension over the years), the part-time pension programme in 1975, and the programme for parental rights to part-time work in 1979.

During the 1990s, employee flexibility was contested in favour of an employer perspective. The new agenda seemed to stress individualism but it was perhaps the other way around, that is, the individual must conform to market forces. The current discussion is characterized by a stress on the need that employees be ready to adapt to economic changes produced by (global) market competition. When individual employee flexibility proposals, such as the recurrent sabbatical year, are brought up, they are dismissed with old work ethic arguments.

This chapter shows that the flexibility concept has had many different meanings. Employees thus have a chance to reclaim the concept, but this requires what could be called a *politics of recognition*, that is, policies (re)introducing the common humanity of various groups and the equal worth of each citizen (Lister 2001: 100). It would mean taking Rehn's view of flexibility one step further and contesting the contemporary market-monopolized conceptions of flexibility. The crucial idea would be to recognize people as *subjects* or agents in policy-making and implementation, as opposed to *objects* of policy (cf. Lister 2001: 101).

Moreover, this perspective requires resources because redistribution goes hand in hand with recognition, for example when it comes to the design of labour market policy. Denmark is hailed as a role model regarding flexibility and flexicurity, but the country also spends more money on active labour market policies than most other countries in Europe. The market will probably always pursue its own flexibility models, in line with the fundamental principles of capitalism. But politics should refrain from reproducing the market's interpretation of flexibility and formulate its own interpretation. Today's lack of confidence among unions, public institutions and government in producing their own interpretation is far more dangerous than the flexibility concept itself.

6

Large Corporations and the Emergence of a Flexible Economic System: Some Recent Developments in the UK

Stephen Ackroyd

Discussion of flexibility by social scientists involves analysis at different levels: the individual, the organizational and that of the socio-economic system. Above the individual it is conventional to consider relationships at the level of the work group (in which case flexible work groups or manning systems are examined) or the level of the organization (where the different designs for the flexible firm and the extent of their adoption are analysed) or the labour market or societal level (where, for example, the type of jobs on offer in the economy as a whole and the responses to them are considered). Of course, discussions at these different levels are important; but at some point we have to consider the interconnections between them. Thus, although this chapter is mainly concerned with flexibility at the highest level, and will consider the emergence of a flexible economic system in the UK, it is recognized that this development rests on considerable adaptation at other levels. The relationship between these levels is not straightforward, however, and there are some unexpected conjunctures. Using Dan Jonsson's analysis in this volume (see Chapter 3), the achievement of a flexible economic system of the kind seen in the UK is at the cost of considerable instability for some firms and many work groups and individuals.

In its beginnings, managerial thinking was focussed on the question of how to obtain more work from employees, and the emphasis in

Note: Thanks are due to the following people for comments on an earlier draft of this chapter: Grahame Thompson, Jan Ch. Karlsson, Bengt Furåker and Kristina Håkansson. Thanks are also due to Paul Thompson and Stephen Procter who have allowed me to rework jointly produced material for this publication.

practice was on job design. Next, knowledge about the way firms are organized and function (as in the traditional orientation of organization theory) came to the fore. It was assumed that the point of organizational design was to render the organization more effectively controlled and directed by managers, and this usually meant more centralization. The end point of this logic of development was the very large firm which undertook all necessary functions for itself under the direction of a centralized management, whose activities and affairs were strongly interlinked with government, which was also bureaucratized. Following the lead of French regulationist writing, this type of socio-economic system is often called 'Fordism' today (Aglietta 1979; Boyer 1988; Peck and Tickell 1994). Another idea for the society based on large-scale organizations, however, coined about the same time but with very different characteristics, is 'corporatism' (Pahl and Winkler 1974; Schmitter and Lembruch 1979). The idea of corporatism includes the implication that the socio-economic system 'incorporates' other collective actors than business, such as the state and the labour interest; but, unlike Fordism, realizing corporatism is the result of deliberate policy by governments. Some countries, including the UK, have failed to approximate either fully developed Fordism or corporatism. However, for all their differences, both Fordism and corporatism suggest a trajectory of development towards a society dominated by large-scale organizations. The sequence is crudely depicted in Table 6.1.

For reasons that will be discussed in this chapter, both the UK and the USA have moved decisively away from the expected path of

Table 6.1 A typology of organized phenomena

'Level' of organized phenomena	Intra-firm organizing (organization behaviour)	Constitution of organization (organization theory)	Socio-economic systems (inter-organizational systems)
Organizational control	Work design Taylorism (1)	Large-scale organizations Fordism (3)	Societal Fordism, or corporate/bureaucratic society (5)
Organizational flexibility	Flexible working (2)	Flexible firms (4)	Flexible economic systems (networks) across industries (6)

development. A switch of track has taken place. One argument which is becoming increasingly authoritative suggests that there is an alternative logic to that underlying the development of the society based on control. This is the development of an economic system based on organizational flexibility. Thus, in parallel with the trajectory towards large organizations and developed regulatory systems, there has been the emergence of an alternative, more flexible mode of organizing and socio-economic configuration. This has developed, somewhat unevenly, initially in the interstices, as it were, of the system based on direct control. At the level of the workgroup, more adaptiveness was sought from employees and/or more autonomy was allowed them in arranging their own work (within specified parameters). At the level of the organization there is much local initiative allowed in work organization and, at the level of the socio-economic system, all centralized command centres supposedly disappear. There are apparently fewer command positions and less direction from the centre; indeed, what is often envisaged by theoreticians is an absence of controlling centres, whether they be political or economic. Instead of approximating Fordism (and still less corporatism), Western societies are likely to arrive, by one route or another, in some arrangement involving flexible economic systems – that is, position 6 as opposed to position 5.

As Table 6.1 may be taken to suggest, the emergence of a flexible economic system involves movement from an emphasis in managerial practice from position 1 to position 6; from a concern about control to a concern about flexibility and adaptiveness; and a movement from a narrow focus on work to a broad concern with economic systems. The implication is that all advanced societies must make a transition of this sort. In principle it is possible to envisage any route from position 1 to position 6, but in practice some routes have been more effective than others, and all have allocated the costs and benefits differently. Hence, if it is widely agreed that the present era is one in which countries must adopt flexible economic systems, it is necessary to think about the following issues: (a) what are practicable routes to realization of a flexible economic system, given that economies will be starting from different configurations? and (b), are there different modes for the development of such systems, involving different allocations of costs and benefits? The pattern adopted by the UK – which has moved with surprising rapidity down a path towards flexible economic systems – is not the only one. Indeed, there are many obvious drawbacks (and some that are not so obvious) to the flexible economic system as it has been realized in Anglo-Saxon economies; that is, Britain and the USA. It is not necessary for other countries to follow headlong and rush to the adoption of the unregulated Anglo-Saxon version of the flexible socio-economic system.

Routes to the flexible economic system

The Fordist or corporatist socio-economic system was based on the achievement of high levels of control vested in obvious centres of power (the large corporations, departments of government, and so on); and markets managed the other allocations beyond the boundaries of these hierarchies. There were, and still are, limitations on the extent to which markets actually determine economic allocations (monopoly, oligopoly, cartels). Fairly obviously large organizations are not necessarily vulnerable to market forces and markets were clearly not the only mode of allocation (as there was state regulation of industry, welfare payments and services, and so on). But, mainly, the spaces outside and between hierarchies were regulated by the price mechanism. At the societal level there were some marked differences in the extent of market allocation. On the one hand there are countries like Sweden in which a remarkable degree of economic centralization goes in partnership with a high level of welfare provision; whilst on the other there is the USA, where economic relations are much more important. In this respect it can be argued that the US economy (today often held up as the model for others) followed a highly untypical developmental route in key respects. The emergence of large industry in that country, for example, was not accompanied by the development of an extensive regulatory and welfare state.

In many ways, where it has emerged at the system level, such as in Britain, the new flexible arrangement does not appear to be very much different from what existed before. However, there has been enough change to cross a critical threshold and to produce a distinctively new pattern of socio-economic relations. The new system of flexible economic relations is not without elements inducing coordination though what these are has changed in emphasis. In the new arrangement, administrative and political coordination has given way to almost exclusive reliance on processes within the economic sphere. For some this is simply a matter of economic maturation, and economic relations are now simply taking an increased importance, amongst other things rolling back the involvement of the state. Another line of argument is that although market-type economic relations have become increasingly important, they are not in a conventional pattern. Market relations, as they have become more extensive, have become augmented by affective ties, so that economic relationships are overlaid by, and increasingly indistinguishable from, community relations. The concept that is used by many here is that of the network, an emergent new type of structure characterized by trust (Thompson 2004). Neither of these positions has much to say about hierarchy. The implication is that it has largely disappeared as an important factor in the equation. It is not that large corporations are no longer with us, but that authority, which is the organizing principle of hierarchy, is no longer important as a mode of coordination.

Against both these positions it will be argued that, in Britain especially, the key relationships, which contribute whatever direction and coordination there is in the socio-economic system, are constituted by the structures of large corporations and their spheres of influence, which extend far beyond their organizational boundaries. In one key respect the British experience turns out to be highly indicative. This is that flexibility at the system level is much more important than other forms. Other societies have approached flexibility by building flexible work groups. However, it seems that even widespread change towards greater flexibility among work groups does not secure flexibility at the level of the organization. Moreover, adoption of widespread organizational flexibility does not necessarily produce flexibility at the level of the economic system. In Britain, formal moves towards the development of flexible work groups were slow and deficient and the adoption of new models of the flexible firm (at least those forms that involve increased employee participation) was also weak (Ackroyd and Procter 1998); and yet, because of the policies and actions of corporations, the economy as a whole has moved rapidly to a new highly adaptable pattern. By contrast with this, in countries like Sweden the adoption of new models for flexibility within the workgroup and the firm have been impressive, though large companies and state regulatory arrangements have been slower to change. Thus, although countries have different starting points it is possible for them to move by different routes and at different speeds towards a flexible economy. In this chapter, the object is to point out some of the characteristics and drawbacks of the British route to the flexible socio-economic system it now has.

The disappearance of the large corporation?

It is perhaps because of the importance of the US in the world that it can be a plausible model of organization and can exert pressure for conformity with its practices – these Smith and Meiksins (1995) have called 'dominance effects' (see also Smith 2005). Certainly, the language of the market is present everywhere in political discourse. It is now widely asserted that market discipline must be allowed to regulate exchanges. But what of the hierarchy? In the socio-economic system based on control, it is clear that the large company is of pivotal importance. What has happened to the large corporation in a flexible socio-economic system? Large organizations have clearly not gone away or diminished in size. Indeed, recent research has suggested that, as aggregations of capital and assets, the largest businesses now bear direct comparison with countries (Anderson and Cavanagh 2000; De Grauwe and Camerman 2002). There are of course problems with such comparisons, most obviously that calculations of national wealth (GNP) measure value added, whilst company performance is measured by turnover. However, given that company value added is commonly about 25 per cent of turnover, this still makes contemporary firms very large economic agglomerations indeed. Hence, large firms remain; but how powerful are they?

Let us consider more carefully the place and role of large companies in economic relationships. Despite their size considered in aggregate, large British companies are now made up of large numbers of small units. Research by the author into major British companies still involved in manufacturing shows that, typically, they now have up to 500 or so major subsidiaries, and, in addition, in some cases, thousands of affiliates and contractual partners. This must be seen as part of a long-term strategy of fragmentation (perhaps better described as parcelization) beginning more than two decades ago (Shutt and Whittington 1987). Even twenty or thirty billion dollars of equity spread through 300 organizations in more than a hundred countries produces an average capital value in any one place that is quite low. Thus, today, corporations take the form of collections of what are, by historical standards, quite small constituent organizations. The development of widespread sub-contracting and other types of inter-organizational relationships, in which whole areas of activity previously undertaken by large organizations for themselves are now outsourced is now commonplace. The development of large numbers of consultancy and other business services organizations suggests that firms also sub-contract much of their non-routine management. Superficially considered, then, the organizational landscape appears as an array of business units, each being quite small. It is easy to conclude that the large firm is no longer a significant economic actor. The falling numbers of direct employees in any one place and the removal of many of the levels in traditional organizational hierarchies also encourages the view that large organizations are no longer significant concentrations of power. British companies have exported a great deal of their capital and a high proportion of their diminished total number of employees (Hirst and Thompson 2000). But none of these trends should be taken to suggest a diminution of the power and influence in the economy of large organizations, it is merely that the way they influence events has changed.

However, large British firms remain formative of wide spheres within the economy. As will now be argued, in many circumstances large businesses are very powerful: they are able to shape the activity of extended groups of firms which they own and other organizations. Some of the advantages of this are obvious. If a business group owns most (or even a high proportion) of the organizations with which it transacts business, as many of them do, in a non-trivial sense it can be said to have become its own business environment. A business group does not, of course, completely relinquish control over its constituent firms, despite an increased willingness to allow many activities to be organized differently in particular localities, and the general extension of operational autonomy to the periphery (Hedlund 1993; Morgan 2005). Where a business does not own all the major companies with which it has collaborative relations, quite high degrees of control are often nonetheless present, such that a major firm defines the nature of the relationship it has with other firms and its purposes. A really surprising development in this respect is the extent to which private corporations have considerable control in their collaborative relations with the state. Even as important contractors and providers, private firms might be expected to be much less influential than they actually are in these relationships, where they clearly often have the upper hand. In short, in a number of ways, major companies often orchestrate collaborative activities well beyond their boundaries and the limits of their ownership. Thus, they can and do shape their environments very effectively despite any limitations in their actual ownership of assets.

New corporate structures and their modes of engagement

It is contended here that there is a new configuration of the British business corporation. This has, so far, been rather inadequately mapped and understood. Hence, an important task undertaken in the next section is to set out, in a synoptic form, what this is. In many ways more significant, however, is the next step in the discussion. Because the new business form, though by historical standards very large, has limitations to its reach if it relies on its own resources, the modes of engagement of such large firms in broader sets of inter-firm relations have become crucial to them. It is contended here that large firms have, in fact, established very much wider affiliations and connections with other firms. These will also be examined. What makes some of these wider patterns distinctive is the directive and controlling role that large firms play in them, either occupying strategic positions in flows of goods and/or in making linkages between related areas of activity not otherwise connected, so bridging what are sometimes called 'structural holes' (Burt 1992). It will be argued that inter-firm structures of these kinds are very common, and indeed that most recognizable inter-firm networks show similarities. As will also be argued, these networks have properties that make them unlike the idealized cooperative networks lionized in some of the literature (Thompson 2004).

A new configuration for the large firm

The existing literature on large firms, which admittedly is not strongly focussed on the UK, generally does not contend that there are widespread changes towards the adoption of a new type of structure. Many authorities actually argue that there is insufficient change towards something new (Heckscher and Donnellon 1994). Alternatively, writers focus on the extent to which the generality of firms do not approximate to the patterns achieved by firms supposedly in the lead of change (Pettigrew and Fenton 2000; Pettigrew et al. 2003). Whittington and Mayer (2002), who undertook an extensive study of large firms in the three largest economies in Europe, also emphasize continuity over change. They argue that large firms in Britain, France and Germany have all continued with variants of the multi-divisional form (M-form) of organizational structure. This is an organizational structure first proposed by Chandler (1962, 1977) and his successors applying the model in other economies (Channon 1973).[1]

---

[1] Whittington and Mayer's thesis is in many ways highly contestable. The extent to which major British companies adopted the multi-divisional structure is a matter of disagreement. Even Chandlerian scholars thought that Britain was slow to develop in what they thought was the expected direction. Actually, the conglomerate form of company persisted in Britain for much of the twentieth century, and a variant of it was the most vital point of economic change in large

Be that as it may, the type of large firm with which we are now confronted in the UK has a highly extensive configuration with many constituent parts. This has been identified in earlier work as the capital extensive firm or CEF (Ackroyd 2002). A similar conception, developed by observers of developments in the US, is the multi-subsidiary firm (Prechel 1997; Zey and Swenson 1999). The most obvious and compelling structural feature of these firms is the sheer number of legally independent subsidiaries comprised by them. They have many more constituent units than multi-divisional companies had in the past, and most if not all of these are very small whether measured in terms of the capital invested or in the numbers of employees. Subsidiaries can and do themselves own other subsidiaries, and there are usually many other entities such as joint ventures and other forms of long-term affiliation such as semi-permanent sub-contraction relationships. Among other things, subsidiarization has the benefit of limiting the legal and financial liabilities of the parent company, and allows a degree of flexibility in the production and distribution of goods and services. As has been said, large British companies still involved with manufacturing have upwards of 200 and sometimes as many as 500 subsidiaries, not to mention other affiliates. Head office is disproportionately small compared with the M-form company. There is no intent to control or direct all activities from the centre, operational autonomy being conceded to management in localities. However, at the same time, the monitoring of key performance measures is retained at head office, as is the capacity for strategic direction.

By contrast with the Fordist firm, and its successor, the multi-divisional company, the CEF spreads out what capital it owns between many sites and locations and so puts less at risk in any one venture. Another feature of CEFs, which again marks them out as an organization with more in common with conglomerates, is their capacity for permanent restructuring and an emphasis on the active pursuit of profit.

---

firms until the middle of the 1980s. Even major British companies which did have some multi-divisional characteristics behaved very much like conglomerates, having diversified portfolios and tendencies to pursue predatory takeovers. The idea that the major British company has continued with the 'M' form is therefore difficult to defend. It is true that most of the larger British firms grouped their activities into 'divisions'. However, these divisions had nothing like the same importance as they did in the classic divisionalized company as outlined by Chandler. In the contemporary large British company, divisionalization is often merely a presentational device and not a significant structural feature.

As in the past large British firms buy and sell other companies frequently; they also readily set up in business in new areas of activity and new places, and disband in others. The characteristics of the CEF, and its differences from the multi-divisional company, are set out in Table 6.2.

Table 6.2 The multi-divisional company and the capital extensive firm (CEF)

	Multi-divisional company	CEF (multi-subsidiary company)
Basic structure	Divisionalized (1–10 divisions)	Diversified (200–700 subsidiaries)
Head office	Large: centralization ++ especially of strategic managerial activities	Small: centralization + Loose/tight mode of coordination and control Capacity for strategic control retained
Component organizations	Relatively few and relatively large	Many and small: operational autonomy plus strategic control from the centre
Capital structure	High capitalization: capital intensive organizations	High aggregate capitalization but capital extensively distributed Numerous profit centres Financial flexibility
Activities	Focussed on an industry and/or location Most activities and support services in house	Extensive, and sometimes very diversified Many activities and support services outsourced at all levels
Strategy	Market domination via market segmentation Strategic development through heavy investment Organic growth	Replication of capacities in different markets Marginal diversification Opportunistic profit-making Growth through acquisition – permanent restructuring
Influence	Market dominance: monopoly/oligopoly Direct control of divisions Strong and continuous links with government	Control through economic spheres of influence Monopsony Strategic positioning of affiliations and alliances, positioning in wider economic relations Sporadic and arms-length links with government

The CEF: a network with special properties

As a set of related organizations a CEF may be considered as a large network in its own right. However, it is clearly a network that has distinctive properties. Despite the apparent decentring of such groups, significant powers are retained at the centre, and there are elements of hierarchy between the constituent organizations that make up the group. The network of firms includes, around the centre, a core membership of firms which are usually wholly owned subsidiaries, but there are also typically many others which are partly owned subsidiaries, joint ventures or other kinds of affiliates. There are yet other firms at the periphery with which there are long-term contract and sub-contract relations with core firms. Depending on the focus of group activities, a large firm which is constituted by a large number of apparently discrete units may nonetheless dominate a whole sector of economic activity or monopolize the supply of a key product to many markets.

A key point is that these are centralized structures in some obvious ways: it is the headquarters to which information routinely flows, and also which retains a capacity (not routinely exercised) to direct or otherwise influence activities. In addition, there are, in contemporary economic circumstances, distinct benefits arising from decentring, so far as selecting possible directions for development is concerned. Thus HQ may itself initiate new areas of activity but also clearly it decides whether any promising local initiatives will become significant activities for the group. In many cases it is not that complete autonomy is granted to constituent units, but that elements of the market are allowed to penetrate the group structure so making marginal entrepreneurship by subsidiaries and affiliates essential. The centre may then decide if local innovation is worth disseminating and, in the right circumstances, may support promising developments with investment. Hence it is argued that elements of hierarchy and direction continue and, indeed, authority invariably constitutes the over-riding logic of allocation. What makes this very clear indeed is the ability of the centre to exercise rights of ownership and to sell off subsidiaries when the need is felt to restructure the organization or realize cash. If this is the case then including market-type relations within hierarchies does not eliminate the principle of hierarchical control. Market-type relations have been allowed to penetrate the organizational boundary, and often also hierarchy has been actively extended outside of it (Loveridge and Mueller 1997). Indicators of hierarchy are the following: the corporate HQ has organizational direction over its subsidiaries and other affiliated companies and beyond this there are extensive and unequal links with subcontractors. There are dense and unequal communications and exchanges between top and bottom network members. Lateral connections between subsidiaries and affiliates are more limited and are often deliberately restricted.

Analytically considered, the kind of network structure constituted by CEFs differs markedly from idealized conceptions of the properties of networks envisaged by some network theorists. In idealized networks, connections are numerous (the network is dense), connections run in several directions and are assumed to be of similar weight. However, considered by this standard, CEFs have rather few connections, they tend to be in a single direction and are not of equal importance. The connections there are, are mainly constituted by hierarchical linkages between units, with an absence of lateral connections. In essentials, they are remarkably like the organizational charts that are used to depict the formal structures of traditional organizations. In a word, like traditional organizational structures, these networks are *imbricated* as opposed to *reticulated*. Imbricated structures are overlaid like the tiles on a roof or the scales on a fish. The point to note about this is that these structures have only a limited degree of variability. To use Dan Jonsson's terms (this volume, Chapter 3), the variability they have is desirable viewed from the controllers' point of view.

Some new modes of engagement by firms in economic processes, and their network properties

But it is as much the way the CEF works in relation to other structures external to it that makes it really distinctive. For Britain, the flexible economic system that has emerged is in many ways like the old, in that it is based on the collaborative production and distribution of goods and services by large numbers of organizations. What is different, however, is that the types of integration and coordination typically found between the firms involved have changed: there has been a shift of emphasis from competition to forms of economic relationship that involve medium-term collaboration. For all the rhetoric of markets, and emphasis on the importance of competition in the new economy, in some obvious ways market relations are being dampened and are receding in importance. The economy no longer resembles the classic structure of markets, in which large numbers of firms competed by placing their marginally differentiated finished products in the market place. Large British firms have a number of characteristic engagements in the new arrangements.

One important development is that a small number of firms now structure many market places in the UK by mediating between producers and consumers. Consumer goods, for example, are delivered in a range of ways, not simply through shops on the high street. Today there are catalogue stores and mail-order organizations, not to mention e-business outlets. All of these, however, are increasingly monopolized by large firms which are eliminating independent high street outlets. The size of such retail and leisure firms allows them to make savings in procurement, distribution and sales. They buy in bulk and supply their own outlets. DuGay (1996) is one of the few commentators to note the increased concentration in retailing and some of its implications. The supply of consumer durables and large products comes along with an array of mediations. Nowadays we see the delivery of financial, insurance and service agreements along with the products themselves. British companies are in the lead in these developments, the UK being the home of numerous world-sized retailing and supply groups. Large retailers can guarantee very large sales and secure low prices from producers. Such firms therefore establish connections with preferred suppliers with whom they have relatively enduring relationships. These arrangements can be changed, but not in the short term. Here again we see flexibility of rather limited degree.

The arrangements that British companies involved in manufacturing have with other companies are another good illustration of new types of organization of the economy. The parts and sub-assemblies of complex products are, of course, produced in many places throughout the world, and they are transported to sites at which they are assembled into finished goods. This sort of arrangement is not properly understood as the extension of market relations, at least not market relations in anything remotely approximating the perfect form. The number of buyers and sellers is very small and getting smaller. From any one supplier's point of view, indeed, continued participation in trading means the commitment of relatively large amounts of capital and other resources to production. This only makes sense against the promise of relatively enduring trading relations, which the majority of such relationships are. What we see are long-term contractual relationships, which are not readily changed. Two branches of manufacturing industry, automotive and computers, provide compelling examples of the processes involved. Although the one has a history of more than 100 years (and much more if you consider that cycle-making and other industries were the precursors of car production) while the other did not get going in a serious way until about twenty years ago, both are now based on a similar system of dispersed manufacture of parts followed by local assembly. As a result of reorganizing manufacturing in this way, commerce has increased greatly also, and here too we see the familiar pattern of stable trading relations sometimes extended over long distances.

British companies are no longer significant final assemblers except of bespoke products. However, many of them do contribute in characteristic ways to supply chains. What they do is seek to occupy strategic positions in the supply of high value added products close to the point of final assembly. The manufacture of industrial seals, the design and supply of control switching and advanced automotive and avionics equipment are all examples of products supplied by the major subsidiaries of large British companies and for which there are relatively high barriers to entry and so little competition. Considered analytically, individual connections between, say, assembler and component producer is a relatively stable *articulation* between trading partners. Chains of articulations are common (as in supply chains), and, although discarding of a subcontractor can occur, when there is actually an absence of alternative suppliers, the possibility of exchanges finding different routes easily or quickly can easily be exaggerated. The word 'articulation' to describe this type of link is chosen advisedly. Linkages between individual units are robust connections which allow a flow of goods/services in one direction and remuneration (plus a degree of control) in the other. Again, this sort of pattern of connections falls far short of the properties of idealized conceptions of networks. The appropriate model here is the articulated truck, or, better still, a railway train. Rather than there being multiple links between points, in which there is no direction to be observed, the actual connections in the new arrangements are quite few and usually not symmetrical. As has been emphasized, though the links between organizations can modify over time, they tend to be relatively enduring. The point to make about this type of structure is precisely that it is flexible; that is, it is not capable of unlimited adaptiveness. The key point is that if large organizations locate themselves at strategic points in wider sets of relations, such as supply chains, they can gain disproportionately whilst not putting much of their own capital at risk. British companies seek to do this by supplying key high value added components supplying many markets.

Thus, it is specifically not claimed here, as is sometimes done, that the changes outlined are so different that entirely new modes of analysis (for example, network analysis, chaos theory) are required to clarify them. On the contrary, the point to make is that the new system of socio-economic regulation is a somewhat different combination of market and hierarchy than has commonly been seen before; that is all. This is the basis on which we have tried to characterize it here, and the aim of the chapter is to suggest some lines of analysis which bring out the character of the new kind of flexible economic system. Both markets and hierarchies continue, but their spheres of operation are no longer so separate as they once were. Ideologists and apologists of capitalism certainly emphasize the continued importance of markets. On the other hand, as has been argued, degrees of hierarchy and control exercised outside the organizational boundary is the dominant feature of these relationships. Hierarchies are more important than they once were as means of economic coordination.

Theoretically, these structures are somewhat like the model of the CEF itself. Flexibility is supposed to arise from the possibility that the flow of exchanges may readily take an alternative route if an existing one is blocked. However, many of the new inter-organizational relationships are basically sets of strongly articulated links. There is a necessary directionality in the connections and they are designed with 'a right way round' (as with an articulated truck). Like the imbricated structure, the structure made from serial articulations is also strong and effective only in particular circumstances – only when the 'right' way round. Indeed, it is easy to exaggerate the degree of flexibility inherent in such structures. Such structures exhibit a requisite degree of variability and no more.

Organizational networks as fields of power

Although business groups may be uncertain of the direction in which they will develop (as is suggested by the tendency to decentre operational decisions and to encourage local entrepreneurship) this is not the same thing as saying they have given up on retaining and developing the strategic control of group resources. For example, when considering the possibility of expansion into a new market or sector, it is almost certain that corporate managers look at strategic considerations, such as the importance to a whole sector or area of activity of the particular business they propose to undertake. They will often make decisions about what to invest in on that basis. It should not pass without remark that the activity of such business groups has enormous effects. Changes in policy by large firms made twenty years ago – to export production and so to employ much less skilled manual labour at home, for example – have profoundly affected the quality of life in British society today.

The move towards new types of relationships between contracting firms does not necessarily imply the loss of many of the traditional features of business organization, such as the capacity to direct business activities and the capacity to exercise other rights of ownership. However, there are several things that make the tentacles of power less obvious when they operate in this way. As has been admitted, more autonomy is allowed to constituent firms in some areas. But this is mainly because the controllers of business groups have come to see distinct advantages in some features of a decentred strategy. Some functions remain centralized and the *potentiality* of directing activities has not changed. It is certainly easy to exaggerate the generality of the tendency to decentre. What is actually happening is that large corporations of British origin often have developed the policy of not being dependent on any one national economy, and to reproduce their most profitable activities in many locations. When they do this, large companies are forced to spread their assets more thinly, to subcontract many of their activities, and to accept local autonomy as the best way to proceed. In this context, debate about organizational change is often conducted without consideration of the systemic features of the policy agendas and motivations that are associated with them. However, in many circumstances policies are discernable, indeed business groups should be thought of as highly potent economic actors, despite the fact that they participate in many local collaborative relationships and their capital is parcelled out into many sites.

Most of the literature in this area is, apart from the idea of the need for more competitiveness, strangely silent concerning the possible reasons for the strategies that businesses are adopting. Authors make insufficient acknowledgement that, if patterns of organization are changing dramatically, this will be reflected in changed motivations on the part of corporate elites (Sklair 2001). In this chapter it is specifically argued that the ideology of shareholder value has given priority to profit-making over reinvestment, as argued by Lazonick and O'Sullivan (2000; see also Lazonick 2005). The pursuit of profits also motivates elite managers, because in Britain and America today they are substantial shareholders too. Also important, the processes that have been identified as 'financialization' are also at work in the UK, pushing companies to seek short-term profits at the cost of long-term growth (Froud et al. 2006). Accordingly, many British businesses are entering into collaborative relationships because by doing so they can use the resources they save to expand into new markets. However, whilst not significantly reducing their profits overall, they have substantially reduced their obligations to the society in which they originally emerged. British companies have moved further and faster in exporting their capital abroad than other countries' companies (Hirst and Thompson 2000). Their policies have not helped government to control them (should it decide to do so) and government capacity to tax them effectively has declined, a factor lying behind state policy towards the welfare state (Hirst and Thompson 1999). Until fairly recently, most British firms saw themselves as being anchored in their economy of origin. They fixed their policy in relation to that of the home market and home government. Today, they show little residual allegiance to their home state. In a direct sense, business had a share in government in this situation. This era is now over.

Conclusions: governance without government

This chapter has considered some hitherto unremarked features of contemporary economic and organizational changes, and their consequences, as they are emerging in Britain. Many observers of both Britain and the USA have remarked on a secular shift in the relative importance of the economy over both civil society and the polity in recent years (Hutton 2002; O'Sullivan 2000). The reasons for these changes being initiated are not obscure. One key source of change, as has already been remarked, is financialization (Froud et al. 2002; 2006). This cites increased pressure from financial institutions on corporations to induce them to pay more attention to the returns they make to capital markets by realizing and distributing higher levels of profit. The result has been not only the pursuit of higher levels of profitability on the part of capitalist enterprises (following the ideology of shareholder value) but the adoption of new policies regarding the utilization of these profits (Lazonick and O'Sullivan 2000). These have brought along with them some considerable changes in the organization of the economy, including especially the new kinds of relationships between organizations that have been analysed here.

Pressures for better financial performance have come at a time when major companies are also seeking to extend their reach by developing wider patterns of international operations. The changes attributed to the organization of the CEF and its characteristic policies are a response to these pressures. Spreading their capital over a larger number of sites – operating on less capital per establishment – and entering into a series of relationships with partner organizations of various kinds to augment their activities are policies aimed at gaining higher returns from capital employed. These kinds of changes have greatly increased the articulated structure of the new flexible economy, and lie behind the emergence of a macroeconomic system that is much more flexible – from the point of view of its owners and controllers. As Jonsson suggests (this volume, Chapter 3) one party's flexibility is another's instability and the flexible economic system involves considerable insecurity so far as some firms and many individuals are concerned. However, a point to note is that there are material reasons why the metaphor of the network has become increasingly influential in discussions of contemporary economic arrangements. But care must be taken to ensure that our chosen models give an accurate picture. Because of the continued presence and influence of very large companies, in many instances change towards more cooperative patterns of organization are more apparent than real. The resources that major firms command have increased rather than diminished, and the extent of their influence, similarly, has also extended. It is correct to regard the articulated economy as more profitable, but it is also important to recognize that it is increasingly infiltrated by hierarchical relations. At the same time, the long-term commitment of corporations to the home economy is in considerable doubt.

The UK never fully embraced corporatism, but the state has nonetheless acquired important regulatory and allocative functions. In the UK it has been traditional for the policy of laissez faire to be dominant, in that the market has been the main process in the allocation of resources and rewards. In the British version of this Anglo-Saxon model, however, the polity (through the agency of the state) has traditionally contributed a minor but highly significant supplementary procedure for allocation (in the shape of the welfare state and progressive taxation system) which throughout much of the last century increasingly mitigated the effects of otherwise unregulated economic allocation. In the process, the state contributed to social integration by sustaining residual elements of civil society. But despite the weakening anchorage of major businesses in the home economy (as indicated by such things as a declining willingness to repatriate their profits, pay corporate taxes or continue with high levels of domestic employment) the policies of governments towards business remains in the traditional mode: laissez faire. More than that, business is so far beyond criticism that what passed for industrial policy a decade ago has been almost completely abandoned. In its place there is a series of positive assumptions about business. In the new interconnected economy, business is seen as making a positive contribution to society as well as realizing more profits. This is because, presumably, the new economy is assumed to operate on cooperation rather than competition. For this reason, business can replace or substitute for the absence of civil society. It is also seen to provide appropriate models for the organization of the state.

In Britain, the policies of the New Labour Government do recognize, in a minimal way, that there is a threat to civil society and to social stability in a society dominated by the flexible economy. Indeed, overestimating the ease with which civil society may be re-invigorated and without much credible idea of the ways to do it, government has copied key aspects of the new economic forms in remaining areas of state provision. Although recent public service reform has often been legitimized through attacks on bureaucracy, the actual thrust of policy is to break down producer control and make public service professionals more accountable to management and funding bodies (Kirkpatrick et al. 2005). The growth of centralized audit and monitoring, with a consequent decline in trust and collegiality, are well remarked outcomes of policy (Clarke and Newman 1997). The attempt to curb the allocative power of private hierarchies is, in this government's view, best met by the development of public sector managerial hierarchies. In the era of the classic welfare state it was bureau-professionals in charge of coordination, now it is more obviously the state, increasingly mediated by private capital. Such policies seem designed to further weaken rather than enhance the possibility of regenerating civil society. It seems very clear that the response of government in the UK has not done anything to improve their effective control of economy or society. Indeed, courtesy of an unacknowledged pact between government and business, we are now entering an era of governance without government.

What is being observed in the UK is a shift of the centre of gravity from polity to economy, in which there has been a decisive loss of control by the former in favour of the latter in the context of a rapidly internationalizing economy. Perhaps the most important conclusion to draw from this analysis is that, in Britain, it is very difficult to locate a stable, let alone a cohesive mode of corporate or societal governance at the present time, at least one that is comparable to the stable system of relationships developed in the period of the post-war settlement (1945–80). Current disputes about the 'nanny' or 'security' state suggest that governance has become a neglected terrain. The best that can be said is that, within the severe constraints represented by the diminished capacity of the state, there remain only a few negotiable governance projects and policy repertoires to be identified. In Britain today even modest reforms to company law and governance arrangements are not negotiable.

There is a real danger that, recognizing the effect of some aspects of change in Britain and the USA, other states will feel themselves under pressure to develop policies with comparable objectives, voluntarily 'liberalizing' economic relationships and dismantling the regulatory powers of the state. However, the extent to which the British path is practical or acceptable for societies with deeper traditions of corporatism is difficult to say and obviously requires further consideration. It is to be hoped that this chapter has indicated the precariousness and potential danger of leaving so much to the machinations of unregulated (and, by now, probably unregulatable) corporate capitalism.

7

Temporary Agency Work in the European Union — Economic Rationale and Equal Treatment

Donald Storrie

Of the various forms of atypical employment, temporary agency work is of most current interest.[1] It has been by far the most rapidly growing contractual form in the last decade and research on agency work is relatively limited. It is also conceptually a very interesting contractual form, being a hybrid of an employment and a commercial contract. It was extensively deregulated during the 1990s and we still await the fate of a proposed EU Directive on agency work.[2] Furthermore, if appropriately regulated agency work may provide some reconciliation of perhaps the major conflict between employer and worker interests in recent years, namely the apparently irreconcilable demand for flexibility for the employers and job security for employees.

Temporary agency work can be defined as follow. The temporary agency worker is employed by the temporary work agency and, by means of a commercial contract, is hired out to perform work assignments at

---

[1] Any views expressed in this chapter are not necessarily those of my employer the European Foundation for the Improvement of Living and Working Conditions.

[2] The main aim of the directive is to establish the *general principle of non-discrimination*, in terms of basic working conditions, of agency workers compared to workers in the *user* firm doing the same or similar work. There are, however, some important exceptions: where a temporary worker has a *permanent contract* and is paid between assignments and where social partners can conclude collective agreements derogating from the principle by providing for alternative means to secure adequate protection and where an assignment or series of assignments with one user firm will *not exceed six weeks*. This was the Commission's original proposal.

user firms. This definition varies between countries only with respect to the employment contract status of the worker.[3]

This chapter starts with some basic empirical facts on agency work in the European Union, and then proceeds with a brief description of the regulation of agency work. It then explores possible reasons for the rapid growth of agency work in Europe, some problems and limitations specific to agency work and concludes with a critical evaluation of policy alternatives.

Empirical background

Data on temporary agency work are generally of very poor quality. In most countries the Labour Force Survey does not ask questions on agency work and even then, research indicates serious reporting errors (see, for example, Burchell, Deakin and Honey 1999 for the UK case). However, while one should be somewhat skeptical as to the accuracy of data on the level of temporary agency work, and comparisons between countries, the rapid increase of agency work since the early 1990s is indisputable. Between 1992 and 1999, agency work at least doubled in practically all EU-15 member states and increased at least fivefold in Denmark, Spain, Italy and Sweden, and just under fourfold in Austria.

Table 7.1 presents the only available data with some degree of measurement consistency between countries and refers to 1999. France, with over 623,000 agency workers, accounts for 30 per cent of the EU total and is followed by the UK. The Netherlands is the most agency work–intensive country, followed by Luxembourg, France, the UK and Belgium (see Table 7.1). In 1999 the intensity was low in Austria, Germany and the Scandinavian and Southern European countries.

Arrowsmith (2006) provides some, less systematic, evidence of trends up to 2004. The major changes since 1999 are: an almost doubling of agency work in Austria, Ireland and Germany and significant growth in Spain. The most notable changes, however, are to be found in Greece and Italy. Agency work recently became legal in Greece and by 2004, 3505 were employed in the sector. The growth in Italy is phenomenal; from 31,000 in 1999 to 153,000 in 2004. Arrowsmith (2006) also provides some evidence on the incidence of agency work in the new member

---

[3] The partial exceptions to this definition are found in Ireland and the UK where the concept of an employment contract is somewhat different from the rest of Europe.

Table 7.1   Temporary agency work in the EU-15 member states in 1999

	Number of agency workers	Share of all agency workers in EU	Rate of agency work
Austria	24,277	1.2	0.7
Belgium	62,661	3.0	1.6
Denmark	18,639	0.9	0.7
Finland	15,000	0.7	0.6
France	623,333	29.9	2.7
Germany	243,000	11.7	0.7
Greece	0	0	0
Ireland	9,000	0.4	0.6
Italy	31,000	1.5	0.2
Luxemburg	6,065	0.3	3.5
Netherlands	305,000	14.7	4.0
Portugal	45,000	2.2	1.0
Spain	109,000	5.2	0.8
Sweden	32,000	1.5	0.8
UK	557,000	26.8	2.1
EU total	2,080,642	100	1.4

Source: Storrie (2002).[4]

states. In most of these countries agency work only became legal after 2000. While the data is exceptionally poor, it is nevertheless clear that agency work is very limited in these countries.

Agency work is highly concentrated among the young in the labour force, with the share of under 25-year-olds ranging between 20 and 50 per cent of all agency workers in the various member states. With the exception of the three Scandinavian member states, the majority of agency workers are men. Male dominance of the sector is most pronounced in Germany and Austria. The gender distribution of agency work can largely be explained by the sectors in which the two sexes work.

The regulation of temporary agency work

Figure 7.1 provides a schematic definition of temporary agency work and the means by which it is regulated. There are two means of regulating

---

[4]This in turn was based on 15 national reports, citing various sources of varying quality, presented to the European Foundation for the Improvement of Working Life and Living Conditions, Dublin, in 2001 and CIETT (2000).

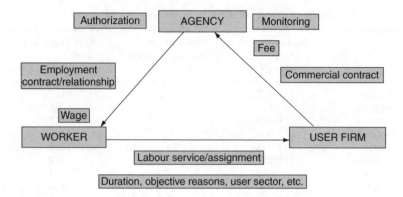

Figure 7.1 A stylised overview of the definition and means of regulating temporary agency work

agency work, the regulation of the business and the labour law regulation of contracts and assignments. The business is primarily regulated by means of licensing and monitoring procedures, and some countries, for example France, curtail the scope of agency activities by legislation which prohibits recruitment services. In many countries, labour law regulates not primarily the contract of employment, but rather the assignment at the user firm. This is typically the case in continental Europe. Collective agreements also play a role in the regulation of assignments and contracts, in particular in the Netherlands and Sweden and, to a lesser extent, in Belgium and France. Within the EU-15 member states we discern three types of regulation.

The continental countries: Belgium, France, Italy, Luxembourg, Portugal and Spain

These countries have detailed regulation of temporary agency work. In both labour and company law, agency work is seen as a distinct activity. Companies must obtain a licence to set up business and are monitored by special institutions. Labour law restricts the type and duration of assignment at the user firm. The objective grounds for assignments are similar to those for limited duration contracts. The legislation must be seen as being amongst the most interventionist in the Union. While the regulation is extensive and detailed, there is considerable evidence of non-observance of the law (Storrie 2002). Collective bargaining is most developed in Belgium and France, beginning to emerge in Spain, Germany and Italy, while in Portugal it remains negligible.

The islands: the UK and Ireland[5]

The UK and Ireland share a common-law system of labour law and this has led to a rather different concept of agency work than in other countries. For example, in the UK those engaged in what is commonly referred to as agency work may be viewed as employed at the user firm or the agency or even self-employed. Despite modest specific legislation of agency work, several laws do make special provisions for agency workers: for example, working time in the UK and unfair dismissals in Ireland. However, as the specific legislation is limited and above all because of the liberal nature of labour law in general – for example, as regards employment security – agency workers are awarded relatively limited legal protection. An unusual feature of agency work in Ireland is that the user firm adopts many of the obligations of the employer and may even be liable for unfair dismissal. In the UK there are only a few minor sectoral collective agreements, most notably in the audio-visual sector. The big companies, such as Manpower and Adecco, have company-wide agreements but as they constitute only a small share of the UK market, coverage is limited.

The Scandinavian countries: Denmark, Finland and Sweden

The Scandinavian countries have practically no special regulation of either the temporary agency business or assignments and the legal treatment of agency work *per se* is probably the least interventionist in the European Union. However, this does not mean that less employment protection is awarded to agency workers than, for example, in the UK, the USA and Ireland. The lack of specific legislation means agency work is not a distinct form of employment and must conform to mainstream labour law. In Finland and Sweden statutory law provides significant protection to all workers and thus even to agency workers. Moreover, in Sweden collective agreements cover the entire sector and, most notably, award workers guaranteed pay corresponding to at least 80 per cent of the monthly wage, regardless of the availability of assignments. Labour law in Denmark, particularly as regards employment protection, is appreciably less strict. However, several collective agreements have specifically addressed agency work and, for example, include special calculations of seniority to accommodate agency work. As prior to the legislation of the 1990s agency work could best be described as illegal, the current legal status of the sector in Scandinavia represents a

---

[5] The United States could also be classified as belonging to this group.

remarkable degree of deregulation and is without doubt the most radical shift among the EU-15 member states in recent decades.

Four EU countries fit poorly into the classifications above. The Netherlands is a mixed model with little regulation of the business but with detailed and specific regulation in statutory law and collective agreements concerning the contract at the agency, with job security increasing with time spent at the agency. Austria and (since legislation in 2003) also Germany shares much of the liberal regulation of the sector in Scandinavia and the island countries (see Weinkopf 2005). In Greece, despite some legislative initiatives in 2003, the status of temporary agency work is still very unclear.

In the continental countries temporary agency work is seen as a distinct phenomenon, as regards both labour and company law. At the other extreme, as perhaps best represented by Sweden and to a lesser extent the UK, agency work is treated like any other form of business and the employment contractual status is regulated no differently than other forms of employment. The Dutch model is somewhere between these two, where only after a period of time at the agency does the worker receive the protection that labour law may provide to all other workers.

Thus, due to the lack of specific legislation in the non-continental countries, the legal status and degree of employment protection of agency workers are dependent on the general system of labour law. For example, the specific legal regulation of temporary agency workers in the UK and Sweden is similar but, due to very different labour law for all workers, the legal status of agency workers in both countries is very different. Thus, it is obviously not possible to assess the employment security awarded to agency workers solely by examining legal aspects of agency work *per se*. In the Continental countries, with their detailed specific regulation of agency work, the impact of the general system of labour law is of somewhat less importance.

On the increase of temporary agency work

There is very limited research that attempts to explain the rise of temporary agency work in Europe. Autor (2003) models the rise of agency work in terms of the decline of employment-at-will in the United States. While a more stringent employment protection may be a reasonable hypothesis in the US, this can hardly be the case in Europe which has seen some relaxation of legislation in the last decade (OECD 1999).

While there is some evidence that some workers express a preference for agency work, not least those at the upper end of the wage distribution (Cam, Purcell and Tailby 2003), most express a preference for a more stable employment status. (See Bergström and Storrie (2003) for some European evidence and Cohany (1998) for the United States.)

The increase in agency work in the 1990s in Europe coincided with the widespread deregulation of the sector. The impact of deregulation on the increase of agency work is indisputable in those countries where agency work has gone from being in practice illegal to almost without regulation at all, as has been the case in Sweden and Finland. Other countries, in particular Italy and Spain, have also seen appreciable deregulation in the 1990s. While there appears to be no obvious relationship between the level of agency work and the type of regulation in various countries, it is, however, quite clear that the current level of temporary agency work in European countries is related to *when* the sector was significantly deregulated. It appears that time is required to both iron out the institutional conflicts that arise from this still relatively new form of employment and to efficiently coordinate the many parties involved. Moreover, the removal of restrictions on agency work only *enables* the increase of agency work. An understanding of what really drives the increase of temporary agency work requires some understanding of the possible economic rationale for agency work.

There are a number of reasons why an employer may hire labour on a temporary basis, such as for a specific task that is limited in duration, to replace an absent employee, and so on. Whatever the reason, the costs of adjusting levels of employment may make frequent open-ended employment contracts for a short duration unprofitable. Here we do not address the issue of why establishments in most OECD countries in the last two decades have, to an increasing degree, used various forms of temporary employment contracts. However, it is relevant to demonstrate that agency work may be a more appropriate means of performing the same functions as other forms of temporary employment contracts, such as fixed-term contracts. The truly distinguishing feature of agency work is that *all adjustment costs are directly borne by the agency*. Of course, the user firm pays for these services, and this is the source of agency profits. These adjustment costs may be grouped as hiring or matching costs and severance costs. I argue that there are reasons to believe that in many situations agencies can perform both these functions more efficiently than user firms.

Severance costs

Severance costs are obviously related to the probability of having to incur these costs at all, that is, to the risk of the employer having to terminate the contract. Early contributors to the theory of the firm, and in particular Knight (1921), focused on the trading of risk and authority between the employer and the employee. The employee's risk is related to the income insecurity that would arise from spot market trading of labour services. Firms, being less risk averse, are willing to take on some of the employee's risk.[6] In return the worker surrenders authority to the employer. The risk adopted is related to the economic viability of the firm. This comprises risks specific to the firm (for example, good or bad management decisions) and product market risks that are largely outside the firm's control. In this context the unique feature of temporary work agencies is that they manage a portfolio of employment opportunities. These opportunities are found in many user firms, which may be located in different economic sectors. This diversity enhances the potential of the agency employer to spread and thus reduce the severance risk. The outsourcing of these functions to the agency may be cheaper than the user firms performing this function in-house.[7]

Furthermore, as the relationship between the user firm and the agency worker is not regulated by any form of employment contract, agency work may provide user firms with a greater degree of numerical flexibility than practically all employment contracts. In this context it may be useful to compare agency work with its closest substitute, namely fixed-term contracts. First, some fixed-term contracts may presume that they will eventually be transformed into an open-ended contract. Such a presumption may be in law (this is the case in some countries as regards, for example, probationary contracts) or by custom or norm. Moreover, an incorrectly applied fixed-term contract (for example, repeated use) may lead to legal sanctions such as fines or the transfer of the fixed-term contract to an open-ended contract. Second, many forms of fixed-term contracts cannot be terminated at will. Indeed the termination of the fixed-term contract in advance of the implied expiry date may require

---

[6] Note that here we are not referring to idiosyncratic risk related to the individual worker as regards, for example, capabilities and effort. This is taken up below when discussing hiring.

[7] However, if risk is related to a macroeconomic shock in all economic sectors there is no potential for risk spreading and thus in this context no benefit in organizing the labour market in temporary work agencies.

stronger grounds in law than for an open-ended contract. The only potential source of numerical inflexibility when using agency work is related to the commercial contract between the agency and the user firm. While it is conceivable that these contracts may include clauses that limit full spot market flexibility, they are unlikely to be particularly extensive.

Hiring and matching[8]

The outsourcing of some functions of the personnel department at the user firm to the agency is most obviously apparent when viewing recruitment. Why and in what circumstances would an agency be efficient at matching workers to a user firm?

Matching in the labour market is one of the classic examples of exchange under asymmetric information (Spence 1973), and is often phrased in terms of job searchers having more information about their capabilities and effort levels than the firm. In this situation, an intermediary can reduce the uncertainty facing the firm, as the agency will have the incentive to accurately report the quality of their workers to the user firm in order to build and maintain their reputation. The agency will be more concerned with reputation than a single job searcher as the agency has a greater number of possible future transactions.

The improvement of reputation has been a very prominent strategy of many agency companies in the last decade and several, such as Manpower and Randstad, have now become recognizable brand names. This is almost certainly related to the information role played by agencies and the recent legal history of agency work. Prior to deregulation, when agencies often operated in a legal grey zone, reputation was poor and some were associated with shady practices. They sought to build reputation with both potential employees and user firms by means of ethical codes of practice, advertising campaigns and the signing of collective agreements (see Storrie 2002). Furthermore, the agency sector underwent considerable market consolidation during the 1990s. According to the International Confederation of Private Employment Agencies (CIETT), by 1998 the top five temporary work agencies accounted for over 50 per cent of turnover in 11 of the 14 member states

---

[8]Matching is the key issue in an equilibrium unemployment model of agency work developed in Neugart and Storrie (2006) upon which this section is based. We argue that matching efficiency may be the major factor behind the growth of temporary agency work.

where agency work exists (CIETT 2000). This process may have further served to push out some of the smaller and less reputable agencies. Improved reputation has presumably served to improve the matching efficiency of temporary work agencies in that they are able to attract better job applicants and to gain acceptance of agency workers with the personnel departments and the trade unions at the user firm.

The rapid growth of agency work since the beginning of the 1990s coincided with the widespread introduction of information and communication technology (ICT). Internet job sites are able to contain appreciably more vacancy and job searcher information at much lower cost than, for example, newspapers. However, the availability of this technology by no means necessarily implies that there will be more direct contact between firms and job searchers without going through a matching intermediary. The fact that the technology significantly lowers the cost for the job seeker to apply for jobs may lead to employers being inundated with job applications. Thus, as argued in Autor (2001a), intermediaries such as temporary work agencies will be required to reap the benefits of the computerized matching technologies.[9] The idea here is that ICT has the potential to increase matching efficiency, but this potential can only be fully realized if it is exploited by matching intermediaries such as temporary work agencies.

There is some evidence (cited in Storrie 2002) that agency work is becoming integrated into management systems of the user undertakings and is thus much more than a one-off measure to cope with unexpected situations. The relationship between the agency and the user firm is becoming comparable to that of supply firms to the user firm. Thus, as temporary work agencies build up business relationships with their user firms and better understand their labour requirements, they may be more able to avoid coordination failure. Coordination failures – that is, the uncoordinated actions of firms and workers – are, according to Petrongolo and Pissarides (2001), a major source of matching inefficiency. This is a process that takes time and may be related to learning-by-doing.

The Industrial Organisation literature is concerned with the boundaries of the firm. When should the firm use the market to acquire the

---

[9] Furthermore, the role of intermediaries in providing high quality information is a much-researched issue in the e-commerce literature (see Malone, Yates and Benjamin 1987; Sarkar, Butler and Steinfeld 1995), which stresses economies of scale and scope and the reputation issue mentioned above.

labour services it needs and when should it acquire these services itself? Note that here we are talking about the outsourcing of the acquisition of the labour services, not their utilisation *per se*.[10] This literature (see, for example, Milgrom and Roberts 1992), suggests that a firm will procure services in the market when the inputs are standardized (in this case the labour services); when there are several competing suppliers (temporary work agencies); if there are economies of scale in the supply firms (temporary work agencies) that are too large to be duplicated by the buyer (user firm); when there are economies of scope that would force the vertically integrated firm (user firm) into unrelated business; and when there are no specific investments on the part of either the buyer or the seller.

The suitability of outsourcing the recruitment function will thus depend on the degree to which the above conditions are met in specific markets. One could expect scale economies to be empirically important. As the agency specializes in recruitment, that is, in search, screening and possibly training, this implies that an agency will recruit more workers than a typical user firm and thus may exploit economies of scale. Indeed, agency work is strikingly concentrated in the major metropolitan areas, where the market is relatively large. Moreover there is some potential for economies of scope. Temporary work agencies are typically also engaged in pure recruitment, without having an employment relationship with the worker and there is some evidence that they also provide some elementary training services.

In the case of a temporary work agency, the uncertainty to the user firm is further diminished by the fact that, unlike a recruitment agency, the user firm does not need to adopt any employment risk and indeed a guarantee of quality may even be stipulated explicitly in the commercial contract between the agency and the user firm for the duration of the assignment.

Agency work also performs a matching role between the agency worker and the user firm, while on assignment. There are good reasons to suppose that search of temporary agency workers may be particularly effective. While on assignment the agency employee may have better access to information on job openings at the workplace than,

---

[10] While the distinctions may not always be clear I argue that the use of agency workers at the user firm is not 'outsourced' labour in the usual meaning of the word. For example, unlike sub-contracted labour the agency worker subjects himself to the authority of the user firm, will generally participate in the usual activities of the firm, will use the user firm's equipment, and so on.

for example, unemployed searchers. Also with the agency worker on location, the employer may more effectively search among the assigned employees. Obviously there may be an efficient exchange of information with the assigned worker revealing ability and motivation while acquiring information on the job and the firm. Moreover the fact that the assigned worker has been screened and assigned by the agency may be a valuable signal to the employer. While one could argue that the assigned worker has less time for search than the unemployed, there is some empirical literature that indicates on-the-job search may be particularly effective.[11]

The limits to temporary agency work

Lest one was led to believe from the previous section that agency work is a suitable means of organizing labour in all forms of economic activity, we should also emphasize that there are a number of economic problems related to agency work, which may limit its use in the labour market. It may also have detrimental consequences for working conditions.

A major economic problem is finding an appropriate means to finance training. As the very idea of agency work is to perform assignments in various firms, the skills required for agency work are obviously not firm-specific. According to human capital theory, firms will not be prepared to fully finance non-firm specific human capital, as they may not be able to reap the return on their investment, as the worker may quit (see, for example, Autor 2001b). Moreover the propensity to quit may be particularly high as the agency worker may be poached while on an assignment at the user firm. There is ample evidence of low training levels for agency workers (Paoli and Merllié 2001).

However, as pointed out by Schmid and Storrie (2001), interest in the acquisition of *specific skills and experience knowledge* was the central argument for the emergence and persistence of internal labour markets. More recent studies have revealed a slight tendency towards the erosion of internal labour markets in favour of network labour markets, as well as a renaissance of occupational labour markets. In both cases it is not length of tenure but experience of a wide range of projects and various

---

[11] While the on-the-job search feature of this idea is similar to the role of probationary fixed-term contracts, the ability of the agency to generate many assignments/probationary jobs will reasonably far exceed those found by an individual searching alone.

forms of cooperation that gives workers the edge in terms of knowledge accumulation (see, for example, Capelli et al. 1997; Marsden 1999).

Working conditions

As opposed to fixed-term contracts agency work does not necessarily mean temporary work. However, in the few countries where there are data, it appears in practice that not only the assignment at the user firm but also the contract at the agency is shorter than for fixed-term contracts (Arrowsmith 2006). Agency work appears to be very sensitive to the business cycle. There is a large body of research that shows that fixed-term contracts are associated with poor working conditions and so there is reason to suppose that this will also be the case for agency work (see, for example, Guadalupe 2001 for quite convincing evidence).

There are two additional features specific to agency work that may be expected to lead to poor working conditions, namely the frequent change of workplace at different user firms and the duality of employer responsibility. This means that all matters that require influence from employee organizations are likely to be difficult to deal with. There is evidence (Storrie 2002) that testifies to the problems in setting up the institutions of social dialogue at the workplace for agency workers.[12] Moreover, the rather fuzzy nature of the three-party relationship may make regulation and its implementation difficult in practice.

Nowhere does the combination of dual employer responsibility and frequent change of workplace combine to such potentially problematic effect than in health and safety at the workplace. Health and safety issues have been regulated in Directive 91/383/EEC, which aims to ensure equal treatment of all working at an establishment, whether they are employees or not. The main thrust of the legislation is to place primary responsibility with the user firm and to require the agency to inform the worker of the risks specific to each assignment. The directive *does* require that the worker be given sufficient training to deal with health and safety matters but *does not* specify who is responsible for the provision of this training. It is far from obvious where the responsibility should lie. Moreover, what does the user firm know about an agency worker's previous training and what does the agency know about the particular

---

[12] However, as argued by Freeman (2002), there is considerable potential through the Internet to modernize union activity. This may be particularly relevant for agency workers who lack continuous contact with a single workplace – 'the web site as a union hall'.

form of training required for a particular user firm? When one also considers the very short duration of a typical assignment, it is far from obvious how these problems can be solved and one should expect some problems with health and safety in agency work.

One could also postulate, but again research is very limited, that the constant change of workplace may be detrimental to psychological well-being. Sociologists, since at least Jahoda, Lazarsfeld and Zeisel (1933), have underlined the social importance of the workplace for individual welfare. With agency work one has several workplaces and it may be difficult to benefit from working together with others towards common goals, observing the fruits of one's labour materializing and receiving support and feedback from one's colleagues. The impact of the lack of such social benefits from work, together with feelings of replaceability, has been graphically described by Sennet (1999).

There is clear evidence of the association of temporary agency work with poor working conditions. The most detailed evidence is to be found in the study by Paoli and Merllié (2001). Compared to all other employment contractual forms, including fixed-term contracts, temporary agency work has the worst record as regards a number of indicators of working conditions, such as information about risks in using materials, products and instruments and repetitive work. Storrie (2002) presents evidence of a lack of employee control over working time not only in terms of involuntary part-time work but also very long hours. Evidence from state inspections, particularly in Southern Europe, indicates illegal practices and abuse as regards, for example, the non-payment of wages.

However, the contractual status and employment conditions may differ appreciably between the various member states. As mentioned above, in Sweden the employment contract is often open-ended and practically all agency work is performed with a collective agreement that provides some working time, and thus also income, security. Isaksson et al. (2001) compare agency workers on open-ended contracts with workers on various forms of temporary contracts in Sweden. They find that agency workers had a greater perception of job security, social support and better health than the others.[13]

---

[13] Storrie (2002) also cites some evidence of better working conditions for agency workers compared to in-house workers. These can be found for high skill and well paid workers and when there is a labour shortage. However, it should be underlined that the limited research performed seldom differentiates between

Finally, it is obvious that the commercial contract between the agency and the user firm has the potential to undermine the pay and working conditions determined by law, collective agreements or norms for workers directly employed at the user firm. This is discussed in more detail in the next section.

Regulation, equal treatment and the flexibility/security trade-off

One of the most important *potential* social advantages of temporary agency work is that it *can* provide an open-ended contract for the worker while contributing to numerical flexibility for the user firm. Any type of limited-duration contract is by definition associated with job insecurity and with probable negative consequences for working conditions (see Benavides and Benach 1999; Paoli and Merllié 2001; Guadalupe 2001). However, in contractual terms employment at a temporary work agency does not necessarily mean employment insecurity and there are some agency workers with open-ended employment contracts. Thus temporary agency work has the potential to contribute to the solution of one of the major conflicts in European labour markets in recent decades, namely to reconcile the firm's preference for flexibility and the worker's preference for job security. While of course there are problems specific to agency work – see above – it does, in principle, provide one means of attaining a positive sum solution to this basic conflict of interests for the types of economic activity for which it is suitable. As such the 'flexicurity' perspective may provide the basis for a compromise with mutual benefits to the social partners. Indeed it was the exploitation of this opportunity that contributed to the Dutch social partners reaching their compromise. Thus, one should explore how, in principle, the regulation of agency work could develop to obtain this dual aim.

However, it must be again underlined that a major concern about agency work *is* related to the precarious nature of agency work, in terms of job security, in practice and in most countries most agency work is not typically performed with an open-ended contract. Moreover, even when agency work is with an open-ended contract, the sector's extreme sensitivity to the business cycle results in considerable *de facto* precariousness (see Storrie 2002).[14]

---

the factors related to the agency work *per se* (the contractual form) and factors related to the job or the worker.

[14] But note that, due to the risk diversification argument stated above, one could argue that agency work may still provide more employment security when business cycle shocks hit the economy asymmetrically.

Equal treatment and standards at the user firm

The regulation of assignments, in duration or objective reasons, is currently the main means of regulating agency work in labour law, particularly in the continental countries. It is far from obvious that regulation of the assignment is in the interests of the agency worker. As regards employment security for the agency worker, regulation of the assignment is not the critical issue, but rather the security of the employment relationship, which, in most EU member states, is with the temporary work agency. The regulation of the assignment at the user firm appears primarily to serve to ensure that agency work does not become widespread in terms of job category and duration at the user firm and thus possibly undermine standards. It is primarily related to the interests of the workers in the user firm. This, while perhaps obvious, should be made explicit. The point here is that if the aim is to regulate working conditions and pay to the benefit of agency workers, the regulation of the assignment, in terms of duration and objective reason, is not the relevant issue.[15]

However, in no way is it implied that the interests of the workers at the user firm are not valid interests. There is clearly potential for agency work to undermine standards as established by employment law or collective agreement, with negative consequences for pay, working conditions and even employment levels for in-house workers at the user firm. This explains why the main issue in the European social dialogue for the unions, who represent primarily the in-house workers, was equal treatment for agency and in-house workers. Moreover it is obviously inappropriate to use agency work only to undermine standards. As outlined above, there are other advantages to using agency work that may make it a profitable enterprise for the agency without having to undercut standards. There are three potential means of ensuring that agency work does not undermine pay and working conditions at the user firm:

1. Legislation can limit the extent of agency work at the user firm through the regulation of assignments, as typically is the case in the

---

[15] However, given that agency work does appear to have negative health and safety consequences, one could consider the prohibition of assignments for particularly hazardous work. We should also note that a longer duration of assignments would serve to diminish the rapid assignment turnover that could be detrimental for agency workers.

continental countries. If agency work does not become widespread, lower standards for agency workers may not impact on the employees of the user firm. However, the growth and current level of agency work in these countries – France, for example – suggests that this may not have been a successful strategy.

2. The proposed EU directive attempts to directly legislate on equal treatment, as exemplified by the wage equalization law in Spain and, more recently, in Germany. However, it is far from obvious what equal treatment should entail and experiences from some member states cast doubt on the effectiveness of statutory legislation. At the European level, agency employer organizations have reacted negatively to the concept of equal treatment. They claim that it is unreasonable that conditions in other firms should determine pay and working conditions in theirs. This is, at least to some extent, a valid concern. Moreover, the intrinsically fuzzy and somewhat complicated nature of the *ménage à trois* that is agency work makes the day-to-day interpretation and implementation of the law rather difficult. In this context, clarity on what equal treatment is supposed to achieve – that is, primarily the maintenance of standards at the user firm – may be helpful. If it is possible to directly and effectively legislate equal treatment this should have most impact in member states which lack other means to ensure equal treatment, such as the UK and Ireland.[16]

3. Another means of achieving equal treatment is through the trade unions at the user firm. In Sweden, trade unions have, under certain circumstances, the right to veto the placement of agency workers at the user firm.[17] In addition practically the entire temporary agency sector is covered by collective agreements. This may also explain why Swedish unions were able to accept the radical statutory deregulation, as they believed – correctly as it turned out – that they could maintain the integrity of the user firm collective agreement. There is little reason to suppose that this is not an effective strategy for protecting

---

[16] Note, however, that in the UK the recent tendency in labour law to use the broad term 'worker' as opposed to 'employee' has served to award the same rights to agency workers, whatever their employment contract status, as employees.

[17] According to paragraph 39 of the Codetermination Act, the trade union may veto the use of outside contractors when it can be assumed to lead to a disregard of law or collective agreement. This is one of the most clearly defined areas of union power in Swedish codetermination law.

the rights of the in-house workers at the user firm.[18] However, the lack of such widespread coverage of collective agreements and trade union presence at the workplace hardly makes this an option in most other member states.[19]

The flexibility/security trade off

As mentioned in the introduction to this chapter, agency work has the *potential* to provide some solution to the security/flexibility trade-off. Policy-makers should pursue the potential of agency work to resolve this seemingly intractable issue.

How then can legislative initiatives be conducive to providing this best of both worlds? As noted above, the regulation of the assignment does not primarily serve the job security interests of the agency worker. Indeed, limitations on the duration and type of assignment may even limit job tenure, and the ensuing benefits of long tenure, at the agency. It is the regulation of the contract at the temporary work agency that should be the focus of attention. Different countries have different levels of protection of employment contracts and it is hardly appropriate to recommend specific proposals for all countries. Nevertheless it appears reasonable to suggest that agency workers should have the same employment protection as other employees. Thus the presumption should be that employment is with an open-ended contract unless there are objective grounds to contract otherwise.[20]

In most countries the repeated use of limited duration contracts is limited and if abused the contract may be transferred to an open-ended contact. The prohibition of a long chain of assignments would presumably lead to more agency workers obtaining open-ended contracts. Longer-term employment contacts may also serve to award agency

---

[18] It may also be a suitable means of guaranteeing working conditions for agency workers, provided of course that the unions are concerned about the welfare of agency workers.

[19] Kahn-Freund was a strong advocate of the effectiveness of trade unions in this context. 'As a power countervailing management the trade unions are much more effective than the law has ever been or ever can be.... Everywhere the effectiveness of the law depends on the unions far more than the unions depend on the effectiveness of the law' (Kahn-Freund 1977).

[20] Of course the terminology does not apply to the UK, Ireland and the USA. In the UK the corresponding presumption would be that agency workers are granted status as employees at the agency in all aspects of labour law and not just in terms of the specific legislation.

workers more seniority rights at the agency. This incorporation of agency work into mainstream labour law entails embracing agency work as a job like any other. Statutory law alone cannot achieve employment protection for agency workers, as Swedish and Dutch experiences indicate. In both these countries there appears to have been a fundamental acceptance of the phenomenon of agency work and a willingness to seek regulation that is not exclusively focused on the risk of agency work in undermining the integrity of the collective agreement at the user firm. In other continental European countries – for example in Germany and Spain – this acceptance has been both reluctant and late. Given that employment protection of agency workers is a valid aim, there is a need for unions to relinquish any remaining reluctance to organize at agencies and to act to provide for employment protection for these workers.

It was argued above that there might be appreciable economic benefits of agency work for user firms and profits to agencies *without having to circumvent the standards of employment at the user firm*. Agency work also provides more numerically flexible labour than limited duration contracts and there are reasons to believe that job matching through agency work may be particularly efficient and thus serve to reduce frictional unemployment. Moreover the risk pooling function of the labour market intermediary may even promote employment creation. From this perspective there may be much to gain from deregulation of the sector along the lines of the Netherlands and Sweden, something that has long existed in the UK and Ireland. The removal of the barriers to entry and monitoring procedures, limitations in scope of the activities of temporary work agencies, and above all the removal of objective reasons for assignments, would almost certainly be of benefit to the sector, the user firms and perhaps the entire economy.

There are thus three principal regulatory issues:

1. to allow temporary work agencies to pursue profitable business activities;
2. to ensure the integrity of the collective bargain at the user firm (to secure decent pay and working conditions for both agency and in-house workers) and finally
3. to ensure some degree of job security for agency workers.

An ideal solution would be one that truly awarded equal treatment to all. *Equal treatment for the temporary agency sector*, in terms of company law, which may be of benefit not only to the sector itself, but also to user firms and the economy as a whole. *Equal treatment for agency workers in terms of employment status in labour law* will provide the same level of employment protection as for other employees, that is, an open-ended contract or, if objective grounds exist, a contract of limited duration. More secure contracts, together with increased employment levels from deregulation, could promote the opportunity for careers for agency workers and enable them to benefit from seniority rights. The final piece of this integrated ideal policy package is to ensure the integrity of standards at the user firm by providing *equal treatment as regards pay and working conditions for agency workers at the user firm*. These three aspects of equal treatment cannot be implemented piecemeal. It would appear that, of the three, the most difficult to achieve, especially through legislation alone, is equal treatment for agency and in-house workers at the user firm as regards pay and working conditions. The role awarded to Swedish unions, as mentioned above, is possibly the most efficient means of regulating this matter but may not be transferable to other countries for institutional and political reasons.

The regulatory proposal broadly sketched above is of course far from fully developed and is written in general, not country-specific, terms and to be successfully implemented would require detailed national adaptations.

While it is argued that agency work is a potential means of ensuring employment security and promoting career development, there is ample evidence to suggest that at present it is not performing this role, and indeed in many countries it is associated with considerable employment insecurity, poor wages and low human capital investment. However, as succinctly put by Deakin (2002): 'The labour law of yesterday issued not from the heads of experts but from engagement, conflict and collective negotiation. There is no reason to think it will be any different in the future'. The role of policy is to provide an enabling legislative framework, not only in terms of labour but also social security law, upon which the involved parties may hammer out the appropriate institutional arrangements. In terms of labour law, the first step in the promotion of agency work conducive to the resolution of the security/flexibility trade-off, should be to provide agency workers with the same employment contract status and other rights as other employees.[21]

---

[21] In this context the exception to equal treatment in the current EU directive for those on open-ended contracts is very unfortunate.

8
Flexibility, Stability and Agency Work: A Comparison of the Use of Agency Work in Sweden and the UK

Kristina Håkansson and Tommy Isidorsson

As both an old and a new phenomenon within the EU community, temporary agency work enjoyed a rapid increase during the 1990s. Among the 14 EU countries, in fact, only Greece, where work agencies were illegal until 2004, has shown no such increase (European Foundation 2005a). Private work agencies were also illegal in Sweden, with minor exceptions, until a 1993 law legalized both private employment agencies and work agencies. The number of employees in temporary work agencies rose rapidly during the 1990s in Sweden and was estimated by the end of the decade to be 42,000. The UK, where temporary work agencies have existed for several decades, also witnessed a considerable increase in the number of agency workers in the 1990s. Although agency workers are increasing in numbers, a recent comparative study on agency work in Europe reveals that they comprise only 1 or 2 per cent of the labour market in most EU countries (Storrie 2002: 31). The impact of these small numbers on the labour market should not be underestimated, however; work organization in user firms has to be adjusted according to the use of agency workers, meaning that the use of a small number of agency workers affects many more employees.

The basic idea of temporary work agencies is to supply workplaces with staff for a limited period. Temporary agency workers differ from other types of temporary staff in that the temporary agency worker is employed by the agency, although the agency sometimes places a

Note: This study was funded by the Swedish Research Council, the Swedish Council for Working Life and Social Research and the Adlerbert Research Foundation through the Royal Society of Arts and Sciences in Göteborg. We want to express our thanks for this support.

manager at the user company to supervize the agency workers and to deal with the user company (Purcell and Purcell 1998).

It has been commonly accepted that employers have increased their utilization of agency workers in order to enhance flexibility: by engaging agency workers, the user organization is better able to adjust its number of workers to match actual demand. In this chapter, we focus on user firms and organizations in order to examine this flexibility argument. Our objectives are to describe the extent to which agency workers are used in Sweden compared to the UK; and, in particular, to analyse the importance of different institutional settings and motives for employers' use of agency workers.

Theoretical framework and research overview

The use of agency workers must be understood in a societal context; employers in different national situations exhibit different behavioural patterns in this regard. For instance, Hall and Soskice (2001) distinguish between liberal market economies, in which employers rely upon highly competitive markets in all types of labour relations, and coordinated market economies, in which employers seek strategic interactions and have a need for institutions that facilitate employment relationships. Coordinated market economies therefore presuppose strong employer associations, strong trade unions and supporting legislation. We consider the UK to be an example of a liberal market economy and Sweden a coordinated market economy. This categorization is in line with other classifications of the two countries (Esping-Andersen 1990; Goodman et al. 2003: 7, 23, 25).

In a highly competitive market situation, all employers seek to stabilize their core workforce and to secure peace on the shopfloor level. Thelen (2001), who also distinguishes between liberal and coordinated market economies, argues that employers seek this stability in various ways. Whereas employers in coordinated market economies rely on encompassing unions and national bargaining structures as stabilizing factors, employers in liberal market economies seek stability in strong internal control. Consistent with the perspective taken by Thelen, these circumstances should indicate different degrees of utilization of agency workers and different conditions for them in the UK in contrast to Sweden.

The agency industry itself is an active force for labour-market deregulation and restructuring (Peck and Theodore 2002: 169). This deregulation has given preferential treatment to agency-mediated staffing of temporary workers. The agency industry also plays an active role in the flexibility discourse. In his analysis of a temporary work agency Walter (2005) discusses how agency salespeople in dialogue with user firms emphasize not only how the agency can solve an urgent need for temporary staffing; they also emphasize how it contributes to an *image* of flexible staffing. 'The user company does not hire workers because somebody is sick, but because the company is a flexible firm' (Walter 2005: 124).

The user firm sees the use of agency work as a means of achieving flexibility (Houseman 2001; Kauhanen 2001; Kalleberg 2001, Kalleberg et al. 2003: 532). Atkinson's (1984) model of the Flexible Firm, although often questioned or modified (Håkansson and Isidorsson 2003; Kalleberg 2001; Nesheim 2004), is a frequently used and influential reference on this subject. In general, the flexibility concept has been well used, if not overused, in discussions of different staffing models, particularly since the late 1980s when 'lean production' concepts, such as 'just-in-time', became popular.

Although just-in-time referred to supplies of parts, it was also a good fit as a human resource concept for flexible use of labour. Just-in-time implies an elimination of all buffers, and leads to a need for capacity flexibility – a need to adjust production to match current demand. Organizations can attain this flexibility in three principal ways. Numerical flexibility can be achieved by varying the number of staff – by using agency workers. It is important to note that production also can be matched to current demand by working-time flexibility and by functional flexibility; the former strategy implies varying working hours, and the latter strategy involves designing the work organization so that employees can vary their work tasks according to current needs. All three strategies – numerical, working-time and functional flexibility – are used to make the organization adaptive to market demands. The main reason for implementing these strategies is not to give employees greater flexibility. In fact, all three strategies lead to an intensification of work for individuals. Because the use of agency work is the focus of this chapter, we refer to our previous research for a fully developed discussion on the relationships among these three strategies for achieving flexibility and their effects on individuals, organizations and the labour market (Håkansson and Isidorsson 2003).

The use of production concepts like just-in-time, production on demand and no buffers implies that fluctuations on the product or service market will precipitate an immediate need for additional staff at peak demand times. Agency workers are then used as a means to achieve numerical flexibility. These production concepts also aim at reducing slack and personnel in the organization, thereby creating a need to replace absent staff immediately. However, the way in which employers implement these production concepts should depend on the societal context faced by the user organization (Rubery and Grimshaw 2003; Lane 1995). Therefore, the effects of the strategies must be analysed in relation to the social and political environment. The different institutional settings in Britain and Sweden would suggest differences in the use of agency workers.

Research questions

Our aim with this chapter is to analyse *to what extent, where* and *why* agency work is used by organizations in the British and Swedish labour markets. This threefold overarching aim can be transformed into more specific research questions. How widespread in Swedish and British workplaces is the use of agency work? What are the employers' motives for using agency workers? What differences and similarities exist in the use of agency workers in the two countries? How does their use vary across workplaces in different regions and industries, and among organizations of different sizes and personnel composition? What factors explain these differences and similarities?

Methods, sources and selection of countries

Labour market regulations have been cited as an obstacle to labour market flexibility (UNICE 2000, SAF 1996). Researchers underline institutional settings, such as legal regulations, as important factors in explaining the use of agency work (Nesheim 2003: 310). In this way they compare countries with different regulatory systems. A comparison between the UK and Sweden gives us two extremes among the EU countries. The UK represents a liberal labour market economy in which employers have a relatively significant influence on employment relations; whereas Sweden represents a country with more regulated employment relations. Sweden is also a highly unionized country, with 78 per cent of the workforce organized compared with 29 per cent in the UK (Kjellberg 2002: 68).

Our most relevant data originate from Swedish and British workplace surveys. We conducted a large survey – the Swedish Agency Worker Survey 2002 – focusing on the extent of the use of agency workers and motives for their use in various workplaces. For information on conditions in Britain, we used data collected by the Workplace Employee Relations Survey (WERS) 1998. Internationally, there is a lack of comparative statistics in this field (Burgess and Connell 2004: 6). Like our Swedish survey, the WERS asks questions about flexibility, making it possible to compare the two. Respondents in both samples are managers or HR personnel at the workplace. These two data sets give us an opportunity to investigate and compare one important aspect of agency work with relatively consistent statistical data.

The Swedish survey was distributed together with Statistics Sweden's (SCB) monthly short-term employment statistics survey and its monthly vacancy investigation. As mandated by government regulations, employers are compelled to answer both these surveys. Our questions, however, were voluntary and printed on a separate sheet consisting of 14 questions on the use of agency workers. Coordination with the two SCB surveys also gives us relevant information on the workplaces that were taking part in the survey. For the UK, the WERS data were collected through interviews conducted with managers.

We complemented our data by using official statistics and other information gathered from unions and branch organizations. We also used legal acts and government documents from both countries and, to some extent, EU legislation.

Sample

The sample frame in our Swedish survey is based on information in the SCB (Statistics Sweden) register of all workplaces in all sectors with a three-month lag factor. The sample is stratified and weighted by SCB and is constructed to give the estimated results at a national level. Our total database includes 3804 workplaces. The response rate for our part of the Swedish survey was 57.5 per cent.

The UK managers participating in the WERS survey were usually the most senior managers at their workplace with responsibility for employment relations. There were 2191 respondents, equivalent to a response rate of 80 per cent (Cully et al. 1999: 9).[1] The two data sets consisted of workplaces with at least 10 employees, representing all industries, with the exception of agriculture, fishing, mining, private households with employed persons, and extraterritorial organizations and bodies. The British survey was conducted in 1998 and the Swedish survey in 2002.

---

[1] See http://www.niesr.ac.uk/research/wers98/ for more information on WERS.

Accordingly, there is a time lag of four years between the surveys, but we contend that this lag does not distort the analysis significantly. Because the use of agency workers is more widespread in workplaces with more than 10 employees, we must bear in mind that the levels of agency work presented in this study are overestimated in relation to the entire labour market (Håkansson and Isidorsson 2004).

The labour market in Sweden and the UK

The Swedish institutions of working-life regulation changed dramatically during the 1990s. In the post-war period up to 1991, unemployment never exceeded and was typically well below 4 per cent. Prior to the dramatic change in unemployment rates at the beginning of the 1990s, the government's understanding of frictional unemployment, though not made explicit, was 2.5 per cent (Bergström, Svensson and Ådahl 2005). In the early 1990s, the unemployment rate increased drastically to a new level of approximately 8 per cent. This figure did not include people in labour market measures. In 2005 open unemployment was at 5 per cent. The present goal of the Swedish government is to decrease the open unemployment rate to 4 per cent, which is considerably higher than it was prior to the 1990 economic crisis (Ministry of Finance 2006).

The high unemployment rate placed the question of employment security on the political agenda and generated considerable discussion among employers and employee organizations. To avoid layoffs in the workplace and to strengthen employment security, the local unions accepted the employers' demands for capacity flexibility. There are several examples of local unions accepting agreements on flexible working hours in exchange for employment security.

The legal regulation of employment in Sweden corresponds to the definition of employment as 'salaried labour in permanent full-time employment with an employer at one place of work belonging to the latter, and where the terms of employment are typically regulated collectively within a certain legal framework' (Norma 1996) . It is possible to employ personnel on a temporary basis for several reasons specified in the Employment Protection Act (LAS). Two of these exceptions are of interest here: (i) the nature of the work and (ii) temporarily high workload. However, the demand for flexibility has produced pressure to change the legal regulation of employment. During the 1990s, the government implemented several deregulations to facilitate flexibility. There have been several changes in the Employment Protection Act (SFS 1982: 80), for instance. In January 1997, a new clause in this

Act gave the employer the right to hire on a temporary basis without stating any specific conditions. However, the clause restricts the period to a maximum of twelve months during a three-year period for individual employees and for a maximum of five employees at the same time. As a way of increasing organizational adaptability to changes in demand, this new clause has significance only for small and medium-sized companies.

Another change has been the deregulation of employment and recruitment services. As mentioned above, the Swedish state's monopoly as an employment agency was abolished in 1993, and it gave way to private work and recruitment agencies. The deregulations have thus facilitated the workplaces to implement strategies for numerical flexibility.

British employment relations changed dramatically at the end of the 1970s. The 'winter of discontent' in 1978–9, when the right-wing government under Prime Minister Margaret Thatcher introduced neo-liberal policies, is seen as the turning point. When the Labour Party returned to office at the end of the 1990s, it was under another brand name: 'New Labour'. Some changes were made in employment relations, but it is not possible to say that employment conditions returned to a pre-Thatcher situation. It is notable that the UK under the Labour government is still blocking the EU directive on equal treatment for temporary agency workers as staff working under traditional employment contracts (European Parliament 2002; European Foundation 2003, 2004). Goodman et al. (2003: 35) characterize developments since 1979 as the decentralization and individualization of the employment relationship aimed at granting greater flexibility to the employer at the expense of job security for employees.

Legal framework for agency work

Compared to most other EU countries, the legal regulations covering work agencies is liberal in both the UK and Sweden (Storrie 2002: 7). The major goal behind the Swedish regulations on agency work, implemented in 1993, was to protect individuals from hindrances they might face when taking employment in the client organization. It is explicitly stressed that no agreement can be made to override this clause, and employers are not permitted to take any fees from employees. The act consists of only seven paragraphs. However, for the work agency industry itself there is no specific regulation in Sweden. There are no clauses on authorization, licensing or permission; work agencies are treated like any other business in this regard. The lack of specific regulation is in line with the Swedish tradition of labour market regulation. This tradition gives the social partners responsibility for regulation via collective agreements. However, another legal framework needs to be mentioned in this connection: the Act on Employee Consultation and Participation in Working Life, or the so-called *Medbestämmandelagen* (MBL; Codetermination Act) of 1976. It includes the explicit obligation for an employer to inform the union holding a collective agreement at the workplace about such work before using external (that is, agency) workers. In some cases there is a right for unions to veto the use of external workers (SFS 1976: 580, para. 38–9).

In Britain recruitment and work agencies have a long history. The leading business organization, the Recruitment and Employment Confederation, dates back to at least 1930. The present legislation on agency work, the Employment Agencies Act, dates from 1973.[2] There are amendments of later date, however. In 2004 the government's Department for Trade and Industry (DTI), in association with the Recruitment and Employment Confederation (REC) and the actors' trade union, Equity, settled 'The Conduct Regulations for Employment Agencies', aimed at helping both agencies and agency workers (DTI, REC and Equity 2003). Also, in British legislation agencies are prohibited from taking fees from workers in exchange for finding them work. There are some minor exceptions to this rule, primarily aimed at models and actors. Recently regulations prohibited agencies in these fields from taking any upfront fees. As in Sweden, it is explicitly stated that agencies are prohibited from restricting their workers in any way from entering the direct employment of a client firm. There are no specific regulations applicable to starting an agency in either of the two countries.

UK regulations state that temporary work agencies must give both client firms and agency workers sufficient information to select a suitable worker for a vacancy and vice versa. However, the enforcement functions under the Act are conducted by visiting inspectors employed by the Employment Agency Standards Inspectorate. There is a penalty of up to £5000 for agencies breaking the rules and the possibility of a

---

[2] The Employment Agencies Act 1973 (as amended by the Employment Protection Act 1975 and the Deregulation and Contracting Out Act 1994) sets minimum standards of conduct for employment agencies and employment businesses operating from premises in Great Britain: http://www.dti.gov.uk/er/agency/regs-pl971.htm#intro; accessed 18/11/04.

10-year ban from the sector (Directgov 2004). In summary, we would characterize the regulations in both Sweden and the UK as liberal. In the EU, discussions on temporary agency work were introduced in 1990. Initially it was seen as one of three different types of atypical work, the other two being part-time work and limited duration contracts. In 1995 the EU Commission launched an EU-level consultation with the social partners to discuss flexibility and security for these three types of atypical work. Agreements were reached on part-time work and limited-duration contracts in 1997 and 1999, and these agreements were also transformed into EU directives. The negotiations on agency work started in 2000, but ended in May 2001 without an agreement (European Parliament 2002). The EU Social Policy and Employment Council also discussed the proposed directive in March 2003 and again in October 2004, without reaching an agreement. The most important divergence is the paragraph on equal treatment on pay for agency workers and workers at the client firm (European Foundation 2003, 2004).

Employment status for agency workers

In order to make meaningful comparisons between Sweden and the UK it is necessary to clarify the employment status and related definitions of agency workers. One must be aware of the various categories of agency workers when discussing regulations on agency work and understand the definitions. The terminology on employment status is not clear-cut in either of the two countries under study. The two legally correct terms in the Swedish context are *tillsvidareanställning* (contract until further notice) and *tidsbegränsad anställning* (limited duration contract) (SFS 1982: 80 para. 4). 'Contract until further notice' is not a common term in English. WERS uses the terms 'open-ended contracts' and 'fixed-term contracts', which are the words we use to describe these two different types of employment relationships. Because agencies in Sweden are treated like any other business, the normal employment contract for an agency worker should be an open-ended contract. It is legitimate, however, to use fixed-term contracts in some act-specified cases – under conditions of temporarily high workload and probationary employment, for example. Because the nature of agency work is to fill in when clients have a demand for temporary staff, the clause 'temporarily high workload' could be said to apply to numerous cases at temporary work agencies. It is quite common for agencies to employ staff on a probationary contract for the first six months. As labour turnover is high in the temporary work agency business, there are a large number of employees on probationary contracts.[3] In other words, both these circumstances – the practice of probationary work and the high turnover in the industry – imply that there is a high proportion of limited duration contracts within the business.

The Swedish act states that open-ended contracts are valid until further notice (SFS 1982: 80). The employer must have fair grounds to dismiss an employee; shortage of work is one such legitimate ground for dismissal. Although the legislation states that the normal employment relationship in Sweden should be open-ended, our interviews at work agencies in Sweden reveal that the employment status for agency workers is not clear cut. In addition to the worker categories mentioned above, there is some but infrequent use of self-employed workers at temporary work agencies in Sweden.[4]

In the UK, the employment status of agency workers is less clear than in Sweden. Storrie (2002) notes that employment relationship statutes in UK work agencies are more intricate than those in Sweden. Law cases play an important role in British labour relations, for instance. There are several law cases in which the employment status of people working through a UK work agency has been denied. There are also examples of previous case law being overruled or changed by subsequent case decisions (IRLB 2003; Mordsley 1995; ELB 2004). There are several categories of workers mediated through work agencies in the UK, including employees at the work agency, temporary work contracts at the user firm, freelance workers and self-employed workers. If there are no significant differences among these groups, this will, among other things, affect the calculation of the number of agency workers in the UK.

As previously mentioned, the difference between agency work in Sweden and agency work in the UK can be understood in terms of Britain's liberal market economy and Sweden's coordinated market economy. In Sweden, the formation of agency work is a result of cooperation between the actors in the labour market, translated into formal rules. In the UK, agency work is formed solely on the basis of market forces, which explains the unclear employment status of agency workers.

---

[3] Based on interviews with a manager at Manpower in Göteborg (10/06/04) and a union representative at Tjänstemannaförbundet HTF (the Salaried Employees' Union) (01/04/04 and 19/05/04) and several case studies at workplaces using agency workers.

[4] Based on an interview with a manager at Manpower in Göteborg (10/06/04).

Statistical evidence for the number of agency workers

International comparisons of agency work are difficult – a problem discussed by Storrie (2002) and by Burgess and Connell (2004). As already mentioned in this chapter, one part of the difficulty arises because of the different definitions of temporary agency worker. There are also differences in the way the data are collected and by whom, resulting in a lack of consistency between the statistics on the number of agency workers in Sweden and the UK. Storrie (2002) presents a recent statistical compilation of international comparisons on the ratio of agency workers to total employment in the labour market. Drawing information from the International Confederation of Private Employment Agencies (CIETT), Storrie (2002: 28) suggests that the percentage of agency workers in Sweden in 1999 was 0.8. However, using information from *Bemanningsföretagen* (the Swedish Association of Staff Agencies) for the same year, we find a lower value of 0.6 per cent. The calculation of the number of agency workers is derived from the average number of payslips in June and December in member organizations in the Swedish Association of Staff Agencies. This method probably implies that the numbers are exaggerated, as it is possible that one person can work at two different agencies during the same month.

The Swedish Association of Staff Agencies estimates that work agencies belonging to the organization count for 80 to 85 per cent of turnover in the sector. Extrapolating to the entire Swedish labour market for 2004 results in a figure of 31,500 agency workers, or 0.7 per cent of all employees. This figure is considerably less than the figure of 42,300 for the peak year of 2000. There was a slight recovery for 2005 (Bemanningsföretagen 2005). The estimate for the UK is better than the Swedish situation; however, it is still confusing. There are several numbers used for the agency worker share of Britain's labour market: 0.9 per cent, 2.1 per cent and 3.6 per cent of the labour force (Storrie 2002: 28, 85). The latter figure for the UK is derived from CIETT's data set.

In a nutshell, these varying figures illustrate the difficulties with statistics in this area of agency workers' proportion of total employment. The CIETT-based calculation of 3.6 per cent or 976,000 agency workers for the UK and 0.8 per cent for Sweden seems, at first glance, to be the most comparable figure. It is based on the number of people on the payroll in temporary work agencies and indicates considerably higher levels of agency workers in the UK. However, it is likely that this method gives a much higher value for Britain. In Sweden the normal situation is that an agency worker works for one agency only. Our interviews with agency workers in the UK indicate that it is common to register at several agencies. Thus the possibility of being counted several times is much higher in the UK than it is in Sweden.

The lowest figure for the proportion of agency workers in the UK – 0.9 per cent or 254,000 – derives from the UK labour force survey (Storrie 2002: 28, 85). According to a report from the Department of Trade and Industry in the UK, this figure underestimates the real proportion (Hotopp 2001). The report suggests three possible reasons: self-employment, second jobs and fixed-term contracts. According to the report, 14 per cent of all placements are self-employed. For our study, the employment status of the placed staff is of minor importance because we are interested in the user perspective. However, compared to the Swedish figure, the UK labour force survey data seem to underestimate the level of agency workers. Another reason for underestimation in the UK labour force survey data is, according to the same report, that questions on second jobs do not fully capture information on agency work.

The figure of 2.1 per cent, or 557,000 agency workers, derives from a Department of Trade and Industry commissioned report on the recruitment agency industry in the UK (Hotopp 2001; Storrie 2002). The information was collected in 1999 via a telephone survey to agencies. One question asked how many individuals, including self-employed people, were placed. This survey indicates a considerably lower proportion of agency workers than the figure presented by the international agency organization, CIETT, and considerably higher than the Labour Force Survey shows. Time series data from both the British recruitment confederation and the Labour Force Survey show that agency work increased by approximately 50 per cent from 1995 to 1999. In conclusion, these issues demonstrate the difficulties in comparing data between countries. The best comparative secondary data show that the proportion of agency workers in 1999 was between 0.6 and 0.8 per cent in Sweden and approximately 2.1 per cent, or three times the Swedish rate, in the UK. Time series data on both countries show that there was a considerable increase in the number of agency workers during the 1990s (Storrie 2002).

The use of agency workers as depicted in the surveys

In this section we present the results of two workplace surveys conducted in Sweden and the UK. The surveys reveal that the use of agency workers in British workplaces is more than twice as common as it is in Swedish workplaces. In the UK, 19.6 per cent of all workplaces with 10 or more employees used agency workers; the corresponding figure for Sweden is 8.2 per cent.

Legal regulations on agency work are, as shown above, liberal in both Sweden and the UK. Regulations are therefore insufficient to explain the differences in the use of agency workers; but other institutional factors may provide valuable explanations. Work agencies and agency work has been legal for decades in the UK and is unquestioned by user firms and trade unions. According to the Koene et al. (2004) study of temporary agency work in Europe, agency work is simply part of the informal rules or shared understandings in the UK – a fact that is embedded in structures of social relations, influencing the national discourse on agency work. The longer tradition of agency work and the institutionalization of agencies explain the more widespread use of agency workers in British workplaces.

In Sweden, agency work is still regarded as a new phenomenon and widely discussed, especially within unions at the national level. The more widespread use of agency work in the UK as compared to Sweden can be understood in terms of liberal versus coordinated market economies (Hall and Soskice 2001). Agency work in Sweden is, to a larger extent, regulated by collective agreements; it is not rare for employees, at least in the larger agencies, to have open-ended contracts. The Swedish tradition in collective wage negotiations, if it has not totally prohibited wage dumping, has at least made it more difficult to use agency work for this purpose. According to a collective agreement signed by unions in the *Landsorganisationen* (LO – the Swedish Trade Union Confederation) on the one side and the employers' organizations on the other side, agency workers' earnings should correspond to wages at the workplace where they do their work. Because of the fees that user firms must pay to agencies, the direct cost for the user firm to use agency workers is higher than for directly employed personnel. However it is possible that the total cost is lower, because an agency worker might be used for a short period. In the UK, which represents a liberal market economy, the working conditions, including wages in some cases, make the direct costs of using agency workers lower than those of employing workers directly (TUC 2005; interview executive director). It is possible, therefore, to use agency work as wage dumping, thereby increasing the utilization of agency workers. However, the use of agency workers at the workplace level is not yet fully institutionalized in Sweden, and we believe that it is plausible that the proportion of employers using agency workers in Sweden will increase. Our analyses show that the proportion

Table 8.1   Workplaces using agency workers, by country, sector and size (%)

No. of employees	Private sector		Public sector	
	Sweden	UK	Sweden	UK
10–19	5.4	7.6	2.6	20.2
20–99	10.8	22.5	5.5	16.3
100	32.2	46.2	22.1	43.2
Total	9.2	19.2	5.7	21.0

Sources: Swedish Agency Worker Survey 2002 and WERS 98.

of workplaces using agency workers is larger in the UK, regardless of sector and workplace size.

As shown in Table 8.1, agency work is more common the larger the workplace. The difference between the two countries is most significant among public sector workplaces with less than 20 employees; the proportion of user organizations in this category is nearly eight times higher in the UK than in Sweden. The agency workers used in this segment of the British labour market belong, to a large extent, to professional and clerical/secretarial occupations, but also to 'personal services'. Members of this latter occupational group cannot be hired as agency workers in Sweden, which could explain some of the public sector difference.

We have shown that use of agency workers is more widespread in the UK than in Sweden. Table 8.2 also demonstrates that the dispersion between different industries is greater in the UK. 'Manufacturing industry' and the 'transport and communications industry' have a high proportion of user firms in both countries. In Sweden, manufacturing tops the list, with 15 per cent of workplaces in the industry using agency workers. In Swedish temporary work agencies, the most expanding group is manual workers to be hired for light assembly work and warehouse work. In the UK the use of agency workers is most widespread in the electricity, gas and water industry; more than half of all workplaces use agency workers, primarily because of the fundamental change from public to private ownership (Purcell and Purcell 1998). Those in permanent employment have been less secure when public organizations have turned private. To a large extent, those organizations use agency workers when they require additional staff.

The similarities between 'manufacturing industry' and 'transport and communication industry' indicate some commonality between the countries, despite their different institutional settings. Production

Table 8.2 Workplaces using agency workers, by country and industry (rank and %)

Industry	Sweden		UK	
	Rank	Per cent	Rank	Per cent
Manufacturing	1	15.0	3	32.1
Transport and communications	2	12.1	2	38.0
Other business services	3	10.2	4	32.1
Health	4	8.6	6	18.3
Hotels, restaurants	5	8.1	11	8.3
Electricity, gas and water	6	7.7	1	54.8
Construction	7	5.9	10	10.8
Wholesale and retail	8	5.0	9	12.9
Financial	9	4.5	5	29.8
Education	10	4.4	7	15.1
Other community services	11	4.0	12	6.2
Public administration services	12	3.0	8	14.3
Total	–	8.2	–	19.6

Sources: Swedish Agency Worker Survey 2002 and WERS 98.

concepts like lean production and just-in-time are widespread in these industries, and seem to provide a key explanation for their disproportionately high use of agency work. However, lean production has been designed differently in Sweden than in Britain. In Sweden, it has been influenced by a long tradition of socio-technical principles with teamwork and team authority, whereas in Britain the tradition of Taylorist principles, with strong internal control, has affected the shape of lean production (Rubery and Grimshaw 2003; Sandkull and Johansson 2000). In both countries, lean production implies teamwork, but the formation of teams in Britain has not increased the skill levels of employees. Lean production usually minimizes staff, which makes the company vulnerable to absenteeism and creates an urgent need for additional staff when demand peaks. The design of lean production seems to influence the degree to which it is possible to use agency workers. If the teams have responsibility and authority for the tasks they perform, and if it takes time to achieve the specific competencies needed, agency workers cannot easily join the team. The use of agency workers is obstructed by teamwork in which the work tasks require firm-specific skills or continuity. These conclusions are supported by data from the WERS survey, which confirm that agency workers in Britain are less often used in companies where the team members jointly decide how the work is to be done. Non-agency work user companies also report more training in teamwork than do user companies. On the other hand, a much greater proportion of user companies report training in computing and quality control, indicating another form of monitoring in user companies.[5]

As shown in Table 8.2, agency work in the UK is also widespread in 'financial services' and 'other business services'.[6] In Sweden, there is a small proportion of workplaces using agency work in 'financial services' – half the Swedish average – yet this industry had the highest increase in the use of fixed-term contracts during the 1990s (Holmlund and Storrie 2002). Furthermore, 'education', 'wholesale and retail' and 'other community services' are the industries least likely to use agency work, but constitute a high proportion of fixed-term contracts. The employers' need for temporary staff may be met by fixed-term contracts rather than agency workers. The use of fixed-term contracts is much higher in Sweden: approximately 15 per cent of all employees compared to about 7 per cent in the UK. These differences can, to a large extent, be explained by different levels of employment protection (see Chapter 1). The protection for open-ended employment is strong in Sweden, enforcing a high use of temporary employees. In the UK, where employment protection is weaker, the benefit for the employer to use temporary employees is lower.

There is a considerable regional difference in the use of agency workers in Sweden: 14 per cent of workplaces in Stockholm use agency workers, for example, compared to 6 per cent outside the big cities. The supply of agency workers is also much larger in Stockholm, facilitating new employment routines; employers who are sure of having access to extra staff can more easily adjust their staffing to a minimum. There is obviously a threshold effect in the use of agency workers.

The logistic regressions in Table 8.3 confirm that sector, size and industry are important variables in explaining the use of agency work. The table also shows that agency workers and workers on fixed-term contracts are used as substitutes in Sweden. In the UK the use of agency workers is more common if the workplace also uses workers on fixed-term contracts; that is, the use of agency workers and fixed-term contracts complement each other. In Sweden, it is the other way around. Workplaces using workers on fixed-term contracts are less inclined to

---

[5] Comparable data for Sweden are not available.
[6] 'Other business services' refers to SIC/NACE Major Group K.

Table 8.3   Odds ratios for characteristics of British and Swedish workplaces using agency workers (logistic regression)

	UK Model 1	Sweden Model 1	Sweden Model 2
Sector			
Public sector (ref.)	1	1	1
Private sector	0.55***	2.14***	1.66***
Size			
10–19 employees (ref.)	1	1	1
20–99 employees	2.11***	2.24***	2.26***
≥ 100 employees	5.62***	10.81***	10.42***
Industry			
Mean (ref.)	1	1	1
Manufacturing	1.98***	1.63***	1.98***
Elect, gas, water	3.18***	0.91	1.04
Construction	0.57***	0.86*	0.96
Wholesale, retail	0.80***	0.74***	0.74***
Hotels & restaurants	0.59***	1.21*	1.21*
Transport	2.14***	1.74***	1.96***
Finance	2.44***	0.58***	0.59***
Other business services	2.53***	1.32***	1.24***
Public admin. services	0.32***	0.53***	0.50***
Education	0.49	0.82**	0.70***
Health	1.02***	2.33***	2.01***
Other community services	0.27	0.65***	0.56***
Workplace uses fixed-term contracts			
No (ref.)	1	1	1
Yes	1.80***	0.61***	0.65***
Male dominance ≥ 60%			
Yes (ref.)	1	1	1
No	0.74***	1.12**	1.12**
Region			
Non-metropolitan area (ref.)			1
Stockholm			2.54***
Göteborg			1.94***
Malmö			1.01
Constant	0.17***	0.03***	0.02***
n	2172	3804	3804

Note: * = p < 0.05; ** = p < 0.01; *** = p < 0.001.
Sources: Swedish Agency Worker Survey 2002 and WERS 98.

use agency workers. Adding the variable region to the analyses in Model 2 affects the odds ratio values in the variables sector and industry. This underlines the importance of taking notice of regions when analysing the use of agency work. Unfortunately we have no equivalent data for the UK.

To sum up, the use of agency workers in both countries is high in industries where lean production has been implemented. Production concepts are therefore one explanation for the use of agency workers. The higher proportion of workplaces using agency work in Britain is due to institutional settings. It is also important to note the differences in the use of fixed-term contracts in the British and Swedish labour markets. In Sweden, industries with a low proportion of workplaces using agency workers have a high proportion of employees on fixed-term contracts. There seems to be a substitution effect between temporary agency workers and temporary employment. This conclusion is also confirmed by logistic regression. Agency workers in the UK usually have fixed-term contracts at the agency for which they work; in Sweden, however, agency workers in the large agency firms are often employed on open-ended contracts. In other words, British workplaces use fixed-term employees, but through an agency. We can conclude, then, that employers in both countries use temporary employees, albeit in different ways.

Motives for using agency workers

As previously mentioned one widespread explanation – and one used as an argument by some employers' organizations – is that the increase in the number of agency workers is due to the workplace need for flexibility or adaptability to changes in demand. The concept of flexibility is widely used in the debate, and a clarification of the real motives is therefore of interest. The questionnaire sent to the Swedish workplaces lists nine possible motives; the British management questionnaire (WERS) lists six. Both surveys comprise questions on numerical flexibility and numerical stability. Some of the motives are equivalent; some are not comparable. In total, the questionnaires give a view of the most important motives for using agency work at the workplace level. Each workplace can select several motives for the use of agency workers. The data are founded on information from the manager or staff responsible for human resources.

As seen in Table 8.4, the most common motive for using agency workers in both Sweden and the UK is to cover for staff absence. One plausible explanation could be an ongoing downsizing. A slimmed-

Table 8.4   Motives for using agency workers by country and sector (%)

	Private		Public		Total	
	Sweden	UK	Sweden	UK	Sweden	UK
Numerical stability	66	60	95	83	72	66
Numerical flexibility	48	43	25	24	43	38
Specialist skills	12	9	5	19	11	12
Difficulties in recruiting	5	20	21	15	8	19
Buffer/freeze on permanent staff	17	11	0	10	13	11

Sources: Swedish agency worker survey and WERS 98.

down organization with no slack is vulnerable to any absenteeism and must replace most of its absent employees in order to maintain production. Thus the replacement of absent personnel is an expression of stability, not, as stated in the public debate, for the purpose of flexibility. This is an issue that is discussed by Jonsson in this volume (Chapter 3) and by Burgess and Connell (2004: 5). A similar result was found in a Norwegian study, indicating that firms put the value of numerical stability above the value of numerical flexibility (Nesheim 2003). In our two surveys the stability motive is mentioned by 72 per cent of Swedish user firms and 66 per cent of British user firms.

The second most frequent motive reflects the employers' need for additional personnel; 43 per cent of the Swedish workplaces and 38 per cent of the UK workplaces using agency workers declare that they use them during peak demand periods. The need for agency workers during these periods indicates that these workplaces adjust the permanent staff to a minimum level, meeting their demands by an increase in temporary staffing. We label this motive numerical flexibility.[7] According to John Atkinson's (1984, Atkinson and Meager 1986) model of the flexible firm, this is how agency workers are supposed to be used. The generalizability of the Atkinson model could be questioned, however, because the prevalence of the flexibility motive is well below the stability motive among users of agency work.

---

[7] This motive is measured by merging two items in the Swedish survey: 'Foreseeable need for extra staff' and 'Unforeseeable need for extra staff'. In the British survey, the flexibility motive is measured by one question: 'Matching staff to peaks in demand'.

Instead of using agency workers during peak periods, workplaces can use agency workers regularly as a buffer because they predict that the number of staff is going to be reduced. This is typically the case after company mergers or massive reorganizations in which extensive reductions have taken place. Case studies indicate that these reductions are sometimes too extensive, implying a need for extra staff. Instead of re-employing people, the company uses agency workers to fill the gaps. The number of employees in the workplace is then dimensioned after a prediction of the future needs, and the agency workers are used during a period of transition. In this case, flexibility is used in a downward direction and the agency workers are used as a buffer. Closely related to this buffer motive is the freeze on permanent staff in the user organization. The employer is not allowed to increase the number of employees (head count) because of cost savings or future reductions. The buffer motive is mentioned by 13 per cent of the Swedish workplaces.[8] In the UK, this motive is formulated as a freeze on permanent staff; 11 per cent of the British user organizations declare this as a motive. Both the buffer motive and freeze on permanent staff motive reflect employers' wish or need for downward flexibility.

Another motive for using agency workers is the need for specialist skills. This motive is mentioned by 11 per cent of the Swedish workplaces and 12 per cent of the British. Finally, the use of agency workers can be the only option when the employer is unable to recruit personnel. Difficulties in recruiting constitute the fifth motive, mentioned by 8 per cent of the Swedish user firms and 19 per cent of the British user firms.

The motives for using agency workers in the public and private sectors show both similarities in and differences between Sweden and the UK. The stability motive is, without doubt, more frequent in the public sector and the flexibility motive more common in the private sector. This result holds true for both countries. Flexibility is the most common motive mentioned by user firms in 'manufacturing' and 'construction' in both countries (for the UK also the electricity, gas and water industry). Because work in the public sector typically is not exposed to fluctuations in demand in the same way as in the private sector, it is not surprizing that flexibility is not as strong a motive in the public sector. On the other hand, the extensive withdrawal of personnel during the 1990s had a large impact on the Swedish public sector, implying a need to

---

[8] The buffer motive is measured by merging two items: 'Manning in the future is uncertain' and 'Avoiding the law on employment security'.

replace absent employees even for short periods. This fact explains the high proportion of workplaces in the public sector using agency workers to replace absent employees: the stability motive. The flexibility motive in the private sector is not surprizing, due to its use of new production concepts such as just-in-time and lean production. Notably, stability is the most frequently reported motive, even in the private sector; despite the fact that an important part of the lean production discourse is flexibility. However, flexible staffing is, to a large extent, used to achieve stability.

In Sweden, the need for specialist skills is more frequent in the private sector, particularly in 'hotels and restaurants' and in 'transport and communication'; in Britain, this motive is more frequent among public sector users, particularly in 'public administration'. In Sweden, recruiting difficulties are primarily a motive in the public sector; in Britain recruiting difficulties are more likely to be found in the private sector, particularly in 'construction' and 'hotels and restaurants'.

In order to obtain a more thorough analysis of where the flexibility and stability motive is used we have executed a logistic regression, enabling us to account for several variables, such as sector, size and industry, in one analysis. Because we have analysed only workplaces using agency work, however, we have grouped some industries in order to obtain sufficient quality in the output data.

As Table 8.5 demonstrates, the probability for the stability motive is four to five times higher in workplaces in the public sector when accounting for workplace size and industry, if the workplace uses employees on fixed-term contracts and if the workplace is male dominated. This finding holds true for both countries. For workplaces in both British and Swedish industries, transport and communication has the highest probability of using agency workers to achieve stability, compared to the mean for all industries.

The flexibility motive also shows similarities and differences when we compare the two countries. Beginning with the similarities, one can see in Table 8.5 that workplaces in the merged industries of 'manufacturing, electricity, gas and water supply, and construction' show higher odds ratios for using agency work to achieve flexibility in both countries.[9] In Sweden, the odds ratio is nearly three times as high as the industry mean, while in the UK it is twice the average. In both countries the

---

[9] Because we have analysed only workplaces using agency work, we have grouped some industries in order to obtain output data of sufficient quality.

Table 8.5 Odds ratios for characteristics of British and Swedish workplaces using agency workers for stability and flexibility reasons (logistic regression)

	User organizations in the UK		User organizations in Sweden	
	Stability	Flexibility	Stability	Flexibility
Sector				
Public sector (ref.)	1	1	1	1
Private sector	0.24***	1.75***	0.20***	0.89
Size				
10–19 employees (ref.)	1	1	1	1
20–99 employees	1.21***	1.21***	0.89	1.51***
≥ 100 employees	1.25***	1.72***	1.26*	2.96***
Industry				
Mean (ref.)	1	1	1	1
Manufacturing; elect., gas, water; and Construction	1.10***	1.92**	0.58***	2.99***
Wholesale, retail; hotel & restaur.; and other com. services	1.11***	0.64***	1.10	0.67***
Transport and communication	1.20***	0.70***	1.68***	1.21*
Finance and other business services	0.89***	1.57***	0.853*	0.98
Public admin. serv.; education and Health	0.76***	0.74***	1.08	0.42***
Workplace uses fixed-term contracts				
No (ref.)	1	1	1	1
Yes	1.14***	1.45***	1.26***	0.46***
Male dominance ≥ 60%				
Yes (ref.)	1	1	1	1
No	1.03	0.88***	1.60***	1.26**
Constant	4.66***	0.25***	8.56***	0.68***
n	822	822	706	706

Notes: * $= p < 0.05$; ** $= p < 0.01$; *** $= p < 0.001$.
Sources: Swedish agency worker survey and WERS 98.

odds ratio that agency work is used for flexibility in our grouping 'public administration, education and health' is well below average. The odds ratio in Swedish workplaces is less than half that of the industry mean; in the UK it is three-quarters.

In the UK the odds ratio is 0.7 of the average in transport and communication; in the Swedish case it is slightly above average at 1.21, yet with a lower probability level. One can also notice that male-dominated workplaces in Sweden have a lower odds ratio for using agency workers to achieve flexibility compared to workplaces not dominated by males; the same goes for stability. In the UK, it is the opposite; among male-dominated users, a higher odds ratio for the use of agency workers is motivated by flexibility compared to workplaces that are not dominated by males. As for the stability motive, there was no significant difference between male-dominated workplaces and other workplaces.

Another difference concerning the flexibility motive is sector. Although the odds ratio is higher in workplaces in the British private sector, there is no significant difference between workplaces in the public and private sectors in Sweden. The Swedish case is explained by the insertion of the industry variable into the logistic regression analysis. Industry levels out the difference between the sectors.

Conclusions

This study shows that the use of agency workers at British workplaces is more widespread than in Sweden. In Britain 19.2 per cent of the workplaces use agency workers, compared to 8.2 per cent for Sweden. The figures on the number of agency workers are higher in the UK than in Sweden. The figures presented in this chapter on the proportion of agency workers in the labour market were 0.8 per cent of employees in Sweden and 2.1 per cent in the UK. There is still some uncertainty about the levels, but there seems to be approximately twice as many agency workers in the UK than in Sweden.

The primary explanation for the different levels of employers' use of agency workers is related to the different institutional settings in the two countries. The higher use of agency work in the UK compared to Sweden can be understood in terms of liberal and coordinated market economies (Hall and Soskice 2001). Agency work in Sweden is, to a greater extent, regulated by collective agreements, including clauses prohibiting wage dumping. Employees, at least in the larger agencies, are employed with open-ended contracts after a six-month probationary contract. There is also a clear employment situation. The formation of agency work in

Sweden is the result of cooperation between the actors on the labour market, accepted in the formal rules in the labour market, but not yet institutionalized in staffing behaviour at workplace level. In the UK, representing a liberal market economy, agency work is based solely on market forces, which explains the unclear employment relationship shown in the different law cases. We have also seen examples of agency workers working under poorer working conditions and at lower direct costs than employees at the user firm. Agency work has been legal for decades in the UK and is questioned by neither user firms nor trade unions. Agency work is simply a part of the informal rules or shared understandings. The longer tradition of agency work and the absence of questioning the work agencies explain the more widespread use of agency staff in British workplaces.

The use of temporary agency workers seems to be influenced by a threshold effect; when agency work reaches a certain minimum level, it is a convenient option for managers. In other words, when agency work is institutionalized, it becomes an everyday alternative in staffing. This situation is most obvious in Britain; however, the phenomenon is visible in Stockholm, where the agency industry is more widespread than it is in other Swedish regions. The threshold effect is also supported by the second model of our logistic regression. Introducing regions into the analyses notably reduces the importance of the two variables, sector and industry, indicating that Sweden will probably see an increase in the use of agency work – if we see agency work as a phenomenon first occurring in Stockholm then diffusing to other parts of Sweden.

The use of agency workers in workplaces in different industries shows a greater dispersion in Britain than in Sweden. In Sweden the values range between 15 per cent for manufacturing and 3 per cent for public administration. In the UK, the corresponding values are 54.8 per cent for electricity, gas and water and 6.2 for other community services. However, even though the level is higher and the dispersion is greater in the UK, there are some similarities in the use of agency workers between the two countries; workplaces in manufacturing and transport and communications are above average. These industries have also implemented lean production and just-in-time production to a greater extent and are therefore more dependent on staffing on demand. These similarities also indicate that production concepts are important in explaining the use of agency work.

Some differences in the use of agency workers between the two countries are related to the different use of fixed-term contracts. In Sweden, 15 per cent of all employees have fixed-term contracts; the corresponding proportion for the UK is 7 per cent. There seems to be a substitution effect between temporary agency workers and temporary employment. Agency workers in the UK have fixed-term contracts at the agency when they are on assignments; whereas in Sweden agency workers in the big agency firms are usually on open-ended contracts after a period of probationary contract. In other words, British workplaces use fixed-term employees, but via an agency.

The need for numerical flexibility is a common motive reported by approximately 40 per cent of the workplaces using agency work in both countries, particularly in manufacturing. This result points to the importance of production concepts like lean production as an explanation for the use of agency workers. The motive of numerical flexibility is more frequent in larger firms in both Sweden and the UK. Temporary agency workers are used not only as a means to achieving numerical flexibility – to adapt to changes in demand by using additional staff in peaks. The most frequently stated motive for using agency workers is stability. This finding holds true in both the private and public sectors and in both countries. In Sweden, 72 per cent of workplaces using agency workers used them to achieve stability – that is to fill the gap caused by absent staff. The corresponding figure for the UK is 66 per cent. This finding indicates that workplaces cannot handle absenteeism, probably because there is so little slack in organizations at a time of ongoing downsizing and intensification of work.

In conclusion, we can say that agency work offers flexible staffing arrangements that are, to a large extent, used to achieve stability. Our results show that the flexibility discussion on agency work is exaggerated, and reflects ideology rather than actual behaviour. Stability is a more common motive for using agency workers than is flexibility. An employer's need for stability is achieved by a flexible work arrangement, which, from the perspective of the individual agency worker, implies instability.

9
Flexible Work Situations and Employees' Thoughts of Leaving the Organization

Tomas Berglund

One important factor in labour market flexibility is the readiness of employees to change jobs and employers. The mobility of employees to growing sectors of the economy is commonly regarded as a sign of a well-functioning labour market. However, flexibility is a complex concept, as demonstrated by Jonsson in Chapter 3 of this volume. Before we can make use of this notion in a stringent and scientific way, we must always ask, 'For whom is flexibility desirable?' Furthermore, flexibility has a conceptual companion in stability through the concept of desirable non-variation. Jonsson stresses the point that variation and change may not always be the ideal for an agent; it could rather be interpreted as instability. From a labour market perspective, therefore, employees' potential for mobility can be regarded as a prerequisite for labour market flexibility; but from the perspective of the employer, employees who want to leave the organization may create instability and potential replacement costs.

In the light of this reasoning, employers may try to structure employee preferences, thereby influencing their employees' desire to stay in or leave the organization. Some segments of the workforce are valuable for the organization and costly to replace; others are more disposable and can function as a buffer in case of reductions. In order to influence employee preferences, the employer can offer more or less favourable working conditions and work situations, creating satisfying jobs that

---

Note: This chapter was written as part of the research project 'Individualisation and Social Comparisons. A Study of Psychosocial Work Environments, Job Satisfaction and Stress', led by Bengt Furåker. The author wants to thank the Swedish Council for Working Life and Social Research for financing the project.

may have retaining effects on employees. On the other hand, less satisfying and insecure working conditions may make employees less prone to stay with an employer, and push them to look for a new job.

To further complicate the situation, it is possible that an organization's internal striving for flexibility plays a role in structuring employee preferences to stay with or leave the employer. In this vein, one can distinguish between *functional flexibility* and *numerical flexibility*. Strategies of functional flexibility can create a core of highly skilled employees with permanent employment. The competencies and skills of the employees become more important factors in the production process, facilitating greater autonomy and allowing for the decentralization of some aspects of decision-making. Functional flexibility has been related to job enrichment, high quality jobs and work autonomy; and to increased demands on achievement in and intensification of work (Gouliquer 2000; Kalleberg 2001; Ramsay et al. 2000; Smith 1997). Such working conditions, which are favourable in many ways, can create a level of job satisfaction and organizational commitment that may induce a willingness to stay with an employer.

Employers use numerical flexibility to adapt to fluctuations in the business cycle. To make it possible to adjust the number of employees to these fluctuations, employers have used atypical employment arrangements like temporary contracts, leaving some employees in a precarious labour market situation (Treu 1992). In an exchange relationship in which the employer cannot offer job security, employees' levels of commitment to their organization may be low. Consequently, employees in atypical employment may be more willing to seek a new job than are core employees with permanent contracts and full-time work schedules.

In this chapter, we focus on employees' thoughts of leaving an employer – so-called withdrawal cognitions – and possible mechanisms behind that preference. Withdrawal cognitions are attitudinal dispositions, which must be distinguished from actual turnover. Social psychology has shown that there is seldom a perfect relationship between attitudes and the actual actions taken by the individual (Ajzen and Fishbein 1980). In the case of withdrawal cognitions and turnover, however, Tett and Meyer's (1993) meta-study has found relatively strong relationships. This chapter examines possible effects of an organizational core or periphery position on employees' withdrawal cognitions. Mediating processes in these relationships are believed to be job insecurity, job satisfaction and organizational commitment. The proposed relationships are tested on questionnaire data collected from Swedish employees during spring 2003.

Withdrawal cognitions in the functional core

The term 'functional flexibility' has been used in the literature to refer to the capacity of an organization to adapt to qualitative changes in demand and methods of production. This capacity depends to a large extent on the organization's success in developing new skills among its employees. Investments in employee competencies and skills through training and learning programmes are costly, which creates an interest in retaining personnel over long periods.

One strategy for creating a motivated and stable core is the use of so-called high-performance work systems (Kalleberg 2001; Ramsay et al. 2000). The purpose of these human resource management strategies is to facilitate innovation and performance in the organization by providing employees with influence, skills and information, and by involving them in teamwork. One central effect of these strategies is believed to be the strengthening of employees' organizational commitment.

This expectation seems to be a reasonable one, given the research on causes of organizational commitment. One well-known model is provided by Mowday, Porter and Steers (1982). In their research, the definition of organizational commitment includes a belief in the organization's values and goals, a willingness to exert extra effort on behalf of the organization and a willingness to remain in the organization. It has been proposed that job satisfaction – an emotional reaction to the fulfilment inherent in job conditions – is one important antecedent of organizational commitment (Lincoln and Kalleberg 1990; Hult 2004). Thus employees maintain their commitment to the organization to the extent that the organization fulfils their values and job expectations. In relation to high-performance work systems, there is some evidence that job satisfaction is positively related to these work practices, even though the results also show an increase in their stress and their workload (Godard 2001; Ramsay et al. 2000).

Studies have demonstrated that job satisfaction and organizational commitment have negative effects on withdrawal cognitions, in that employees become less inclined to leave the organization if they feel satisfied with their job or if they are highly committed to the organization. However, some studies have shown separate effects of organizational commitment and job satisfaction on withdrawal cognitions (Tett and Meyer 1993). This finding suggests that organizational commitment and job satisfaction are different attitudinal reactions to working conditions, with different causal relationships to thoughts of quitting. Other studies have demonstrated a causal chain in which job satisfaction is antecedent to organizational commitment, meaning that organizational commitment mediates the effect of job satisfaction on withdrawal cognitions (Tett and Meyer 1993). Consequently, the effects of working conditions on job satisfaction constitute the primary relationship, and organizational commitment is merely a by-product. Other antecedents to organizational commitment, such as work ethic, are exogenous to work.

If we attempt to relate these considerations to the characterization of functional flexibility, however, it is reasonable to believe that working conditions in the functional core are related to increased job satisfaction and organizational commitment. It is therefore expected that a low prevalence of withdrawal cognitions exists among core workers and that this relationship is mediated by job satisfaction and organizational commitment.

Numerical flexibility and thoughts of leaving

Numerical flexibility refers to an organization's ability to adjust the size of its workforce to accommodate environmental changes – particularly to fluctuations in the demand for services or products. The use of agency workers, discussed in Chapters 7 and 8, is one method for creating numerical flexibility and externalizing parts of the workforce (Kalleberg 2001). In another strategy, certain segments of the employee pool are not offered permanent contracts; rather an attempt is made to couple employees to the organization on a much looser basis through various forms of temporary contracts.

There is a common agreement among researchers that temporary employees experience higher job insecurity than permanent employees do (de Witte and Näswall 2003). However, the concept of job insecurity is ambiguous; it can refer to the subjective perceptions that one is at risk of losing one's job (Burchell 2002) or to objective involuntary job-loss rates. Furthermore, the subjective perception of job insecurity can be distinguished by its cognitive and affective component (Guest 2004). The cognitive component refers to knowledge about the security of one's job. The affective component refers to emotional responses to that information, which can be due to one's judgement about one's labour market opportunities. It is reasonable to believe that employees with temporary employment are aware of their precarious situation in relation to the organization in which they are working. In this regard, there should be a clear association between employment status and the cognitive aspect of subjective job insecurity.

Because of their job insecurity, temporary employees may be less inclined than permanent employees are to stay in an organization. However, the affective and cognitive dimensions of subjective job security could have different relationships to thoughts of quitting. On the one hand, the worry of losing one's job may originate from a strong commitment to the position in which one is currently employed. It is not obvious, therefore, that worry is linked to withdrawal cognitions. On the other hand, information about one's job security may be used as a basis for rational calculations about one's future in the organization. Withdrawal cognitions would be a logical consequence for people in insecure jobs.

The use of part-time employment is sometimes included in the model of numerical flexibility (Atkinson 1985). This decision has been disputed by researchers who look at part-time work as a more permanent type of employment status and as a typical employment status for many women (Furåker and Berglund 2001; Kalleberg 2001; Tam 1997). Consequently, part-time workers may not create numerical flexibility in the way in which theory proposes. On the other hand, there is some evidence for looking at part-time workers as being more peripheral to the organization than full-time workers are. Studies in Britain show that part-time employees have lower wages and poorer promotion prospects and fringe benefits than full-time workers do (Tam 1997). Labour legislation in Sweden promotes equal treatment of full- and part-time workers (Kalleberg 2000), however, which implies that these effects of exclusion may not be as salient in the Swedish context.

At least from a theoretical point of view, the possible effects of full-time versus part-time employment on such work attitudes as organizational commitment can be explained by the theory of partial inclusion (Katz and Kahn 1978). This theory explains reduced organizational involvement through the partial inclusion of part-time workers in the social system of the organization and, consequently, their lower levels of socialization into the value system and role behaviours of their workplace. However, there is no obvious reason for believing that a relationship exists between working time and withdrawal cognitions. If it does, one possible mediating variable could be organizational commitment. Part-time employees, who enjoy less organizational integration than their full-time peers do, may have more thoughts of quitting their jobs.

Data and method

In the analyses to follow, we use a data set originating from a postal survey collected during spring 2003. The sampling frame comprised 16- to 64-year-old participants who were employed at the time of the survey. They were all participants in the Swedish regular labour force survey, administrated by Statistics Sweden and randomly selected through the central population register. A total of 4558 participants were asked on the telephone if they were willing to receive a postal questionnaire, and 460 declined. Of the remaining 4098 employees, 3286 returned the questionnaire, yielding a 72 per cent response rate.

To test the hypothetical reasoning above, we use a method that separates direct and indirect relationships that have been proposed in theory by analysing them through various steps and models (Aneshensel 2002; Baron and Kenny 1986; Chirumbolo and Hellgren 2003). Theoretically, we believe that there are relationships between work situations characterized by a core versus a peripheral position on the one hand and withdrawal cognitions on the other hand. These are the focal relationships for the study.

A core position is characterized by functional flexibility through the use of so-called high-performance work systems. In previous studies, the prevalence of high-performance work systems has been measured on an organizational level, by asking management; and on an individual level, by asking employees. Ramsay et al. (2000) measured these practices on an organizational level, but studied the consequences on an individual level. Their focus was on the organizational practices that enhanced employee involvement (for example, job control, team autonomy), created motivation (that is, incentive schemes), and aimed at skill-development. Godard (2001) measured the prevalence of high-performance work practices by directly asking employees. A distinction was made between on-line and off-line practices. On-line practices focused on the presence of teamwork, multi-skilling and job rotation; and off-line practices focused on such participatory practices as quality circles and committee systems.

In the present study, no direct information about the prevalence of high-performance work practices in the workplace is available, either at an organizational or an individual level. Instead, these practices are measured indirectly through their presumed effects on two indicators. The first indicator measures the extent of employee discretion over central aspects of the work situation. Employees are asked about the extent to which they have discretion in five aspects of their work: the planning of their work day, the performance of work tasks, their working hours, their salary, and further education or training during paid working time. Reponses are given on a 5-point scale (to a very large extent, to a large extent, to a certain extent, to a small extent, not at all). The summation of the responses to these five questions constitutes the discretion scale, the range of which is 0–20, where higher values indicate greater influence over the work situation ($\alpha = 0.79$). In the logistic and multinominal regressions performed on these data, only scales with a linear relationship to the dependent variable in the logit model meet the conditions for use as independent variables (Menard 1995). This condition is not met for the discretion scale in some of the analyses below. To handle this problem, the discretion scale has been reduced to a categorical variable by dividing it into three parts: small influence (0–5), medium influence (6–13) and large influence (14–20).

The second indicator of high-performance work practices is an approximation of the extent of teamwork in the employees' work situations, measured by asking employees about the extent to which their jobs involve cooperation with workmates. The response alternatives to this question are the same as those in the 'extent of discretion' questions.

Peripheral positions, believed to be characterized by numerical flexibility, have been described as atypical employment. In this study, a direct indicator of atypical employment is the type of employment contract and the distinction between permanent and temporary contracts. Temporary contracts include fixed-term contracts, seasonal work, substitutes, on-demand employment, probationary employment and participation in labour market programmes. Another indicator of a more peripheral position is weekly working hours. In this study, we differentiate among full-time (35 hours or more), long part-time (21–34 hours) and short part-time (20 hours or less) work.

The central dependent variable for the analyses is an indicator of withdrawal cognitions. The variable is constructed by a question in which employees are asked: 'Over the recent period, have you thought about or decided to change workplace?' The response options were 'No', 'Yes, I have thought about changing workplace' and 'Yes, I have decided to change workplace'. The last two options have been collapsed into one category indicating withdrawal cognitions.

Theoretically, we believe that there are mediating mechanisms between the central independent variables and the dependent variable (see Figure 9.1). Core workers characterized by discretion and close cooperation are believed to be less inclined to have withdrawal cognitions than are workers with less influence and no cooperation with

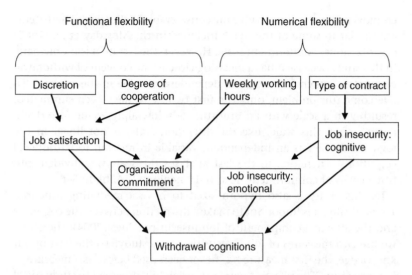

Figure 9.1   Hypothetical model of factors affecting withdrawal cognitions

workmates. These relationships are believed to be mediated by job satisfaction and organizational commitment. Furthermore, a possible effect of weekly working hours – part-time workers' greater inclination to change workplaces – is due to the mediating effect of organizational commitment. The hypothesized effect of type of contract on withdrawal cognitions is believed to be mediated by job insecurity. Temporary workers are believed to have a greater inclination to change their workplaces than are workers employed on a permanent basis. The mechanism mediating this effect is primarily a cognitive experience of job insecurity and, secondarily, an emotional response to that information.

To obtain a general or 'global' measure of job satisfaction, employees were asked to describe, using a 5-point ordinal scale, how satisfied or dissatisfied they were with nine facets of their job (pay, working times, work tasks, work load, physical work environment, psychosocial work environment, possibilities for further training, career opportunities and extent of codetermination in management of work activities). The resulting measure ($\alpha = 0.84$) was constructed by summing the responses to these nine items.

Three questions in the survey measured organizational commitment: 'I am proud of my workplace'; 'In order to make my employer successful, I am willing to work harder than is normally required'; and 'I would rather work for my present employer than take a job with another employer who is willing to give me considerably higher pay'. These items are similar to some of the items included in the Mowday et al. (1982) organizational commitment scale. However, the last item is problematic in this study because it has a meaning close to the concept of withdrawal cognitions, which is the central dependent variable in the analysis. To overcome this problem, only the first two items have been summated, resulting in a scale with an unfortunately low alpha value ($\alpha = 0.57$). Furthermore, this scale, like the discretion scale, is not linear in the logit when used as an independent variable in relation to withdrawal cognitions. Therefore, in the last analyses the scale was divided into three levels of commitment (low: 0–1; medium: 2–4; high: 5–6).

Job insecurity is also hypothesized to have a mediating function. Theoretically, it is important to make a distinction between the cognitive and the affective component of job insecurity (Guest 2004); therefore, we use two measures of job insecurity in this study. To the best of our knowledge, the first measure has never been used before as a measure of job insecurity. The questionnaire was originally designed to study social comparisons in working life. Many of the questions varied according to the referent group and comparison attributes. In one battery of questions, employees were asked: 'Compare the following facets of your job with those of your closest workmates. In comparison, how do the following appear in your job?' Various facets of the job were then listed, one of which was 'job security'. The response options were: 'I have it much better', 'I have it slightly better', 'We have it approximately the same', 'I have it slightly worse' and 'I have it much worse'. The variable used in the analyses comprised the response options collapsed into three categories: 'better', 'equal', 'worse'.

Because social comparisons are used by the individual to find information about his or her situation by contrasting it to important referent groups (Festinger 1954), this job security comparison brings the cognitive aspect of job security to the forefront. However, the social comparison can also produce emotional effects that could stem from such information: feelings of injustice and dissatisfaction (Adams 1965) or, something which could be an effect of this particular information, worrying about losing one's job. To measure the possible affective component of job insecurity, a second variable was created from the question: 'To what extent do you worry about losing your job?' The response options were collapsed into categories representing three degrees of worry: great worry/some worry; little worry; no worry.

In order to examine the direct effects of the central independent variables and the relative importance of the mediating variables, the analyses were conducted in several steps (Aneshensel 2002; Baron and Kenny 1986; Chirumbolo and Hellgren 2003). In the first step, the focal independent variables were regressed on the mediating variables, allowing us to study any relationships that might exist among the independent variables of discretion, degree of cooperation, weekly working hours and type of contract; and the mediating variables of job insecurity, job satisfaction and organizational commitment. Because different levels are employed in the dependent variables, we have had to use different forms of regression techniques to conduct the analyses. The reasons for the differing techniques are explained subsequently.

In a second step, the direct effects on withdrawal cognitions of discretion, degree of cooperation, weekly working hours and type of contract are studied. In a third step, the mediating variables (job insecurity, job satisfaction and organizational commitment) are inserted into the regression analysis. The purpose of this procedure is to determine whether the insertion of the mediating variables affects the estimates of the relationships among the central independent variables and withdrawal cognitions. If the estimates are reduced by the insertion of the mediating variables, a mediating effect is confirmed. Perfect mediation occurs if the central independent variables no longer predict withdrawal cognitions (see Chirumbolo and Hellgren 2003).

Some background variables are also included in the regressions: gender, age, country of birth, employment sector, occupational group, supervisory tasks, number of employees at the workplace, tenure at present workplace and union membership. In Table 9.1, frequencies, means and standard deviations for the variables are presented.

Table 9.1 Descriptive statistics (dependent and independent variables)

Central dependent variable			
Withdrawal cognitions	%		
No	54.7		
Yes	45.3		
Total (n)	100 (3259)		

Central independent variables			
Weekly working hours	%	*Discretion*	%
<21 hours	27.6	Small (0–5)	15.6
21–34 hours	19.4	Medium (6–13)	64.6
>34 hours	53.0	Large (14–20)	19.8
Total (n)	100 (3286)	Total (n)	100 (2896)

Table 9.1 (Continued)

Central independent variables

Type of contract	%	Cooperation with workmates	%
Temporary	12.2	To a very large extent	40.2
Permanent	87.8	To a large extent	33.6
Total (n)	100 (3286)	To a certain extent	17.9
		To a small extent/not at all	8.3
		Total (n)	100 (3193)

Mediators

Better or worse job security	%	Worry about losing one's job	%
Better	8.4	Great/some worry	14.9
Worse	9.3	Little worry	21.4
Equal	82.3	No worry	63.7
Total (n)	100 (3102)	Total (n)	100 (3205)

Organizational commitment	%	Job satisfaction (scale 0–36)	M = 21.2; sd = 5.9
Low (0–1)	10.9	n	2743
Medium (2–4)	71.6		
High (5–6)	17.5		
Total (n)	100 (2986)		

Organizational commitment (scale 0–6)	M = 3.2
	sd = 1.4
n	2986

Background variables

Gender	%	Country of birth	%
Male	44.9	Sweden	91.4
Female	55.1	Outside Sweden	8.6
Total (n)	100 (3286)	Total (n)	100 (3286)

Age	%	Occupational group	%
16–34	28.4	Managers	4.3
35–49	38.6	Professionals	20.2
50–64	33.0	Semi-professionals	20.1
Total (n)	100 (3286)	Service workers	34.7
		Manual workers	20.7
		Total (n)	100 (3274)

Employment sector	%
Public	39.4
Private	60.6
Total (n)	100 (3282)

Union member	%
No	17.3
Yes	82.7
Total(n)	100(3286)

Supervisor	%
Yes	19.7
No	80.3
Total (n)	100 (3220)

Tenure at present workplace	%	Number of employees in the workplace	%
≤ 6 months	8.6	<10	17.4
> 6 months ≤ 2 years	18.2	10–19	14.6
> 2 years ≤ 5 years	24.3	20–49	20.5
> 5 years ≤ 10 years	15.9	50–99	13.4
> 10 years	33.0	100–499	17.8
Total (n)	100 (3156)	≥500	16.3
		Total(n)	100(3097)

Results

The starting point for the analyses is the relationships between the central independent variables and the variables that are believed to have a mediating function. The focus in the first analyses is the two measures of job insecurity. Because of the character of the variables measuring job insecurity, we use multinominal regressions to study the effects of the independent variables. Multinominal regressions are suitable when the dependent variable is represented by a nominal scale and there are more than two response categories (Long 1997). In our case, it would have been possible to argue that the dependent variables are ordinal, which made it more correct to use ordinal regressions. But one condition was not met: the parallel regression assumption that the regression estimates should remain the same over the different thresholds in the dependent variable (Long 1997). Therefore, multinominal regressions are more suitable.

Table 9.2 presents the results of the analyses of the two measures of job insecurity. The first regression is on job security in comparison to close workmates. Although we find few statistically significant effects of the central independent variables on the dependent variable, there is one important effect of type of contract: higher odds of temporary than permanent employees describing their job security as being worse than that of close workmates. This is an expected effect if we look at the dependent variable as more a cognitive than an emotional aspect of job insecurity. Obviously, one might expect most temporary employees to be prone to judging their job security as being worse than that of their workmates because there is a high probability that their close workmates are permanently employed.

There are some notable results among the background variables that are statistically significant. Men more than women and private employees more than public employees are inclined to see their job

Table 9.2 Better or worse job security compared to that of close workmates (0 = equal job security) and worry about losing one's job (0 = not worried at all) (multinomial regressions; odds ratios)

		Job security in comparison to workmates		Worry about losing one's job	
		Better job security	Worse job security	Great or some worry	Small worry
Gender	Male	1.63**	1.23	1.31+	1.20
	Female (ref.)	1	1	1	1
Age	16–34	1.64*	1.69+	0.89	0.97
	35–49	0.88	1.84*	1.06	0.98
	50– (ref.)	1	1	1	1
Country of birth	Outside Sweden	1.74*	1.45	2.50***	1.48*
	Sweden (ref.)	1	1	1	1
Employment sector	Public	0.60**	0.84	0.50***	0.50***
	Private (ref.)	1	1	1	1
Occupational group	Managers	1.07	3.38**	1.25	1.88*
	Professionals	1.19	1.71+	0.99	1.28
	Semi-professionals	0.99	1.09	1.17	1.00
	Service workers	1.10	1.49	1.05	0.96
	Manual workers (ref.)	1	1	1	1
Supervisor	Yes	1.36+	0.82	0.77	0.66**
	No (ref.)	1	1	1	1
Number of employees in workplace	<10	2.49**	0.85	0.78	0.89
	10–19	1.63+	0.99	0.50**	1.12
	20–49	1.84*	0.86	0.71+	1.04
	50–99	1.46	0.87	0.77	0.92
	10–499	1.75*	0.82	0.88	1.22
	≤ 500 (ref.)	1	1	1	1
Tenure at present workplace	≤ 6 months	0.52	4.85***	1.07	1.14
	> 6 months ≤ 2 years	0.64+	4.87***	1.27	1.03
	> 2 years ≤ 5 years	0.81	2.62**	1.40+	0.97
	> 5 years ≤ 10 years	1.03	2.61**	1.12	0.95
	> 10 years (ref.)	1	1	1	1
Union member	No	1.14	1.72**	0.61*	0.80
	Yes (ref.)	1	1	1	1
Weekly working hours	< 21 hours	0.78	1.30	1.18	0.88
	21–34 hours	0.80	1.49+	0.84	0.95
	> 34 hours (ref.)	1	1	1	1
Type of contract	Temporary	0.67	9.01***	1.87**	1.45+
	Permanent (ref.)	1	1	1	1
Discretion	Large	1.45	0.54*	0.57*	0.86

	Medium	0.96	0.61*	0.89	1.26
	Small (ref.)	1	1	1	1
Cooperation	To a very large extent (ref.)	1	1	1	1
with	To a large extent	1.44*	0.95	0.96	1.25+
workmates	To a certain extent	1.12	1.56+	0.85	1.29
	To a small extent/not at all	0.77	1.09	0.77	1.05
Better or worse	Better	–	–	1.07	0.93
job security	Worse	–	–	6.66***	2.20***
	Equal (ref.)	–	–	1	1
Nagelkerke R^2		0.24		0.14	–
n		2472		2436	

Notes: Levels of significance: + = p < 0.10 ; * = p < 0.05; ** = p < 0.01; *** = p < 0.001.

security as being better than that of their close workmates. Furthermore employees in small workplaces are more likely to experience better job security than are employees in larger workplaces. Somewhat unexpectedly, employees born outside rather than within Sweden are more likely to judge their job security as being better than that of their workmates. Compared to the oldest age group, the youngest age group is more inclined to report that they have both better and worse job security than that of their workmates; whereas employees in the middle age category are significantly more likely to report that they have worse job security than do members of the reference category.

Length of tenure with one's employers is an important variable in explaining employees' judgement of their job security. Employees who have worked for a short period are more likely to see their job security as poor than employees who have worked for a long time. This result probably reflects some of the regulations in the Swedish labour market, especially the employment protection legislation (LAS; see also Chapter 10). This legislation stipulates, with some exceptions, that last employed must be first to go during reductions, which explains why tenure determines employee evaluations of their job security. Some further notable results are that the odds are higher for managers than for manual workers and for non-union members than for union members when judging their job security to be poor.

In the analysis of the affective component of job insecurity, there are higher odds for temporary employees than for permanent employees to worry about losing their jobs. The cognitive aspect of job insecurity was also inserted into the analysis, and the odds are higher of worry among employees who believe that they have lower job security than their close workmates than for employees who believe that they have equal job security. This result shows that there is a relationship between the cognitive and affective components of job insecurity. However, the cognitive aspect does not explain all the variation in the affective component of job insecurity, which indicates that the two measures are not the same construct.

As for the background variables, there are some relationships to the affective component that are puzzling in contrast to the foregoing analysis. First, people born outside of Sweden report greater worry about losing their jobs than do people born in Sweden. This finding contradicts the analysis of the cognitive side of job insecurity, in which we find significantly higher odds for foreign-born Swedes than for those born in Sweden of perceiving themselves as having better job security. Second, in the analysis of the cognitive aspect we found that public employees had lower odds than did private employees for perceiving their job security positively. In this second analysis, public employees are less worried than are private employees about losing their jobs. In the former analysis, we found that tenure at one's present workplace had a strong effect on the perception of having poorer job security than one's close workmates. However, in the second analysis there is no relationship between the same independent variable and worry about losing one's job. This finding underlines the indication that the first analysis of job insecurity comparisons is a cognitive rather than an affective aspect of job insecurity.

To sum up the results of the first analyses, type of contract appears to be the most important of the central independent variables related to job insecurity. Temporary employees believe that their situation is more insecure than permanent employees do, and are more worried about losing their jobs. As for the other central independent variables (that is, weekly working hours, discretion and cooperation), there are small or no effects.

The second analysis concerns the effects of the central independent variables on job satisfaction (Table 9.3). The regression method used is ordinary least-square regressions, and unstandardized slope coefficients are presented. In Model 1, there are some results that are in line with the theoretical reasoning. First, there is a strong and positive relationship between discretion and job satisfaction. Second, cooperation with workmates is clearly related to job satisfaction. For the two other central independent variables, only small or no effects are revealed. Furthermore the two measures of job insecurity are related to job satisfaction: employees who perceive themselves as having poorer job security or are

Table 9.3 Effects on job satisfaction (OLS regression; unstandardized regression coefficients)

		Model 1	Model 2
Gender	Man	−0.41	−0.35
	Woman (ref.)	0	0
Age	16–34	−1.07**	−1.07**
	35–49	−0.79**	−0.74**
	50– (ref.)	0	0
Country of birth	Outside Sweden	0.18	0.40
	Sweden (ref.)	0	0
Employment sector	Public	−1.03***	−1.20***
	Private (ref.)	0	0
Occupational group	Managers	1.85**	2.04**
	Professionals	0.03	0.11
	Semi-professionals	0.19	0.23
	Service workers	−0.10	−0.05
	Manual workers (ref.)	0	0
Supervisor	Yes	0.44	0.34
	No (ref.)	0	0
Number of employees in workplace	<10	−0.08	−0.18
	10–19	−0.10	−0.23
	20–49	−0.64+	−0.76*
	50–99	−0.86*	−0.95*
	100–499	−0.75*	−0.82*
	≥ 500 (ref.)	0	0
Tenure at present workplace	≤ 6 months	0.21	0.31
	> 6 months ≤ 2 years	0.38	0.55
	> 2 years ≤ 5 years	0.11	0.20
	> 5 years ≤ 10 years	−0.10	−0.09
	> 10 years (ref.)	0	0
Union member	No	0.89**	0.91**
	Yes (ref.)	0	0
Weekly working hours	< 21 hours	−0.47+	−0.41
	21–34 hours	−0.03	−0.01
	> 34 hours (ref.)	0	0
Type of contract	Temporary	−0.46	0.43
	Permanent (ref.)	0	0
Discretion	Large	8.82***	8.68***
	Medium	4.04***	4.01***
	Small (ref.)	0	0
Cooperation with workmates	To a very large extent (ref.)	0	0
	To a large extent	−0.42	−0.44+
	To a certain extent	−0.49	−0.47
	To a small extent/not at all	−1.38**	−1.41**
Better or worse job security	Better	−	0.09

	Worse	–		−1.61***
	Equal (ref.)	–		0
Worry about losing one's	Great/some worry	–		−1.52***
job	Little worry	–		−0.61*
	No worry (ref.)	–		0
Intercept			18.40***	18.80***
R^2_{adj}			0.26	0.27
n				2194

Notes: Levels of significance: + = p < 0.10; * = p < 0.05; ** = p < 0.01; *** = p < 0.001.

worried about losing their job are more dissatisfied than are employees who do not have these perceptions.

There are also some effects regarding the control variables. Older employees are more satisfied with their jobs than are younger employees; private employees more satisfied than public employees; non-unionized more satisfied than unionized employees; and managers more satisfied than manual workers. There is also a significant pattern regarding size of workplace. Employees in the largest workplaces are more satisfied than are those in medium-sized and large workplaces.

We now continue with the third analysis. This analysis examines the relationship between the central independent variables and organizational commitment, which is also believed to have a mediating function. The variable measuring organizational commitment is an index construction and we therefore continue to use ordinary least-square regressions in the analysis. Furthermore, the analysis is performed on two different models. In the first, the central independent variables and the two measures of job insecurity are inserted, as well as the background variables. In the second model, job satisfaction has been added.

The results of the analysis are shown in Table 9.4. Two of the central independent variables have significant effects on organizational commitment. The discretion variable has a positive relationship to organizational commitment: the higher the influence, the higher the commitment. The variable measuring cooperation is also related to organizational commitment. Both these results point to the fact that work situations that imply influence and close cooperation – work situations that we believe characterize core employees – have a positive impact on organizational commitment.

Job satisfaction was added to the analysis in Model 2, and it had a strong positive effect on organizational commitment. When this

Table 9.4 Organizational commitment (OLS regression; unstandardized regression coefficients)

		Model 1	Model 2
Gender	Man	−0.04	−0.00
	Woman (ref.)	0	0
Age	16–34	−0.23**	−0.11
	35–49	−0.16*	−0.07
	50– (ref.)	0	0
Country of birth	Outside Sweden	−0.03	−0.07
	Sweden (ref.)	0	0
Employment sector	Public	−0.37***	−0.23***
	Private (ref.)	0	0
Occupational group	Managers	0.60***	0.38**
	Professionals	0.19+	0.17*
	Semi-professionals	0.20*	0.18*
	Service workers	0.17+	0.17*
	Manual workers (ref.)	0	0
Supervisor	Yes	0.35***	0.31***
	No (ref.)	0	0
Number of employees in workplace	<10	0.09	0.12
	10–19	−0.13	−0.09
	20–49	−0.21*	−0.12
	50–99	−0.11	−0.01
	100–499	−0.17+	−0.07
	≥ 500 (ref.)	0	0
Tenure at present workplace	≤ 6 months	0.01	−0.02
	> 6 months ≤ 2 years	0.16+	0.09
	> 2 years ≤ 5 years	0.12	0.10
	> 5 years ≤ 10 years	0.11	0.12
	> 10 years (ref.)	0	0
Union member	No	0.25**	0.16*
	Yes (ref.)	0	0
Weekly working hours	< 21 hours	−0.14*	−0.09
	21–34 hours	−0.01	−0.01
	> 34 hours (ref.)	0	0
Type of contract	Temporary	0.12	0.07
	Permanent (ref.)	0	0
Discretion	Large	1.13***	0.17+
	Medium	0.58***	0.13+
	Small (ref.)	0	0
Cooperation with workmates	To a very large extent (ref.)	0	0
	To a large extent	−0.08	−0.03
	To a certain extent	−0.26**	−0.21**
	To a small extent/not at all	−0.37**	−0.23*
Better or worse job security	Better	0.04	0.01

	Worse	−0.17	−0.01
	Equal (ref.)	0	0
Worry about losing one's	Great/some worry	0.02	0.18*
job	Little worry	0.01	0.08
	No worry (ref.)	0	0
Job satisfaction	Scale	–	0.11***
Intercept		2.83***	0.78***
R^2_{adj}		0.16	0.32
n			2082

Notes: Levels of significance: $+ = p < 0.10$; $* = p < 0.05$; $** = p < 0.01$; $*** = p < 0.001$.

variable has been controlled, then, it also appears a positive effect of the affective job insecurity variable on organizational commitment. Employees who are worried to a high or to some degree are more committed to the organization than are employees who are not worried at all. Notable also is the effect of discretion disappearing in Model 2, which indicates that the effect of discretion is mediated by job satisfaction. However, the effect of cooperation on organizational commitment remains even in Model 2, indicating that there is a relationship that was not hypothesized in the model (see Figure 9.1). Close cooperation and team work may create organizational commitment in ways other than job satisfaction, presumably more social psychological in nature.

For the two other central independent variables – type of contract and weekly working hours – we find a significant effect only for weekly working hours. In line with the theory of partial inclusion, employees working short part-time are less committed to the organization than are full-time employees. This effect is no longer significant when the job satisfaction variable is inserted into the analysis.

For the background variables, there are some noteworthy results. The youngest employees are less committed to the organization than older employees are. Private employees are more committed than public employees, which is in line with earlier findings (Furåker and Berglund 2001). Furthermore, union members and non-supervisory employees are less committed to the organization than are non-union members and supervisors, and managers are more committed than manual workers.

To sum up, we have found that discretion and cooperation are related to job satisfaction and organizational commitment. As for weekly working hours, there is a significant relationship with organizational commitment and a tendency for it to be related to job satisfaction.

However, there are only small or no effects on these mediating variables by type of contract. On the other hand, type of contract is clearly related to both aspects of job insecurity. Theoretically, we only expected that there should be a relationship with the cognitive side of job insecurity, but this was not the case. To a great extent, the picture follows the theoretical reasoning about the relationships between the central independent variables and the mediators presented in Figure 9.1.

After these analyses of the relationships among the central independent variables and the mediators are completed, we are in a position to carry out the final analysis, which examines the effects of the central independent variables (discretion, cooperation, type of contract and weekly working hours) on withdrawal cognitions; and any mediating effects of job insecurity, job satisfaction and organizational commitment. The variable measuring withdrawal cognitions is a dichotomy, which makes logistic regression the proper statistical method to use (Menard 1995). In Table 9.5, the odds ratios are presented and, as in the analysis above, the regressions are performed in different models, subsequently introducing the mediators in the analysis.

If we first look at Model 1, we find some effects of the central independent variables on withdrawal cognitions. The effects of the variables measuring discretion and cooperation on withdrawal cognitions imply that more influence and greater cooperation make employees less inclined to quit. Of the two remaining central variables, only type of contract has significant effects on withdrawal cognitions. We find no effect of working time.

If we then follow the analysis through the different models, it is possible to conclude that the negative effects of discretion have to do with job satisfaction and organizational commitment. The proof is that the effects of discretion disappear in Model 3 when job satisfaction and organizational commitment variables are inserted – variables that, by themselves, have strong negative effects on withdrawal cognitions. This finding implies that the effects are mediated and that, in essence, discretion in the work situation increases employee job satisfaction and organizational commitment and therefore decreases the desire to change jobs.

As to the effect of cooperation with workmates on withdrawal cognitions, the same reasoning applied in the discussion of discretion is not valid in this case. The effect is reduced by job satisfaction and organizational commitment, but the difference between employees who cooperate to a small extent or not at all in comparison to the reference

Table 9.5 Withdrawal cognitions (logistic regression; odds ratios)

		Model 1	Model 2	Model 3
Gender	Man	1.12	1.10	1.06
	Woman (ref.)	1	1	1
Age	16–34	3.35***	3.37***	3.25***
	35–49	2.72***	2.69***	2.68***
	50– (ref.)	1	1	1
Country of birth	Outside Sweden	0.98	0.93	0.99
	Sweden (ref.)	1	1	1
Employment sector	Public	1.09	1.15	0.92
	Private (ref.)	1	1	1
Occupational group	Managers	1.79*	1.68*	2.60**
	Professionals	1.74**	1.70**	1.93***
	Semi-professionals	1.50*	1.49*	1.69**
	Service workers	1.18	1.16	1.25
	Manual workers (ref.)	1	1	1
Supervisor	Yes	0.98	1.01	1.10
	No (ref.)	1	1	1
Number of< 10		1.16	1.19	1.20
employees	10–19	1.11	1.13	1.14
in the workplace	20–49	0.98	1.01	0.89
	50–99	1.11	1.14	1.02
	100–499	1.16	1.18	1.04
	≥ 500 (ref.)	1	1	1
Tenure at present	≤ 6 months	0.91	0.87	0.89
workplace	> 6 months ≤ 2 years	0.96	0.91	1.04
	> 2 years ≤ 5 years	1.32*	1.30+	1.38*
	> 5 years ≤ 10 years	1.64***	1.64***	1.76***
	> 10 years (ref.)	1	1	1
Union member	No	0.94	0.92	1.07
	Yes (ref.)	1	1	1
Weekly working	< 21 hours	1.07	1.06	0.96
hours	21–34 hours	0.84	0.83	0.84
	> 34 hours (ref.)	1	1	1
Type of contract	Temporary	1.46*	1.14	1.26
	Permanent (ref.)	1	1	1
Discretion	Large	0.30***	0.31***	1.10
	Medium	0.68**	0.68**	1.24
	Small (ref.)	1	1	1
Cooperation with	To a very large extent (ref.)	1	1	1
workmates	To a large extent	1.13	1.13	1.05
	To a certain extent	1.37*	1.32*	1.19
	To a small extent/not at all	1.86**	1.88**	1.58*

Better or worse job	Better	–	1.01	1.05
security	Worse	–	1.78**	1.52+
	Equal (ref.)	–	1	1
Worry about losing	Great/some worry	–	1.37*	1.15
one's job	Small worry	–	1.25+	1.15
	No worry (ref.)	–	1	1
Job satisfaction	Scale	–	–	0.87***
Organizational	Low (ref.)	–	–	1
commitment	Medium	–	–	0.63*
	High	–	–	0.40***
Constant		0.34***	0.30***	5.70***
Nagelkerke R^2		0.14	0.15	0.28
n				2073

Notes: Levels of significance: + = $p < 0.10$; * = $p < 0.05$; ** = $p < 0.01$; *** = $p < 0.001$.

category (very high extent) remained significant in Model 3. Therefore, we can conclude that the effect of cooperation also involves some mechanism other than job satisfaction and organizational commitment. One possible explanation is that there are other forms of commitment that are not included in the concept of organizational commitment. Workmates often develop internal forms of solidarity and loyalty, which could have an effect on the inclination to stay (Goldthorpe et al. 1968; Lysgaard 1985). However, this dimension is not measured in the present study.

In the case of type of contract, we believed that the mediator should be job insecurity. If we look at Model 2, where the variables measuring job insecurity are inserted, we can see that both variables have effects on withdrawal cognitions. Employees who experience less job security in comparison to their close workmates or are afraid of losing their job are more inclined to have withdrawal cognitions. In Model 1, temporary employees have significantly higher odds of wanting to quit than do permanent employees. In Model 2, with the insertion of the variables measuring job insecurity, the odds ratio for temporaries dropped and no longer represents a significant effect. This pattern supports the reasoning concerning the relationships among type of contract, job insecurity and withdrawal cognitions. However, this analysis does not directly show which of the variables of job insecurity reduce the effect on withdrawal cognitions. To study this relationship, a special analysis (not shown here) was performed in which the change in effect of type of contract on withdrawal cognitions was studied by varying the insertion of the two insecurity variables in Model 2. The result showed that both variables are important mediators, but that job security in comparison to close workmates had a greater mediating effect than did the variable measuring worry about losing one's job.

There are some other results to report concerning the background variables. Age decreases the tendency to have withdrawal cognitions. As for the variable measuring tenure at present workplace, an inclination towards withdrawal cognitions seems to increase after 2–5 years and 5–10 years, but then drops again when the employee has been at the workplace for more than 10 years. The variables in this study provide no explanation for this pattern. It cannot be explained by the mediating variables, for example through decreasing job satisfaction. One possible explanation is that most jobs do not live up to employees' expectations. As this insight comes to the employee's attention over time, thoughts of quitting may become more persistent. But employees who do not quit may have to adjust their expectations in order to avoid feelings of dissonance (Festinger 1957). After this adjustment, withdrawal cognitions may not be that persistent.

A last result from the analysis that must be mentioned is the effect of occupational group on withdrawal cognitions. The results show that employees in higher-level positions are more inclined to have withdrawal cognitions than are manual and service workers. This finding may be an indication of the greater labour market possibilities that higher-level occupational groups perceive.

Conclusion

In this chapter, we have examined circumstances in employees' work situations that make them more or less prone to thoughts of leaving their present jobs – so-called withdrawal cognitions. The overall question has been: 'Can employers structure or influence employees' withdrawal cognitions through the work situations they offer them?' One such factor can be the organization's internal striving for flexibility, which could structure the workforce in terms of a functional core and a periphery that are more or less numerically flexible.

This study shows that work situations with a high degree of discretion or cooperation among workmates render employees less likely to have thoughts of leaving their jobs – through the mechanisms of job satisfaction and organizational commitment. Consequently, the results imply that the favourable working conditions that often characterize the functional core of the organization can have a stabilizing effect on the core workforce.

The effects of peripheral positions on withdrawal cognitions are not clear-cut. Temporary employees are more prone to thoughts of leaving the organization than are permanent employees, and this difference appears to be due to the temporary workers' higher level of job insecurity. This result implies that the contractual relationship with the employer has consequences for an employee's potential for mobility. To use concepts from the introduction of this chapter, to offer temporary contracts to employees is a way of creating flexibility for the employer. For the employee, it may, in many cases, create instability and a preparedness to look for a new job. The other indicator of a peripheral position – working time – has no effects on withdrawal cognitions: part-time workers do not have higher levels of withdrawal cognitions than full-time workers. At least in a Swedish context, it is difficult to infer that part-time workers are atypical or non-standard employees.

From a macroeconomic viewpoint, it may be important that employees are willing and prepared to change jobs because it is a prerequisite for labour-market dynamics and flexibility. More than 45 per cent of the Swedish employees in this study have thoughts of changing their workplaces. This finding may indicate that a large proportion of the Swedish workforce is aware of the situation on the labour market and has some potential for labour market mobility.

However, strategies and practices of flexibility on a meso level or organizational level may have consequences for the potential for flexibility in the labour market as a whole. If there develops an A-team of core workers and a B-team of more or less peripheral workers, new rigidities on the labour market and in the economy could be created. A selection process may emerge whereby the most qualified and motivated employees are dragged into the organizational core and sheltered from the dynamics of the economy. The potential for mobility must come from more peripheral workers, who are prepared to change jobs because of job insecurity or unfulfilling working conditions.

From a justice perspective, a segmentation of labour markets into a core and periphery may be regarded as unfair by many employees. In this data set, 91 per cent of Swedish employees think that a job with high job security is very or quite important. This finding suggests that job security is a value held by a large majority of Swedish employees. If the labour market develops into segments in which some employees find job security, while others remain relatively unprotected from the dynamics of the market, there is a potential for serious tension in Swedish society.

A further issue is the economic soundness of such segmentation of labour markets. The creation of a core segment of job-secure, loyal and committed employees can destroy some of the rationality of the economy and hamper the allocation of qualified workers to new and growing sectors of the economy.

10
Type of Employment Contract and Attitudes to Flexibility: An Analysis of Data from Three Swedish Surveys

Bengt Furåker

Workers' flexibility is important for economic development and growth. In modern capitalist countries, it happens all the time that some workplaces are closed down or are subject to downsizing, whereas others expand their workforce and new ones are established. All changes do not have to be positive for the economy as a whole, but a positive development requires change. This in turn means that workers must be prepared to make adjustments; thus, now and then, they are expected to switch jobs, work tasks or occupation, to commute, to move geographically, agree to working hours suited to business activities, make wage adjustments, and so on.

Flexibility, or the lack of it, is also important in relation to unemployment. When people look for vacancies as new entrants or re-entrants in the labour market or after having lost their job, it is likely that they will become unemployed for a while. To improve their chances of getting work they can go through retraining, start commuting, move geographically, and so on, depending on the situation. Moreover they must be willing to take the jobs offered. Employers can in turn contribute to the matching process by allocating their activities to places or regions with a surplus of labour (regional policies are aimed at helping them in that respect). Measures taken at the workplace itself may also help the

Note: This chapter is a revised version of a contribution to a book in Swedish (Furåker 2005a). The work on the original paper was funded by the Swedish Institute for Growth Policy Studies, whereas the three surveys were made possible by grants from the then Swedish Council for Research in the Humanities and Social Sciences (the 1991 and 1993 surveys) and the Swedish Council for Working Life and Social Research (the 2001 survey). I want to express my thanks for all this support.

recruitment of unemployed individuals. A simple example is when the management at a workplace with only men (or women) wants to recruit unemployed persons from the absent sex and for that purpose makes arrangements with respect to changing rooms and the like.

The discussion about labour market flexibility is very much focused on workers' attitudes and behaviour and this is also the point of departure for the analysis to follow. Older workers are, for several reasons, less inclined to move geographically and to switch jobs. When individuals have lived in a place for a long time, they tend to be tied to it. The number of years left to retirement is also important for whether one or the other type of adjustment is meaningful. It may not make sense to start training for a new occupation (if that is required) when the time of gainful employment is close to its end. Other explanations as to the lack of flexibility are related to the individual's family situation or to reduced working capacity. When both spouses in a family are gainfully employed it becomes more complicated for them to move geographically; if one of them is unemployed but has a chance to get a job in another place it may be difficult for the whole family to move. People with reduced working capacity frequently have rather limited possibilities of switching to other jobs.

Another type of obstacle may be found in the institutional arrangements in the labour market. It is often argued that employment protection legislation prevents desirable adjustments. The purpose of such legislation is to give employees a certain degree of employment security; it is supposed to reduce arbitrariness and to prevent too quick dismissals. It can define legitimate reasons for dismissals, the length of notice periods, notification procedures and terms for severance pay. The critics of employment protection legislation argue that it decreases flexibility and mobility in the labour market. Seniority is commonly given a significant role in this kind of legislation. It thus pays to stay long in a job and those who change to something new will always start out as being the last employed.

The arguments against strict employment protection legislation also focus on the prerequisites for recruitment to jobs and the impact on unemployment and employment levels. It is often maintained that if it is difficult to get rid of personnel, employers become more cautious about whom they employ. They are supposed to become both more restrictive and more selective. These mechanisms are considered to be particularly important for smaller firms, for which every single new entrant means a great deal. Thus, with strict legislation, total employment is assumed to be lower than it would otherwise be and certain categories such as young people, women and handicapped individuals are expected to have greater difficulties in getting a foothold in working life at all. Whether or not these critical opinions are supported by empirical research is something that I will come back to. Anyway, this chapter starts out from these assumptions but formulates the research question somewhat differently. Employment protection legislation allows a specific way of getting around some of the problems just indicated, namely fixed-term jobs. It is common to distinguish different subtypes, such as project work and seasonal work (Storrie 2003). The risks for employers of hiring people on such contracts are less because a time limit is defined which makes it relatively easy to get rid of employees if they turn out not to be needed any more or not to fit in with work tasks and workmates. We can then ask whether temporary workers are more inclined than other employees to adjust to demands for flexibility. By analysing data from a few surveys, I want to throw some light on this issue.

In the next section the complex concept of flexibility will be touched upon. Without differing from the definition spelled out by Dan Jonsson (see Ch. 3), I will add certain things to the discussion through a comparison with the concept of mobility. Thereafter I shall present some facts about the employment protection legislation in Sweden and take a look at some of the international research on the impact of such legislation. The focus will mainly be on how strict rules affect labour market flows. Having provided this background, I will turn to my empirical data that come from three surveys carried out in 1993, 2000 and 2001. These data contain answers on questions about people's willingness to move geographically in case of unemployment (all three surveys) and to agree to a wage cut to save their job (two of the surveys). An important task is to see whether permanent and temporary workers differ from one another in these respects or whether other factors such as age and family situation are more important.

The concepts of flexibility and mobility

It is obvious that the concept of flexibility can have different meanings and we therefore need to specify how we use it. As mentioned above, I generally adopt the definition suggested by Dan Jonsson (see also my discussion in Furåker 2005b: Ch. 8). One important issue is whether flexibility refers to potential or actual adjustments. When we, for example, characterize an individual as 'spatially flexible', the reason may be that he or she has moved geographically once or several times, but we can also use this label if he or she is merely capable or willing to move. By making a comparison with the concept of mobility – which is close to that of flexibility and often used synonymously – I want to give some further illustration of this.

In a presentation of American labour mobility research more than 50 years ago, Herbert Parnes (1954: 13–22) claims that the concept of labour mobility can have three different meanings. The first stands for individuals' capacity to move between jobs, between employment and unemployment, and in and out of the labour force. Second, the concept of mobility refers to people's willingness to move; this is, in other words, an entirely subjective dimension. Finally, it can signify actual change. Parnes makes the comment that most researchers – no matter how they define their concepts theoretically – have to rely on actual mobility when it comes to providing empirical data. He points out, however, that if we can decide whether individuals have quit their jobs voluntarily – in contrast to when they have been dismissed – at least some element of positive motivation is included. There are also (mainly since the 1950s) many studies in which people have been asked about their willingness to accept one or the other kind of mobility (cf. Parnes 1968: 483). In this chapter, such data will be used.

The first two dimensions of the concept of mobility suggested by Parnes imply potential change; they do not refer to actual change but give an indication of certain preconditions for it to take place. With respect to the capacity dimension it may be difficult to decide what people are really able to do. If changes of occupation – to take just one simple example – are to be successful, the individuals concerned must be capable of acquiring the knowledge and skills demanded in the new occupation. Whether or not they will succeed in this is ultimately determined only when they actually take on their new work tasks. Still, some actors, the individuals themselves and perhaps also others, must decide in advance if it is meaningful to spend energy on the retraining required.

Regarding the subjective dimension – willingness or readiness to accept various kinds of mobility or flexibility – there are similar difficulties to determine its implications. For example, even if individuals in a survey assure us of their willingness to move geographically, we cannot be sure that they will actually do so in a real situation. We must count on the possibility of some gap between words and deeds. Nonetheless individuals' answers to such questions are often likely to be positively correlated with their actual behaviour. For example, we know that young people move geographically to a larger extent than older individuals and this is also reflected in research on attitudes (see, for example, van den Berg, Furåker and Johansson 1997: 183–5). Another point to be made is that the subjective dimension probably also tells us something about the capacity for flexibility/mobility. People expressing their willingness to switch to another job, go through retraining, move geographically, and so on, are likely to believe that they can realize their intentions. Again, we must be aware of the possibility of a gap between the subjective and the objective dimension – in this case between subjective assertions and objective capacities – but the individuals in question are probably the best persons to decide (or at least no worse than others to do it) what they are capable of doing.

Actual adjustments can be treated as the most important indicator of flexibility. Regardless of the preconditions in respect of capacity and willingness, it is in the end actual change that matters. By studying workers' changes of employers and of jobs, patterns of migration, and so on, we can see what actually happens in the labour market. However, these kinds of information do not necessarily tell us anything about certain things that can also be interesting. If, for example, a firm has a low level of personnel turnover, we may be interested in knowing whether this is due to its jobs being attractive or to a generally low demand for labour. In such a situation, knowledge about potential flexibility might tell us something about what would happen if more jobs (similar, better, worse – however these categories are defined) became vacant. Moreover there are changes that presuppose individuals' positive participation, that is, require both capacity and willingness to adjust. Without a genuine will behind them such changes may quickly come to nothing. For example, when people have been forced to move geographically, it quite often occurs that they move back again as soon as they get the chance.

Another point in relation to the concept of flexibility is that we must specify what unit we take as our point of departure. Is it individuals, wages, capital, firms, the labour market as a whole or something else? This chapter is about individuals' attitudes toward certain types of flexibility, but the attitudes can be aggregated to the labour market level. In addition, although we are dealing with a subjective dimension – individuals' acceptance of adjustment – it is likely to have some positive correlation with capacity. There are many aspects to examine regarding attitudes toward flexibility, but my empirical analysis is limited to two dimensions only. I will analyse data on individuals' willingness to move geographically in case of unemployment and on their acceptance of wage cuts to save their jobs.

Labour law and labour market

The Swedish employment protection legislation (LAS) came into existence in 1974 (for an overview and comments on the rules, see Bylund et al. 2004; Göransson 2004; Lunning and Toijer 2002; Sigeman 2001). Before 1974 there was for some time a law aimed at providing protection for employees aged 45 years and above. The point of departure for LAS is the assumption that an employment contract normally has no time-limit, but it allows temporary contracts under certain circumstances. Dismissal must be based on just cause and the individual should be informed by letter. Lack of work is a just cause for dismissal, which means that when firms have no more need for an individual he or she can be laid off. Personal reasons can also make up a legitimate ground for dismissal. At the minimum, the notice period has to be one month and it is increased stepwise with time of employment. It is two months if the individual has been employed at least two years but less than four years, it is three months if the individual has been employed at least four years but less than six years, and so on, up to six months when employment has lasted more than ten years. In case of dismissal certain rules of priority are applicable; the main principle is that an individual with the shortest length of service will have to go first ('last in', 'first out'). It should be mentioned that people can be fired immediately for gross misconduct.

Moreover, LAS is to some extent optional, which means that the rules can be partly redefined through agreements between employers and unions. This has been regarded as necessary to provide rules adjusted to the specific circumstances in certain areas of the labour market. Another important piece of legislation related to employees' job security is the codetermination law. The latter requires that employers inform unions, and negotiate with them, when planning to carry out important changes at the workplace and lay-offs of course belong to that category.

Since LAS was adopted in 1974, it has been revised in certain respects. The law was controversial from the beginning and it has repeatedly been subject to political debate and conflict. A first significant modification was carried out in 1982 and thereafter several changes have been made (besides the above-mentioned sources, see also OECD 1999: 52–3, 66: OECD 2004b: Ch. 2). Nevertheless, there is considerable continuity between the rules existing today and those that were created more than 30 years ago. Among the most important changes we must mention that it has become easier to establish temporary employment contracts. Notice period is calculated differently today than before, but the minimum and maximum periods remain the same. We should also observe that in 1993 temporary work agencies were allowed in Sweden. Because LAS is applicable also to employees in such agencies, this reform has no direct impact on employment protection, but it has unquestionably created new possibilities for flexibility in the labour market (cf. Storrie 2002). Another important change is that, in certain cases, in firms with ten employees or less, two individuals can be exempt from the rules of priority.

Labour market flexibility in terms of changes of employer is strongly business cycle–related (cf., for example, AMS 2003; Björklund et al. 2000: 213–14; Furåker 2004). This pattern holds for the whole period during which LAS has existed; the proportion of changes of employer was much lower during the recessions of 1982–4 and from 1992 and some years ahead, but after these troughs it has turned upward again. Despite the continuity of employment protection legislation we thus find significant variation in terms of flexibility, which implies that there are other factors to take into account. The mechanisms behind the correlation with business cycles seem to be simple. The more job openings there are, the less important it is for employees to stick to what they have and the more willing they become to try another job that may also be associated with a wage increase and other improvements.

The OECD has paid a great deal of attention to the role of employment protection legislation in the labour market. In the most recent study, a large number of countries are compared regarding strictness of the law (OECD 2004b: Ch. 2). The total index is made up of a number of indicators referring to individual protection against dismissal, additional regulation in case of collective dismissals and legislation on temporary employment and temporary work agencies. With the index used – which has to some extent been revised over the years – in 2003 Sweden shared 19th or 21st place (due to the fact that two versions of the measure are used) out of 28 countries and 28th place means the most restrictive legislation (OECD 2004b: 117). The last in the ranking are above all Southern European countries, while at the opposite end of the scale we find the United States, Canada and the United Kingdom.

The comparison also covers the changes that have occurred since the late 1980s and the late 1990s respectively (besides OECD 2004b, see also OECD 1999: Ch. 2). Although we also find examples of the opposite, several countries have gone through a process of liberalization, mainly with respect to the possibilities of establishing temporary employment contracts. As to permanent employment contracts we discover only minor changes and the overriding conclusion is therefore that employment protection legislation shows strong continuity over time. Sweden scores the same on the index in 2003 as in the late 1990s but still gets a lower rank in 2003 (OECD 2004b: 117). For the late 1980s, the Swedish score is higher, giving it 16th place out of 20 countries compared.

Another conclusion drawn by the OECD is that strict rules slow down the flow of labour from employment to unemployment. This is simply in line with the purpose of the law, that is, to give workers some protection against quick and arbitrary dismissals. Except for the Nordic countries, there is a similar indication regarding flows from unemployment (to employment or out of the labour force), but it is not statistically significant. Unfortunately, in the OECD report, transitions from unemployment to jobs are not kept separate from transitions from unemployment out of the labour force. The theoretical assumption, anyway, is that strict rules make employers more restrictive with hiring. Consequently, all in all, the impact on the level of unemployment can be expected to be low because two forces are supposed to be in operation and they go in opposite directions. According to the OECD (2004b: 81), it cannot be verified that the strictness of employment protection legislation is associated with high overall levels of unemployment. However, it seems that the incidence of long-term unemployment is increased.

We need to observe that fixed-term jobs are to some extent functional alternatives to liberal legislation. Given that the possibility of establishing temporary employment contracts is not too limited, we can expect it to be used more often in countries where employment protection legislation is generally strict. There is empirical support for this assumption (OECD 2004b: 87; see also Hudson 2002a: 40–2). Moreover, the step from temporary to permanent employment contracts is negatively correlated with the strictness of legislation regarding open-ended employment (OECD 2004b: 87–8). When, in the latter respect, liberalization has taken place, it seems that the proportion of fixed-term contracts decreases.

In Sweden the proportion of temporary employment among all employees has been around 15 per cent over the last few years. It is often mentioned that in 1990 this share was only about 10 per cent, which implies that there has been a rather large increase. However, some observations must be added to give a fuller picture. Figure 10.1 shows the proportion of temporary employment for all the years since 1987, when this kind of information started to be collected in the Swedish labour force surveys. The diagram also includes a curve over unemployment rates (standardized according to the OECD) for the same years.

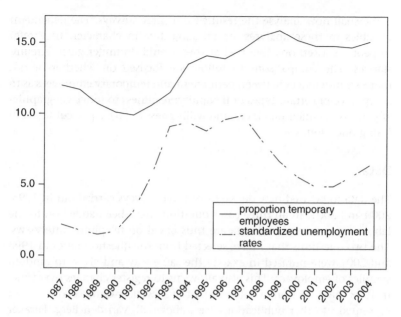

Figure 10.1 The proportion of temporary employees and standardized unemployment rates in Sweden, 1987–2004 (annual averages; %)

Sources: OECD *Employment Outlook* (various years) and SCB (Statistics Sweden) database.

There is a positive although not very strong correlation between level of unemployment and the proportion of temporary employees. When considering the period as a whole, certain features – not so commonly mentioned in the public discussion – become visible. First, we find that the proportion of temporary employment was higher in the late 1980s than in the early 1990s. There was a clear decline in the years when the labour market was overheated; it seems that when it was difficult to recruit workers, employers were relatively willing to offer permanent jobs. In 1987 the proportion of temporary employees was 12 per cent and it went down below 10 per cent in 1991, when the turning point came as the business cycle bent downward and unemployment started to rise. Second, the top level was reached in 1999 with 15.9 per cent; thereafter figures have been lower or, rather, stable. Those who predicted that the proportion of temporary employees would continue to increase successively have not been entirely right. On the other hand, it can be pointed out that the decline in unemployment after 1997 was larger than the decline in the proportion of temporary employees.

We shall now analyse the results from three surveys. The dependent variables in these analyses are all subjective in character; they refer to people's assertions about what they would do under given circumstances. The comparisons to follow are focused on whether or not there are differences between permanent and temporary employees as to acceptance of certain types of flexibility: readiness to move geographically in case of unemployment and willingness to take a pay cut to avoid losing one's job.

Data

The data to be used here derive from three surveys carried out in 1993, 2000 and 2001. In all three cases questions have been added on to the labour force surveys and data are thus based on telephone interviews. The two questions that I have selected from the questionnaires in 1993 and 2001 were phrased in exactly the same way and given to random samples of employees. This also allows us to register changes over time. In 1993 the collection of data was part of a Sweden–Canada comparison presented in other publications (see, above all, van den Berg, Furåker and Johansson 1997). For the reason that the Canadian study involved only blue-collar workers in certain industries – and not all categories of employees – I have refrained from using it here. Moreover, the Swedish survey in 1993 was basically a replication of a study carried out in 1991. Because the number of individuals with temporary jobs was very small in the 1991 dataset, I have decided not to bring in this (for a comparison of the Swedish data from 1991 and 1993, see Furåker and Johansson 1995). The response rates in the two surveys from 1993 and 2001 are high, about 90 and 86 per cent respectively. It should be noted that the proportion of temporary employees is somewhat lower than the national averages in 1993 and 2001. The national averages were then 11.5 and 14.8 per cent respectively, while the figures among our respondents are 8.4 and 13.9 per cent (see Table 10.A in the appendix). The difference is not that large and it is not unexpected as response rates are likely to be higher among permanent employees than among temporary employees.

In 2000 some colleagues and I carried out another survey on people's knowledge about and attitudes toward the rules of unemployment insurance. It was again done in connection with the labour force survey – which means telephone interviews – and was based on a random sample but this time drawn from the whole working-age population. The response rate was lower compared to the 1993 and 2001 surveys – about 67 per cent – which is partly due to the fact that various categories of non-employed individuals were also included. We have not found very great differences between respondents and non-respondents, but women are somewhat over-represented among the former. The proportion of temporary workers is in this case 15 per cent, which is almost the same as the national average in 2000 of 15.2 per cent. From this dataset I have picked one question that is not identical with those in the surveys from 1993 and 2001 but is still rather close. Because I am interested in type of employment contract, I have analysed only the answers provided by employees, thus leaving out the answers from the self-employed, the unemployed and people outside the labour force.

The 1993 and 2001 surveys

In the surveys from 1993 and 2001 there are two questions that I consider particularly relevant for my purpose. They deal with attitudes toward spatial or geographic flexibility and wage flexibility respectively. The first one was formulated in the following way. 'What would you choose if you had to: remain unemployed for a year waiting for a job in your present place of residence or move to another place where you immediately could get an equivalent job?' The idea is to get some indication of people's propensity to move. The second question deals with another type of adjustment: 'If your workplace was threatened with closure, would you then accept a wage cut if that was the only way to save your job?' In this case, it is a matter of the willingness to defend one's job through wage flexibility. One point with this question is that it can reveal the existence of a functional alternative. It may be possible to avoid flexibility in one respect by accepting it in another.

The answers to the questions mentioned may tell us something about people's readiness to make adjustments and they thus fit in with the second dimension in Parnes's categorization of mobility dimensions. However, his first dimension is arguably also involved, insofar as people who declare themselves willing to do something probably also consider themselves capable of doing it. Yet we cannot be sure whether people would actually act in accordance with their answers, although it seems generally reasonable that words and deeds are positively related to each other. Let us now take a look at the first empirical picture (Table 10.1).

For both years we see that slightly more than 30 per cent answered that they – in case of unemployment – would be willing to move to another place to get a job. Accordingly, a good two thirds answered that they would not move or that they did not know. I have collapsed the two latter categories into one as the opposite pole to those inclined

Table 10.1   Responses as to whether people on different types of employment contract in case of unemployment would wait for a job in their present place of residence for a year or move to another place where they could immediately find an equivalent job, 1993 and 2001 (%)

	Move	Stay or don't know	Total and numbers
1993			
Permanent employment	30.6	69.4	100 (867)
Temporary employment	44.3	55.7	100 (79)
Total	31.7	68.3	100 (946)
$Chi^2 = 6.31$; $p = 0.012$* (df 1)			
2001			
Permanent employment	29.5	70.5	100 (1903)
Temporary employment	36.8	63.2	100 (307)
Total	30.5	69.5	100 (2210)
$Chi^2 = 6.60$; $p = 0.010$** (df 1)			

to move (the proportion saying 'don't know' is just 6 and 7 per cent respectively for the two years). As we can see, the proportion expressing a willingness to move is clearly lower among the permanent employees than among those temporarily employed. There was a gap of almost 14 percentage points between the two categories in 1993. For 2001 we find a much smaller difference, but it still amounts to about 7 percentage points. Thus, so far we have some support for the thesis that temporary employment is associated with greater willingness to move. The question is whether these differences remain when we control for other factors.

Before that, however, we will first look at the outcome on the second survey question, the one giving an indication of whether people are inclined to accept a pay cut in order to save their jobs. Table 10.2 shows the distribution of answers in this respect for permanent and temporary employees in 1993 and 2001. Again, there is a distinction between those who are willing to make adjustments and those who have said no or who do not know (the latter category is about 8 and 7 per cent for the two years). It should be added that those who answered 'yes' were also asked how large a reduction they would agree to. Most respondents turned out to accept a reduction of up to 10 per cent of their present wage and only a small minority agreed to a larger cut. There is no reason to go into detail on this issue; I will just stick to the distinction between

Table 10.2 Responses as to whether workers on different types of employment contract would accept a wage cut to save their job, 1993 and 2001 (%)

	Yes	No or don't know	Total and numbers
1993			
Permanent employment	61.1	38.9	100 (866)
Temporary employment	51.3	48.7	100 (78)
Total	60.3	39.7	100 (944)
$Chi^2 = 2.87$; $p = 0.090^*$ (df 1)			
2001			
Permanent employment	36.6	63.4	100 (1905)
Temporary employment	32.9	67.1	100 (307)
Total	36.1	63.9	100 (2212)
$Chi^2 = 1.60$; $p = 0.205$ non-sign. (df 1)			

the two main categories, those willing to reduce their wage and those unwilling or undecided.

In total, about 60 per cent in 1993 but only 36 per cent in 2001 agreed to a wage cut to save their job. This difference is somewhat surprising but possibly has to do with differences in the labour market situation. Respondents in 1993 had in a short time experienced a dramatic increase in unemployment (the survey was carried out in February and March that year), after several years of exceptionally high demand for labour. Although unemployment was high also when the survey was done in 2001, it was the fourth year in a row with decreasing rates.

The proportion answering yes is larger among permanent employees than among temporary employees for both years, although the difference is statistically significant only for 1993. Permanent employment seems to be associated with a greater willingness among people to defend their jobs and therefore with greater concessions in terms of wage cuts. It remains to be seen whether this interpretation can be sustained when other variables are controlled for. If supported, it is an indication of something crucial in all discussions on flexibility, namely that different forms of flexibility can be alternative solutions to one another. It is now time to introduce other variables in the equations.

Multivariate analyses

In the following treatment of data, I use logistic regression because the dependent variables are dichotomized. Regarding the issue of geographic flexibility – besides type of employment – I include sex, age, marital

status, children in the household and socioeconomic position as independent variables. The choice of these control variables is based on
the analyses that have been done previously on the same datasets (see,
for example, van den Berg, Furåker and Johansson 1997; Soidre 2001,
2004; Gustafson 2003). We know that geographic flexibility is related
to age; young people are more inclined to move and they actually do
so to a larger extent than older individuals. Sex, marital status and children (up to 18 years of age) in the household can be other important
factors. Family obligations are likely to lower the willingness to move
geographically and women generally take more responsibility than men
for children and family. Moreover we also know that higher ranking
white-collar workers are more inclined than other employees to switch
place of residence for their job.

Whether these control variables are relevant also with respect to the
wage reduction issue is less obvious. I have nonetheless decided to use
them also for those analyses. It makes sense to assume that the financial
situation – that is often related to sex, age, family situation and socioeconomic position – is important for the acceptance of a wage reduction.
However, I want to add another aspect. Our previous analyses indicated
that willingness to take a wage cut to save the job is clearly associated
with whether respondents regard their relationship with management
as good and whether they think they have a say when management
wants to carry out significant workplace changes. Positive experiences
of this kind make it more important to defend one's job, even at the
price of a lower wage. Thus they need to be taken into consideration
also here. Because the two variables are correlated with one another and
we need to keep down the internal falling off, I have included only
one of them, the perception of the relationship with management. An
overview of the independent variables in the analyses of the 1993 and
2001 data is given in the appendix (Table 10.A).

We shall now examine the first logistic regressions regarding
the issue of geographic flexibility in the event of unemployment
(Table 10.3). Model 1 includes only one independent variable, namely
type of employment. The results for both years are in line with the
bivariate associations shown in Table 10.1. Respondents on temporary
contracts have higher odds than respondents on permanent contracts
of answering that they would move if they became unemployed.

When in Model 2 our control variables are introduced, the associations between type of employment and the dependent variable
are no longer statistically significant. For 1993 we find clearly higher
odds for temporary employees, but this result does not fulfil statistical

Table 10.3 Effects on odds of respondents answering 'move' as to whether in case of unemployment they would wait for a job in their present place of residence for a year or move to another place where they could immediately find an equivalent job, 1993 and 2001 (logistic regression; odds ratios)

	1993	1993	2001	2001
	Model 1	Model 2	Model 1	Model 2
Type of employment				
Permanent (ref.)	1	1	1	1
Temporary	1.81**	1.22	1.39**	0.93
Sex				
Woman (ref.)		1		1
Man		1.81****		1.54****
Age				
16–24 years		5.77****		4.23****
25–39		2.63**		2.74****
40–54		2.12**		1.61***
55–64 (ref.)		1		1
Marital status				
Married/cohabitant (ref.)		1		1
Single		2.05****		1.84****
Children in the household				
Yes (ref.)		1		1
No		0.97		1.82****
Socioeconomic position				
Manual worker (ref.)		1		1
Lower- or middle-level white collar		1.77***		1.75****
Higher-level white collar		3.34****		3.30****
Constant	0.44****	0.79****	0.42****	0.07****
Nagelkerke R^2	0.009	0.151	0.004	0.158
n	946	944	2210	2207

Notes: Levels of significance: * = $p < 0.10$; ** = $p < 0.05$; *** = $p < 0.01$; **** = $p < 0.001$

requirements and for 2001 the odds ratio is even below 1. Other factors are apparently more important than type of employment contract for workers' readiness to move geographically in case of unemployment.

With only one exception, sex, age, family situation (marital status and children in the household) and socioeconomic position are all clearly significant variables in the two analyses. Women turn out to be less prepared to move than men, whereas the opposite holds for younger individuals compared to middle-aged and older people. Singles show a higher propensity to move than married/cohabiting individuals. There is a significant association between having children in the household and the dependent variable for 2001 but not, somewhat surprisingly, for 1993. Socioeconomic position appears to be important in the way we expected; compared to manual workers, white-collar workers, and especially higher-level white collars, are more often positive towards geographic flexibility in case of unemployment.

Turning to Table 10.4 and the issue of wage reduction, Model 1 shows a significant outcome for 1993 but not for 2001, which is in line with the Chi^2 tests presented in Table 10.2. We also see that the original association from 1993 remains basically intact, when in Model 2 the other variables are introduced. Among the control variables, this year only socioeconomic position and perceived relationship to management appear important. Lower- and middle-level white-collar workers are to a larger extent ready to accept a wage cut to save their jobs than are manual workers. The odds ratio for higher-level white-collars is also relatively high but not statistically significant. Perceived relationship to management turns out to have a strong effect. Respondents who think of this relationship as neutral or negative are less prone to accept a wage reduction than the reference category, regarding it as 'very good'. The fact that certain categories of employees are more inclined than others to answer in the affirmative can be taken as an indication that they regard a loss of their job as particularly negative, but also that they have some financial scope for making do with a lower income. In this connection, it seems that permanent employment contracts have a role to play as well as the relationship to management.

The outcome of Model 2 for 2001 is partly different. First, there is no significant difference at all between individuals on permanent contracts and individuals on temporary contracts. If the threat of unemployment was not regarded as severe in 2001 as in 1993 (see above), we have a possible explanation for this. However, there are also some other results to report. Males appear more willing to accept a wage cut than females and the same holds for the age categories 25–39 years and 40–54 years (above all for the latter) compared to the reference category. The opposite holds for singles compared to married/cohabiting individuals, whereas socioeconomic position is not a significant variable. People's

Table 10.4 Effects on odds among respondents of answering 'yes' as to whether they would accept a wage cut to save their job, 1993 and 2001 (logistic regression; odds ratios)

	1993	1993	2001	2001
	Model 1	Model 2	Model 1	Model 2
Type of employment				
Permanent (ref.)	1	1	1	1
Temporary	0.67*	0.63*	0.85	1.01
Sex				
Woman (ref.)		1		1
Man		1.08		1.57****
Age				
16–24 years		1.33		1.20
25–39		1.30		1.32*
40–54		1.06		1.80****
55–64 (ref.)		1		1
Marital status				
Married/cohabitant (ref.)		1		1
Single		1.17		0.82*
Children in the household				
Yes (ref.)		1		1
No		1.03		1.18
Socioeconomic position				
Manual worker (ref.)		1		1
Lower- or middle-level white collar		1.79****		1.11
Higher-level white collar		1.46		1.15
Perceived relationship to management				
Neither good nor bad, rather bad, and very bad		0.57***		0.58****
Rather good		0.89		0.75***
Very good (ref.)		1		1
Constant	1.57****	1.20	0.58****	0.38****
Nagelkerke R^2	0.004	0.046	0.001	0.045
n	944	929	2212	2163

Notes: Levels of significance: * = $p < 0.10$; ** = $p < 0.05$; *** = $p < 0.01$; **** = $p < 0.001$.

perceptions of their relationship to management turn out very much the same as for 1993, but this time there is even a significant difference between the two positive categories, answering 'rather good' and 'very good' respectively. The outcomes taken together can possibly be interpreted in a similar way to what I did with respect to 1993, that is, acceptance of a lower wage is more frequent among those who have good reasons to defend their present job and who also have some financial margins. At the same time, in this case there is no difference related to type of employment contract.

In sum, the results presented so far leave a somewhat divided impression, but it is possible to interpret them in a meaningful way. There is so far nothing to indicate that – when other factors are controlled for – workers on fixed-term contracts would be more inclined than workers on open-ended contracts to be flexible as regards the dimensions studied. In one respect it is even the other way around; in 1993 permanent employees were more willing to accept downward wage adjustments. It remains to be seen whether this picture will be sustained when we analyse the third dataset.

The 2000 survey

As pointed out above, the survey from 2000 deals with people's knowledge about and attitudes toward unemployment insurance issues. The question selected here is the closest we can get to one of those analysed above and it is formulated in the following way. 'If you became unemployed, what would you think of doing to get a job? Would you take a job, if you then had to change place of residence?' This question was asked because there is an unemployment insurance rule saying that people on benefits must be prepared to move geographically to take employment. It is obviously quite close to the question already dealt with on change of place of residence, although the two are not identical. We should, in addition, note that the respondents in 2000 had the opportunity not only to answer 'yes', 'no', or 'don't know', but also 'perhaps'. Table 10.5 shows how permanent and temporary workers responded to the question.

It appears that about one fifth were positive towards a change of place of residence if they became unemployed. Around 16 per cent answered 'perhaps' and the remaining 63 per cent said 'no' or 'don't know' (the latter answer is given by less than 2 per cent). There is a clear difference between permanent and temporary workers; relatively fewer among the former chose 'yes'. However, the outcome on

Table 10.5 Responses among permanent and temporary employees as to whether, in case of unemployment, they would take a job implying a change of place of residence, 2000 (%)

	Yes	Perhaps	No or don't know	Total and numbers
Permanent employment	18.9	17.0	64.1	100 (1138)
Temporary employment	28.7	12.4	58.9	100 (202)
Total	20.4	16.3	63.4	100 (1340)
$Chi^2=11.08$; $p=0.004***$ (df 2)				

the 'perhaps' alternative goes in the opposite direction, which means that the remaining difference in terms of 'no' and 'don't know' answers is not that great but still as we would expect, if type of employment contract is to mean anything. We will next control for other variables.

Multivariate analysis

The multivariate analyses to be presented next basically correspond to the analyses of willingness to move in the 1993 and 2001 surveys. In Table 10.6 the same control variables are included and Table 10.A in the appendix presents the distributions of the independent variables in the survey of 2000. We should note that – due to technicalities – the categorization of age is done in a slightly different way, but this is of no great consequence. Another aspect is, however, important. As the respondents in the survey carried out in 2000 had the option to answer 'perhaps' we must reconsider the issue of dichotomization. After due consideration, instead of choosing multinomial regression, which would be one option, I decided to draw the dividing line between respondents answering 'yes' and those saying 'perhaps', 'no' or 'don't know'. It seems that the answer 'yes' is a better indication than the combination of 'yes' and 'perhaps', if we want to predict people's actual mobility in case of unemployment. I also tried the other solution, collapsing respondents answering 'yes' or 'perhaps' into one single category. However, as there was then no association with type of employment contract to begin with, I have refrained from showing these regressions.

As previously, I start with one independent variable only, that is, type of employment (Model 1), and we then find a significant difference between permanent and temporary workers. Temporary workers are more inclined to declare their willingness to take a job implying a switch of place of residence. Moreover, we discover that the original association

Table 10.6   Effects on odds of respondents answering 'yes' as to whether, in case of unemployment, they would take a job implying a change of place of residence, 2000 (logistic regression; odds ratios)

	Model 1	Model 2
Type of employment		
Permanent (ref.)	1	1
Temporary	1.73***	1.42*
Sex		
Woman (ref.)		1
Man		1.33*
Age		
16–24 years		2.61***
25–34		2.41***
35–54		2.28***
55–64 (ref.)		1
Marital status		
Married/cohabitant (ref.)		1
Single		2.32****
Children in the household		
Yes (ref.)		1
No		1.58***
Socioeconomic position		
Manual worker (ref.)		1
Lower- or middle-level white collar		1.34*
Higher-level white collar		3.60****
Constant	0.23****	0.04****
Nagelkerke R^2	0.011	0.133
n	1340	1339

Notes: Levels of significance: * = $p < 0.10$; ** = $p < 0.05$; *** = $p < 0.01$; **** = $p < 0.001$.

remains when other independent variables are introduced (Model 2), although it becomes much weaker. This weakening is, of course, due to the impact of other factors: sex, age, marital status, children in the household and socioeconomic position. The results for all these variables basically look the same as in the previous analyses, although there are differences in the size of the coefficients and in statistical significance.

These differences are not that important for the present discussion and will therefore not be dealt with any further here. We thus have a significant difference between permanent and temporary employees to report in the 2000 survey; the latter appear to be more inclined to move geographically in the event of unemployment. At the same time, we should keep in mind that whereas the variable 'type of employment contract' has not produced any consistent results, all other factors considered have turned out to be important in basically all the regressions.

Conclusion

In this chapter I have studied the role of type of employment, that is, fixed-term and open-ended employment contracts, for employees' attitudes toward certain forms of flexibility. The starting point is employment protection legislation that is often assumed to reduce labour market flexibility. If this legislation has such an impact, we might expect to find differences in terms of flexibility between employees on permanent contracts and those on temporary contracts. It is the stricter rules associated with permanent jobs – in respect of notice periods, priorities in case of dismissals, severance pay, and so on – that are assumed to reduce flexibility. In the light of this, I have found it relevant to make comparisons between individuals with different types of employment contracts.

Before summarizing my findings and trying to draw conclusions from them, I want to recall the limitations of my analysis. To begin, the concept of flexibility covers a wide range of phenomena and I have only dealt with a few aspects. Another limitation is that my data provide information on what people say they would do and not on what they actually will do or have done. The data utilized are limited to a subjective dimension and it is obvious that attitudes and action may diverge. Still, this kind of information is of interest, if we can assume a positive correlation between words and deeds. From other studies we can conclude that such an assumption is reasonable. For example, we know that young people are more apt than middle-aged and older people to say that they want to move geographically and they actually also move more often.

Well aware of what the empirical data presented here can and cannot tell us, we can look at the patterns that appear. First, I have studied whether type of employment contract has some impact on people's willingness to change place of residence in the event of unemployment. In three different surveys we asked employees about this. The wording of questions was twice (1993 and 2001) identical and on one occasion (2000) it was different but yet quite similar. Second, I have also studied the attitudes among permanent and temporary workers toward wage reductions, if that was the only way to save their job. This was done in two of the surveys (1993 and 2001), again with identical wording of the question.

Some results are particularly interesting. There is generally a significant bivariate association between type of employment contract and attitudes to change of place of residence, but when we control for other factors – age, sex, family situation and socioeconomic position – this association ceases to be statistically significant or even disappears completely except in one of the three surveys. In other words, the empirical support for the hypothesis that fixed-term contracts would make people more willing to move geographically is not very strong. Other factors, such as age and family situation, seem to be much more important. We should note that temporary workers are often young and less tied to family obligations. It is therefore relatively easy for them to move and type of employment contract is thus in itself less significant.

With respect to willingness to take a wage reduction to save one's job, we also find a statistically significant association with type of employment contract in one of the surveys and it remains statistically safe even when other variables are controlled for. It, however, points in the opposite direction, that is, those with permanent jobs are more often inclined to agree to a wage cut to secure their jobs. Apparently people with permanent positions have more to lose by being laid off and they are therefore more apt to accept other changes to defend their jobs. Now, this result was not significant in one of the two surveys and we must accordingly be cautious with our conclusions; the data do not really confirm my interpretation, although there is some evidence in favour of it.

It is possible that type of employment contract has some role to play regarding geographic flexibility, but this conclusion is not very robust. In contrast, it is very clear that other factors are very significant. Young employees, compared to older employees, are generally more positive towards moving and the same goes for men relative to women and for white-collar workers (particularly at higher levels) relative to manual workers. Certain aspects of the family situation – such as marriage/cohabitation and children in the household – tend to reduce the willingness to move. In light of this, it is very unclear whether increased possibilities for employers to hire people on temporary contracts would have any significant impact on geographic mobility patterns.

Our data also suggest that employees in permanent positions may be more interested in lowering their wage to save their job. The support for this hypothesis is not consistent, but we have some indication for 1993 when, less than ever, people could feel safe in their jobs due to a dramatic deterioration of the labour market. A possible explanation is that workers on permanent contracts have more to defend, but in addition they must also have the financial possibilities to get by on a lower income. Of course, also in this case it may not be type of employment contract in itself that is the important thing. It may just be the other way around, namely that those who have the strongest reasons to defend their jobs also relatively often have permanent contracts.

Still this discussion illustrates one aspect of the complex of flexibility problems that I have repeatedly come back to here, namely that there are functional alternatives. When demands for adjustment are put forward, adjustment can take different forms. If one type of flexibility is not feasible, there may be other possibilities. In the end the outcome may be very much the same.

Appendix

Table 10.A Distribution of variable values for independent variables used in the analyses of data from 1993, 2000 and 2001 (%)

	1993		2000		2001	
	%	n	%	n	%	n
Type of employment	100	1019	100	1354	100	2216
Permanent	91.6	933	85.0	1151	86.1	1909
Temporary	8.4	86	15.0	203	13.9	307
Sex	100	1112	100	1354	100	2216
Woman	48.3	537	47.5	643	47.0	1041
Man	51.7	575	52.5	711	53.0	1175
Age	100	1112	100	1354	100	2216
16–24 years	13.4	149	9.7	131	10.8	239
25–39 (2000 = 25–34)	35.3	393	23.7	321	36.1	801
40–54 (2000 = 35–54)	37.6	418	49.8	674	36.6	833
55–64	13.7	152	16.8	228	15.5	343
Marital status	100	1080	100	1354	100	2216
Married/cohabitant	69.9	755	70.3	952	70.9	1571
Single	30.1	325	29.7	402	29.1	645

Table 10.A (Continued)

	1993		2000		2001	
	%	n	%	n	%	n
Children in the household	100	1080	100	1354	100	2216
Yes	69.9	755	46.0	623	70.9	1571
No	30.1	325	54.0	731	29.1	645
Socioeconomic position	100	1054	100	1354	100	2213
Manual worker	52.7	555	46.2	625	45.5	1007
Lower- or middle-level white collar	36.4	384	39.1	529	40.0	886
Higher-level white collar	10.9	115	14.8	200	14.5	320
Perceived relationship to management	100	932			100	2169
Very good	32.9	307			31.5	683
Rather good	40.5	377			43.2	936
Neither good nor bad, rather bad, or very bad	26.6	248			25.4	550

11
Time-related Flexibility and Stability for Employees

Dan Jonsson

Theoretical background and empirical focus

Increasing demands on employees from their employers with regard to working time flexibility and other forms of flexibility are often justified as responses to increasing demands for flexible supply of goods and services from customers. According to this narrative, customers are demanding an ever-greater variety of goods and services, and demand fluctuates more and more strongly and quickly. The era of mass production and stable demand is over. To survive in an increasingly competitive market-place, producers must meet demands for increased flexibility. Therefore, employees have to be more flexible as well. In short, demands for increased flexibility on employees derive ultimately from customers' demands for increased flexibility.

Part of this argument is no doubt true. As an example, unquestionably, working hours that can be easily changed and represent flexibility for employers *can be used* to increase product volume flexibility for customers, and, *other things being equal*, increased flexibility of employees results in increased flexibility for customers. This does not mean, however, that increased flexibility of employees is always associated with increased flexibility for customers.

It is important to understand that employer-assessed employee flexibility can be a means of attaining other goals than customer-assessed vendor flexibility. Customer-assessed vendor flexibility need not even be the main goal sought by increasing employer-assessed employee

Note: The author wishes to thank the Swedish Council for Working Life and Social Research that funded the work on this chapter.

flexibility, contrary to what seems to be an implicit assumption in the flexibility narrative. Instead, increased flexibility for the employer can be used, partly or exclusively, to reduce labour costs by reducing the volume of paid working time.

When there is stable demand for products and services, or when variation in demand is absorbed by a stock of completed products, as in traditional mass production, an even production pace can be maintained, and as a consequence it is relatively easy to fill the entire paid working time with work. When the demand for products and services fluctuates strongly and stocks of completed products are kept small, on the other hand, some paid working time during which the employee is present at the workplace may not be used for working, because there is no work to do at the moment – on some occasions, no more products or services are needed. In other words, there will be some *slack*, that is, paid working time not fully used for working.

Slack can be reduced, however, by increased flexibility for the employer in terms of employment flexibility, workplace flexibility, working time flexibility or work flexibility as defined in Chapter 3. For example, if the working times of employees or the number of employees can be quickly adapted to variation in demand for products, or if employees can be easily transferred from direct production work to indirect work or from the production of less-in-demand products to that of more-in-demand products, little paid working time is wasted due to a lack of work to perform when demand is slow. In other words, such flexibility can be used to reduce labour costs by reducing slack so as to reduce the volume of paid working time.

Flexibility for employers may thus be regarded as a rationalization strategy, or a strategy to reduce labour costs, and as such it makes sense to consider flexibility for employers in the context of other strategies for reducing labour costs. These further strategies seem to belong to two main categories.

One general strategy aims at increasing *work efficiency*. This concern was systematically addressed already in the writings of Frederick Taylor (1911) on so-called Scientific Management. Taylor gives several examples of how labour productivity could be increased dramatically by using the tools provided by Scientific Management. For example, he tells the story of how a colleague, Frank Gilbreth, managed to increase the number of bricks laid per man per hour, while erecting a factory wall, from 120 to 350 (Taylor 1961: 81). This was accomplished, in this case as in others, by combining three kinds of changes. First, new work methods were developed and taught to employees; second, new tools and implements, designed to suit these new work methods, were introduced; finally, only the most able workers were employed.

Another general strategy for reducing labour costs aims at increasing *work intensity*. Even if employees use efficient work methods, and work efficiency is optimal for this and other reasons, there may exist a potential for increasing labour productivity and decreasing labour costs by increasing work intensity. Taylor suggested that time measurement methods, used to determine the 'ideal' time needed to perform a work task, as well as economic incentives based on the employee's performance, should be used to prevent work intensity from slipping.

In this chapter, some results from a survey of Swedish employees relating to the theoretical issues outlined above will be presented. For reasons already indicated, items that concern work efficiency, work intensity and slack are included, as well as items about flexibility and stability for employees. Since the questionnaire is directed to employees, there is unfortunately no direct indicator of flexibility for employers available. However, since instability for employees may be caused by flexibility for employers and stability for employees may cause inflexibility for employers, the indicators available may provide some indirect information about flexibility for employers. Similarly, flexibility and inflexibility for employees may be related to instability and stability for employers, respectively.

A further limitation of the study is that it focuses on time-related flexibility and stability for employees, mainly working time flexibility and stability. This means that the variation, flexibility and stability of working times are all considered, and in addition two items relating to time flexibility during work are also analysed.

Data collection, data analysis and main variables

The empirical results reported in this chapter are based on a survey conducted by Statistics Sweden from September to October 2005. The study population was defined as all employed persons in Sweden from 25 to 65 years of age. Questionnaires were distributed by mail to a random sample of 2505 persons, drawn from Statistics Sweden's Employment Register. 1681 usable questionnaires were returned, resulting in a response rate of 67.1 per cent. Information about each respondent's sex, age, income, education and whether the respondent's employer belonged to the private or the public sector was available from Statistics Sweden's registers, and was added to the data from the questionnaires.

Education was coded according to SUN 2000, a Swedish statistical standard based on ISCED 1997.

The approach chosen for multivariate analysis of the main variables is SEM, structural equation modelling (see, for example, Kline 2004). SEM may be described as a generalization of multiple linear regression analysis, where also other variables than error terms may be regarded as latent (unobserved) variables, and where constraints other than those pertaining to error terms can (and sometimes must) be imposed on parameters such as means, standard deviations and regression coefficients.

Because the 'factors' obtained through factor analysis are latent variables, SEM can also be used to perform confirmatory factor analysis, where the indicators associated with a particular factor – but not their factor loadings – are selected based on theoretical arguments. This is analogous to multiple linear regression analysis, where the independent variables are specified in advance, but their regression coefficients with regard to the (similarly pre-specified) dependent variable remain to be estimated.

In the multivariate analyses presented below, SEM will be used to implement a combination of confirmatory factor analysis and multiple linear regression analysis. The models used will have specifications like those in Figure 11.1. Each model contains a latent variable which is a summarizing factor based on two or more indicators. At the same time,

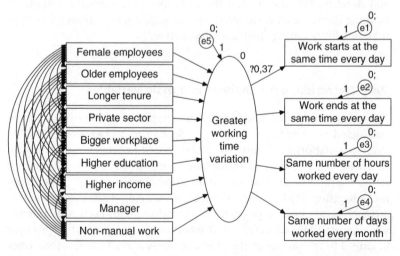

Figure 11.1   Specification for the structural equation model in Figure 11.2

this factor is regarded as the dependent variable in a multiple linear regression analysis.

Apart from assumptions concerning error terms, the structural equation model in Figure 11.1 includes two assumptions about parameter values which are needed to identify the remaining parameters. First, it is assumed that the mean of the latent working time variation variable is 0; second, the unstandardized regression coefficient for the indicator 'Work starts at the same time every day' is assumed to be –0.37. The sign of this parameter is negative because the indicator refers to a *lack* of variation; its size (0.37) is chosen so as to normalize the variance of the latent working time variation variable.

Based on the theoretical dimensions outlined above and the indicators available in the data collected, six work-related factors were identified and will be subjected to multivariate analyses using structural equation modelling. These factors are working time variation, working time flexibility, time flexibility during work, working time instability, work intensity and temporary slack in workload. For one theoretical dimension, work efficiency, it was not possible to create a suitable corresponding factor based on available indicators.

The independent variables used in the structural equation models are sex, age, tenure, private vs public sector workplace, size of workplace, education, income, managerial vs non-managerial occupation and occupation with non-manual vs manual work. Age, tenure, size of workplace, education and income have been dichotomized into high and low, or long and short, with the dividing lines close to the medians of the frequency distributions.[1] On the basis of textual descriptions by the respondents, their occupations were coded by Statistics Sweden according to the Swedish statistical standard SSYK, which is based on ISCO-88. Employees belonging to the first main group, 'legislators, senior officials and managers', were classified as having managerial occupations. In addition, employees belonging to the first main group, the second main group, 'professionals', or the third main group, 'technicians and associate professionals', were classified as having non-manual occupations. It should be noted that since non-manual occupations include managers, managerial occupations are contrasted to other non-manual

---

[1] The median age of employees was 45 years and the median income approximately SEK 250,000. Median tenure was approximately 10 years, median size of workplace was between 30 and 40 employees and median educational accomplishment was upper secondary level of education (level 3 according to SUN 2000).

occupations rather than to non-managerial occupations in the regression analyses.

Since the independent variables are all dichotomous or have been dichotomized, the unstandardized regression coefficients for these variables have a simple interpretation as differences between means. For example, an unstandardized regression coefficient of 0.5 for sex can be interpreted as representing a difference of 0.5 between the means for men and women with respect to the factor considered. Thus, comparisons of regression coefficients within the same model are meaningful.

Comparisons between models, for example between the regression coefficients for sex across different structural equation models, are more problematic, however, since the size of unstandardized regression coefficients are affected by legitimate measurement scale transformations of the dependent variables – in this case, the six factors listed above. To make comparisons between regression coefficients in different models more meaningful, measurement scales have been normalized by introducing assumptions in the models so as to make the variance of all factors approximately equal. (As noted above, it was partly for this reason that a particular regression coefficient was set to –0.37 in Figure 11.1.)

Finally, the 'factor loadings' reported for the indicators are standardized regression coefficients, thus compensating for possible differences between the variances of the indicators. Thus, the parameters shown in the structural equation models below are unstandardized regression coefficients for the links between the independent variables and the factor but standardized regression coefficients for the links between the factor and the indicators. To reduce clutter, correlations between the independent variables will not be reported, and the small circles representing error terms shown in Figure 11.1 are also omitted.

Specific results

Working time variation

Two questions were asked about the variation of the *length* of working time, namely 'Do you normally work the same number of hours every day?' and 'Do you normally work approximately the same number of days every month?'. Response frequencies are shown in Table 11.1.

Thirty six per cent of the respondents indicate that they do not normally work the same number of hours every day, which may be seen as evidence of considerable short-time (intra-day) variation in the length of working time. Long-term variation in terms of days worked per

Table 11.1 Length of working time (%; n = 1395)

The same number of hours every day	Approximately the same number of days every month		
	Yes	No	Total
Yes	62.7	1.4	64.1
No	30.4	5.5	35.9
Total	93.1	6.9	100.0

month, on the other hand, seems to be a rare phenomenon, comparatively and absolutely.

Two other questions concerned not only the length of working time but also the *location* of working time, namely 'Do you start your work at the same time every day?' and 'Do you finish your work at the same time every day?'. The response alternatives were 'Yes, at exactly the same time every day', 'Yes, at approximately the same time every day' and 'No, at different times on different days'. Response frequencies are reported in Table 11.2.

The impression conveyed is, again, that there is considerable short-term variation in working times. For 42 per cent of the respondents, work ends at substantially different times on different days, and for 27 per cent it starts at substantially different times on different days.

Interestingly, employees affected by short-time variation in working times are more likely to be affected by long-term variation as well, and vice versa; there is a positive correlation between the two items (r = 0.25; p < 0.001). Similarly, employees who start their work at different times on different days are more likely to end their work at different times as well, and vice versa. As evident in Table 11.2, there is

Table 11.2 Daily working time (%; n = 1397)

When each day's work starts	When each day's work ends			
	At exactly the same time	At roughly the same time	At different times	Total
At exactly the same time	11.0	8.7	3.1	22.8
At roughly the same time	0.4	36.6	13.1	50.1
At different times	0.2	0.9	26.0	27.1
Total	11.6	46.2	42.2	100.0

a strong positive correlation between the two variables ($\tau_b = 0.85$, $\gamma = 0.87$; $p < 0.001$).

When interpreting these correlations one should keep in mind the possibility that different modes of variation of working times could be substituted for each other. For example, if it is possible to change the time when the workday starts, it is not necessary to change the time when the workday ends in order to change the length of working time. If only one of these methods were used in most cases, there would be a negative correlation between the two items, reflecting a *substitution effect*. In reality, however, we find positive correlations between different modes of working time variation. This suggests a predominant *polarization effect*. Maybe some workplaces demand or allow variation in working times much more than others, and different modes of variation are used simultaneously to achieve that goal at these workplaces. Another possible explanation is that certain categories of employees are required to vary their working times much more than others, or have the opportunity to do so much more than others. Again, these employees would be affected in multiple ways. For example, 31 per cent of female employees report that their work *starts* at different times on different days compared to 22 per cent of male employees; at the same time, 46 per cent of female employees report that their work *ends* at different times on different days, compared to 38 per cent of male employees.

It should be emphasized that at this point we do not know whether the working time variation observed is desirable or undesirable for the employee. For example, we do not know whether an employee who leaves the workplace at different times on different days does so because she *has to* or because he *wants to*. This question concerns flexibility vs instability and will be addressed later.

As shown in Figure 11.2, the four items considered above can be used as indicators of a working time variation factor. This factor is most strongly associated with the items 'Work starts at the same time every day' ($\beta = -0.75$) and 'Work ends at the same time every day' ($\beta = -0.92$). It is more weakly associated with the two items that concern only the length of the working time in terms of hours worked per day ($\beta = -0.55$) or days worked per month ($\beta = -0.23$).

According to the SEM analysis, working time variation as measured by the working time variation factor is greater for women than for men ($b = 0.24$) and also greater for younger employees than for older ones ($b = -0.30$). In addition, working time variation is greater for more highly educated employees ($b = 0.29$).

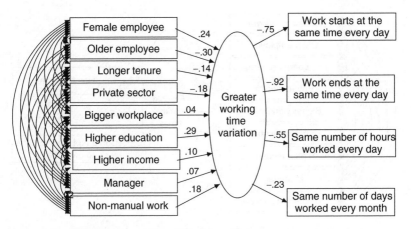

Figure 11.2   SEM analysis of working time variation

Working time flexibility

Two questions were designed to provide information about the *flexibility* (desirable variability) of working times from the employee's point of view. One question simply asked whether the employee had 'flexitime'. While flexitime may be understood in different ways, the most common meaning seems to be an arrangement where employees can decide within limits when to begin and end their work each day. The other question was phrased 'Are you able to change and adapt your working times according to your own needs?' Both questions thus concerned variability that may be assumed to be desirable for the employee.

Working time flexibility seems to be widespread (see Table 11.3). Some 20 per cent of the respondents say that they are 'often' able to change their working times in accordance with their own needs, and in addition 29 per cent say that they have flexitime and that they are 'sometimes' able to change their working times in accordance with their own needs (see Table 11.3). There is clearly

Table 11.3   Flexibility of working time (%; n = 1383)

Flexitime	Working times adapted to own needs			
	Often	Sometimes	Never	Total
Yes	15.0	29.0	3.5	47.6
No	5.4	25.6	21.5	52.4
Total	20.4	54.6	25.0	100.0

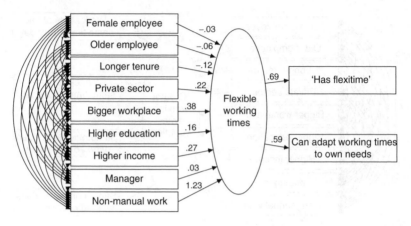

Figure 11.3   SEM analysis of working time flexibility

a conceptual overlap between the two items, so it is not surprising that there is also a positive correlation between them ($\tau_c = 0.43$, $\gamma = 0.67$; p < 0.001).

The two flexibility indicators can be combined into one flexible working time factor (see Figure 11.3). This factor has a moderately strong loading on the flexitime item ($\beta = 0.69$) as well as the item about whether working time can be adapted to the employee's own needs ($\beta = 0.59$).

Working time flexibility is strongly associated with occupation; employees with non-manual work are much more likely to have flexible working times, other things being equal (b = 1.23). In addition, high income *per se* is positively related to flexible working times (b = 0.27). Two workplace variables are also associated with working time flexibility. Other things being equal, flexible working times are more common at big workplaces than small (b = 0.38), and also somewhat more common at workplaces in the private sector than in the public sector (b = 0.22).

Time flexibility during work

The formal right or informal possibility to take a pause from work when the need arises can be seen as providing work flexibility for the employee, but it can also be seen by an employer as facilitating work avoidance. The answers reported in Table 11.4 show that there is nevertheless substantial scope for employee-initiated pauses. Thus, about 78 per cent of the respondents tend to agree that they are able to briefly interrupt their work if they want, for example, to make a telephone call,

Table 11.4 Indicators of time flexibility during work (%)

	Entirely correct description	Rather good description	Neither good nor bad description	Rather bad description	Entirely incorrect description	Total (n)
Possible to briefly interrupt work	40.8	37.4	9.2	7.9	4.6	100 (1386)
Possible to leave the workplace part of the day	24.3	25.7	13.6	14.1	22.3	100 (1384)

and 50 per cent tend to agree that they are able to leave their workplace 'part of the day' if required.

As shown in Figure 11.4, time flexibility during work was thus measured by means of two items. The item most closely associated with this factor was 'I can leave my work part of the day to perform an errand' ($\beta = 0.97$). The item 'I can take a short break during my work to make a phone call' was also positively associated with this factor ($\beta = 0.55$).

Time flexibility during work was higher among employees with non-manual work (b = 0.26), managers (b = 0.30) and employees with high

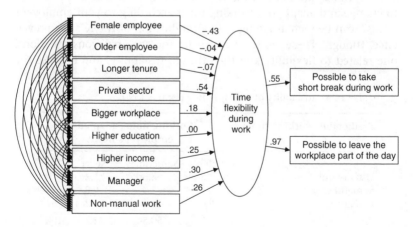

Figure 11.4 SEM analysis of time flexibility during work

wages (b = 0.25). In addition, female employees were less likely to have time flexibility during work than male employees (b = –0.43), and private sector employees had more flexibility than public sector employees (b = 0.54). Somewhat unexpectedly, the last-mentioned effects were even stronger than those associated with occupation and income.

Working time instability

Two questions were related to the *instability* (undesirable variability) of working times from the employee's point of view: 'Do you have predictable working times?' and 'Do you have to change and adapt your working times according to your employer's needs?' It is reasonable to assume that unpredictable working times are in general undesirable. Thus, a question about unpredictable working times can be used as an indicator of instability of working times. Similarly, if working times are adapted primarily to the needs of the employers rather than the employees, this variability is likely, although not certain, to be regarded as undesirable by employees, so a question about this can be used as another indicator of instability of working times.

Approximately 27 per cent of the respondents say that they 'often' adapt their working times to their employers' needs, while 16 per cent of the respondents do not agree that their working times are 'usually' predictable.

It is clear that instability, like flexibility, is fairly widespread, but it is difficult to compare the prevalence of desirable and undesirable variability in working times. The row marginal frequencies in Table 11.3 and Table 11.5 for the questions 'Are you able to change and adapt your working times according to your own needs?' and 'Do you have to change and adapt your working times according to your employer's needs?' can be seen as giving a rough indication of the relative prevalence, though. These are the frequencies for two analogous questions, one related to flexibility and the other to instability, and because the

Table 11.5 Instability of working time (%; n = 1390)

Predictable working times	Working hours adapted to employer's needs			
	Often	Sometimes	Never	Total
Usually not	4.5	3.3	1.2	9.1
Sometimes	3.7	2.9	0.2	6.9
Usually	18.6	44.2	21.2	84.0
Total	26.8	50.5	22.7	100.0

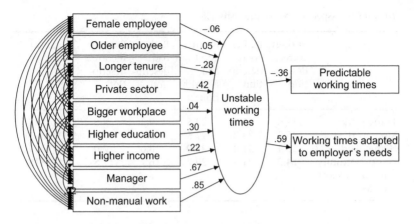

Figure 11.5   SEM analysis of working time instability

frequencies are roughly the same in both cases, one can draw the tentative conclusion that the flexibility and instability of working times are roughly equally widespread.

Finally, there is a positive correlation between the variables in Table 11.5 ($\tau_b = 0.22$, $\gamma = 0.50$; $p < 0.001$), suggesting the existence of a moderate polarization effect for instability of working times. These two indicators can be combined into a common unstable working times factor, as shown in Figure 11.5. Predictable working times are negatively associated with this factor ($\beta = -0.36$), while working times that are adapted to the employer's needs are positively associated with unstable working times ($\beta = 0.59$).

Other things being equal, working time instability is greater among employees with non-manual work than among those with manual work ($b = 0.85$), and such instability is greater for managers than other employees with non-manual work ($b = 0.67$). Highly educated ($b = 0.30$) and highly paid ($b = 0.22$) employees also tend to be subjected to more working time instability than less highly educated and paid employees. In addition, working times are especially unstable among private sector employees ($b = 0.42$) and to some extent also among employees with shorter tenure ($b = -0.28$).

Work intensity

Work intensity was measured by four items. Respondents were asked if they regarded their work as tiring and also if the number of work tasks had increased, if their work pace had increased and if their opportunities

Table 11.6 Aspects of work intensity (%)

	Entirely correct description	Rather good description	Neither good nor bad description	Rather bad description	Entirely incorrect description	Total (n)
Tiring work	21.6	41.1	23.5	9.3	4.5	100 (1387)
More work tasks	35.8	34.2	17.5	5.4	7.0	100 (1381)
Higher work pace	26.4	31.0	27.0	8.6	7.0	100 (1379)
Less opportunity to take a short break	14.7	21.4	29.7	16.7	17.5	100 (1375)

to take a short break during the work had decreased. (The questions about changes referred to 'the last 5–10 years'.) As shown in Table 11.6, approximately 63 per cent of the respondents regarded their work as tiring, 70 per cent said they had received more work tasks, approximately 57 per cent answered that their work pace had increased and approximately 36 per cent said they had less opportunity than before to take a short break during the work.

Confirmatory factor analysis showed that the four items in Table 11.6 can be regarded as indicators of a common work intensity factor. As shown in Figure 11.6, this factor has strong or moderately strong associations with tiring work ($\beta = 0.68$), increased number of work tasks

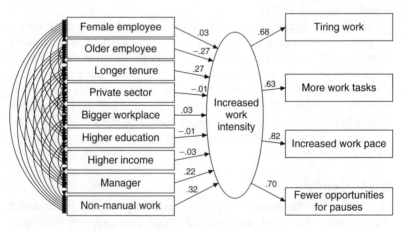

Figure 11.6 SEM analysis of work intensity

($\beta = 0.63$), increased work pace ($\beta = 0.82$) and reduced opportunity to take a break from work ($\beta = 0.70$). Since three of these factors concerned changes relating to work intensity, it seems appropriate to talk about an *increase* in work intensity.

Work intensity is reported to have increased somewhat more among employees with non-manual work ($b = 0.32$) than among those with manual work, and more among managers ($b = 0.22$) than other employees with non-manual work. In addition, work intensity tends to decrease with age ($b = -0.27$) when controlling for tenure, but to increase with increasing tenure ($b = 0.27$) when controlling for age.

Work efficiency

It should not come as a big surprise that a majority of employees, in fact 83 per cent of the respondents, considered themselves to work efficiently. On more specific questions, about 61 per cent of the respondents said that they had changed their work methods 'during the last 5–10 years' in order to work more efficiently, while approximately 38 per cent said new tools and implements had been introduced in the same time frame to make the work more efficient. Thus, contrary to old notions of rationalization through technology, more employees seemed to be affected by changed work methods than by introduction of new technology.

Unfortunately, it did not prove possible to create an adequate work efficiency factor based on the items in Table 11.7. The pattern of correlation among the three items did not allow a common factor to be created, not even a factor based on two items.

Table 11.7 Aspects of work efficiency (%)

	Entirely correct description	Rather good description	Neither good nor bad description	Rather bad description	Entirely incorrect description	Total (n)
'Working efficiently'	22.8	60.1	15.0	1.8	0.3	100 (1380)
New work methods	20.4	40.4	24.6	7.8	6.7	100 (1379)
New tools and implements	11.9	26.2	25.2	15.2	21.4	100 (1380)

Table 11.8 Workload variation and slack (%)

	Entirely correct description	Rather good description	Neither good nor bad description	Rather bad description	Entirely incorrect description	Total (n)
Not fully occupied part of the day	4.7	13.9	15.2	25.4	40.8	100 (1281)
Not fully occupied part of the year	5.6	13.7	10.6	22.0	48.2	100 (1383)

Temporary slack

A widespread use of 'downsizing', 'lean production' and related 'flexibility strategies' can be expected to result in rather low levels of temporary slack in companies. As shown in Table 11.8, this is also what employees reported in response to items allowing them to agree or disagree that they were sometimes not fully occupied during part of the day or part of the year. For example, less than 20 per cent of the employees tend to agree that they are not fully occupied part of the day, while more than 40 per cent strongly disagree with this assertion.

As shown in Figure 11.7, the two temporary slack items could be

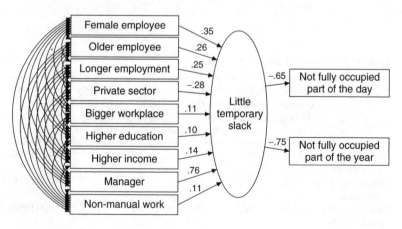

Figure 11.7 SEM analysis of temporary slack in workload

combined into a common factor. This factor was positively associated with the 'slack during the day' item ($\beta = 0.65$), as well as the 'slack during the year' item ($\beta = 0.75$). To obtain consistency with the analysis of work intensity, the slack factor has been inverted in Figure 11.7 so that high values on this variable imply high workloads.

Managers report considerably less temporary slack than do other employees with non-manual work ($b = 0.76$). There are also substantial differences according to sex, age, tenure and workplace affiliation. Temporary slack is experienced less by women than by men ($b = 0.34$), and slack tends to decrease with increasing age ($b = 0.26$) and with increasing tenure ($b = 0.25$). Finally, private sector employees report more temporary slack than do public sector employees ($b = -0.28$).

General results and discussion

Table 11.9 summarizes the most important results from the multivariate analyses above. The independent variables can be characterized in terms of favourable and unfavourable outcomes with regard to variability-related factors and workload-related factors. With regard to variability factors, great working time flexibility, great time flexibility during work and little working time instability represent favourable outcomes, whereas little working time flexibility, little time flexibility during work and great working time instability represent unfavourable outcomes. With regard to workload factors, increased work intensity and little temporary slack represent unfavourable outcomes, whereas non-increased work intensity and much temporary slack represent favourable outcomes.

Table 11.9 Substantial associations between factors and independent variables

	Greater working time variation	Flexible working times	Time flexibility during work	Unstable working times	Increased work intensity	Little temporary slack
Female employee	0.24		−0.43			0.35
Older employee	−0.30				−0.27	0.26
Longer tenure				−0.28	0.27	0.25
Private sector		0.22	0.54	0.42		−0.28
Bigger workplace		0.38				
Higher education	0.29	0.27	0.25	0.30		
Higher income				0.22		
Manager			0.30	0.67	0.22	0.76
Non-manual work		1.23	0.26	0.85	0.32	

Employees with *non-manual work* and in particular *managers* tend to have mixed outcomes for variability factors – they report high flexibility but also high instability. At the same time, they tend to have unfavourable outcomes with regard to workload factors – they tend to report high work intensity and little temporary slack.

Compared to public sector employees and employees with lower education, *private sector* employees and employees with *higher education* also tend to have mixed outcomes with regard to the variability factors. Like employees with non-manual work and managers, they report high flexibility but also high instability. Private sector employment and high education are not associated with high workloads, however. In fact, other things being equal, private sector employees report more temporary slack than public sector employees.

Controlling for age and other independent variables, employees with *longer tenure* tend to receive favourable outcomes for variability factors but unfavourable outcomes for workload factors. These employees were less likely to report working time instability than employees with shorter tenure, but more likely to report increased work intensity and little temporary slack. The effects of tenure on these factors were not strong, however.

Compared to male employees, *female employees* tend to suffer negative outcomes for variability factors as well as workload factors. They report little time flexibility during work and little temporary slack. According to the multivariate analyses, there are virtually no differences between male and female employees with regard to working time flexibility, working time instability and work intensity, however.

The age of the employee and the size of the workplace did not exhibit consistent patterns of association with the factors considered.

It may seem paradoxical that employees who have particularly flexible and unstable working times and hence more of desirable as well as undesirable variability in working times – for example, employees with non-manual work – in most cases do not report more variation in working times than other employees. However, if we look at the indicators for the variation in working times factor, we find that they refer to *actual* variation in working times, for example whether work starts at the same time every day or not. The indicators of working time flexibility and stability, on the other hand, refer to *potential* variation in working times – for example, if it is *possible* to adapt working times to suit the employee. These two types of factors are analytically distinct and not necessarily closely associated empirically.

Table 11.10   Correlations among additive indices used as proxies for factors

	Working time flexibility	Time flexibility during work	Working time instability	Increased work intensity
Time flexibility during work	0.46**			
Working time instability	0.27**	0.09**		
Increased work intensity	–0.13**	–0.28**	0.17**	
Little temporary slack	–0.05	–0.19**	0.01	0.23**

Note: ** Correlations are significant at the 0.01 level (two-tailed test).

Finally, we shall look at a simple correlation analysis of our data. To keep things simple, five additive, unweighted indices have been created, based on the indicators used above for working time flexibility, time flexibility during work, working time instability, increased work intensity and little temporary slack. Overall correlations for these indices are reported in Table 11.10.

Two interesting patterns can be seen in this table. First, working time instability is positively correlated with both working time flexibility ($r = 0.27$) and time flexibility during work ($r = 0.09$). Thus, desirable and undesirable variability tend to be associated.

Second, increased work intensity is negatively correlated with both working time flexibility ($r = –0.13$) and time flexibility during work ($r = –0.28$), but positively correlated with working time instability ($r = 0.17$). Little temporary slack is similarly negatively correlated with time flexibility during work ($r = –0.19$). In other words, inflexibility as well as instability are in general associated with increased work intensity and little temporary slack. Thus, unfavourable outcomes with regard to variability factors are in general associated with unfavourable outcomes with regard to workload factors; conversely, favourable outcomes with regard to variability factors are in general associated with favourable outcomes with regard to workload factors.

A positive correlation between two variables may be due to a common influence from a third, exogenous variable. Thus, one way to try to account for the positive correlation between flexibility and instability as well as that between undesirable variability outcomes and high workload is to look for some common independent variable or variables.

With regard to the positive correlation between flexibility and instability, Table 11.9 shows that some of the independent variables used in the multivariate analyses above were indeed associated with dependent variables in a way which could explain the correlations between these dependent variables. Specifically, non-manual work, managerial occupation, higher education and private sector employment are all positively associated with flexibility as well as instability. The reasons for these empirical associations are not obvious, but the identification of these common factors nevertheless represents some progress in explaining the correlations among the dependent variables.

On the other hand, the positive associations between unfavourable variability outcomes and high workload cannot easily be explained by both variability outcomes and workload being influenced by one or more common independent variables included in the SEM analyses above. While female employees did to some extent suffer both low time flexibility during work and high workloads, this pattern is confined to one background variable. By contrast, employees with non-manual work, for example, reported both high working time flexibility and high workloads.

However, another approach may be tried. Instead of looking for *characteristics of employees* that tend to be associated with both unfavourable variability outcomes and high workloads, one could look for *traits of work situations* that create both unfavourable variability outcomes and high workloads. For example, increased performance demands on employees may not only lead to increased work intensity, but can also lead to unplanned overtime, thus creating working time instability for employees. Similarly, increased demands on employees may prevent them from occasionally shortening their working time to suit their own needs, thus creating working time inflexibility for employees.

In terms of cause–effect relations between variables, the general idea is that if employees are faced with increasing performance demands they tend to change their way of working to meet these increased demands. This not only leads to increased work intensity but also reduces the scope for both working time flexibility and working time stability as well as other forms of flexibility and stability related to time and work.

To test this idea, a structural equation model was devised, using available indicators. While the latent variables 'overall performance demands' and 'overall work effort' in this model are conceptually broader than the corresponding factors 'temporary slack in workload' and 'work intensity' used in previous analyses, no additional indicators were available, so the operationalization of the new latent variables is open to some doubt. With this reservation, the results of the SEM analysis are unequivocal. The structural equation model in Figure 11.8 does indeed suggest that greater performance demands lead to greater work efforts ($\beta = 0.32$) and that greater work

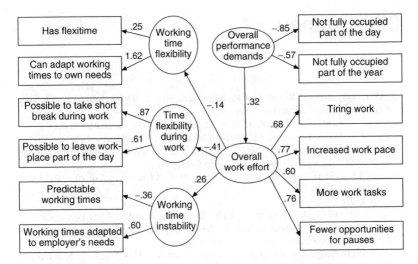

Figure 11.8 A structural equation model for the causal relations between flexibility, stability and workload

efforts in turn lead to less flexible working times ($\beta = -0.14$), less time flexibility during work ($\beta = -0.41$) and more unstable working times ($\beta = 0.26$).

In conclusion, I would like to point to a paradox in recent developments with regard to work organization. On the one hand, the importance of 'flexibilization' is emphasized, but on the other hand 'downsizing' and 'lean production' are also emphasized. These latter developments tend to lead to higher performance demands on employees. This, the analysis above suggests, is not entirely consistent with 'flexibilization', since higher performance demands tend to create inflexibility and instability for the employees, contrary to the 'flexibility rhetoric'. If 'flexibilization' has created increased flexibility, it is probably mainly flexibility for employers that has been created.

Bibliography

ACAS (2004) *Annual Report and Resource Accounts, 2003/04.* London: Advisory Conciliation and Arbitration Service.

Ackroyd, S. (2002) *The Organization of Business.* Oxford University Press.

Ackroyd, S., and S. Procter (1998) 'British Manufacturing Organization and Workplace Industrial Relations: Some Attributes of the New Flexible Firm'. *British Journal of Industrial Relations*, 36 (2): 163–83.

Adams, J.S. (1965) 'Inequity in Social Exchange'. *Advances in Experimental Social Psychology*, 2 (2): 267–97.

Affärsvärlden.

Aglietta, M. (1979) *A Theory of Capitalist Regulation.* London: New Left Books.

Ajzen, I., and M. Fishbein (1980) *Understanding Attitudes and Predicting Social Behavior.* Englewood Cliffs, N.J: Prentice-Hall.

AMS (2003) *Geografisk rörlighet och arbetsgivarbyten.* Ura 2003: 1. Stockholm: Arbetsmarknadsstyrelsen.

Anderson, S., and J. Cavanagh (2000) *Field Guide to the Global Economy.* New York: New Press.

Aneshensel, C.S. (2002) *Theory-Based Data Analysis for the Social Sciences.* London: Pine Forge Press.

Aronsson, G. (1999) 'Arbetslivets förändring – flexibilitet på gott och ont', in *Den gamla socialförsäkringens nya kläder: rapport från forskarseminariet i Umeå*, 27–45. Stockholm: Försäkringskasseförbundet.

Arrowsmith, J. (2006) *Temporary Agency Work in the Enlarged European Union.* Dublin: European Foundation for the Improvement of Living and Working Conditions.

Atkinson, J. (1984) 'Manpower Strategies for Flexible Organisations'. *Personnel Management*, 16 (8): 28–31.

Atkinson, J. (1985) 'The Changing Corporation', in D. Clutterbuck (ed.), *New Patterns of Work*, 13–34. Aldershot: Gower.

Atkinson, J., and N. Meager (1986) *Changing Working Patterns. How Companies Achieve Flexibility to Meet New Needs.* London: National Economic Development Office.

Autor, D. (2001a) 'Wiring the Labor Market'. *Journal of Economic Perspectives*, 15 (1): 25–40.

Autor, D. (2001b) 'Why Do Temporary Firms Provide Free General Skills Training?' *Quarterly Journal of Economics*, 116 (4): 1409–48.

Autor, D. (2003) 'Outsourcing at Will: The Contribution of Unjust Dismissal Doctrine to the Growth of Employment Outsourcing'. *Journal of Labor Economics*, 21 (1): 1–42.

Bamber, G.J., and R.D. Lansbury (eds) (1998) *International and Comparative Industrial Relations. A Study of Industrialised Market Economies.* 3rd ed. London: Sage.

Barnard, C., S. Deakin and R. Hobbs (2003) 'Opting Out of the 48-Hour Week: Employer Necessity or Individual Choice? An Empirical Study of the Operation of Article 18(1) (b) of the Working Time Directive in the UK'. *Industrial Law Journal*, 32 (4): 223–52.

Barnett, Daniel (2005a) *Employment Law Bulletin*, 03/05/05.
Barnett, Daniel (2005b) *Employment Law Bulletin*, 14/07/05.
Baron, M.B., and D.A. Kenny (1986) 'The Moderator-Mediator Variable Distinction in Social Psychological Research: Conceptual, Strategic, and Statistical Considerations'. *Journal of Personality and Social Psychology*, 51 (6): 1173–82.
Bemanningsföretagen (2005) *Statistik 2004*. *Statistikuppgifter januari–december 2004*. www.almega.se/Files/ALMEGA/Caradoc_Members/%D6vrig_handling/Fil_till_hemsidan_B.DOC; accessed 20/09/05
Benavides, F., and J. Benach (1999) *Precarious Employment and Health-related Outcomes in the European Union*. Luxembourg: Office for Official Publications of the European Commission.
Bergström, O., and D. Storrie (eds) (2003) *Contingent Employment in Europe and the United States*. Cheltenham: Edward Elgar.
Bergström, V., A. Svensson and M. Ådahl (2005) 'Riksbanken och sysselsättningen'. *Penning- och valutapolitik*, 1: 5–19.
Björklund, A., P.-A. Edin, B. Holmlund and E. Wadensjö (2000) *Arbetsmarknaden*. 2nd rev. ed. Stockholm: SNS.
Blackburn, R., and M. Hart (2002) *Small Firms' Awareness and Knowledge of Individual Employment Rights*. Employment Relations Research Series, No. 14. London: Department of Trade and Industry.
Blyton, P., and P. Turnbull (2004) *The Dynamics of Employee Relations*. 3rd ed. Basingstoke: Palgrave Macmillan.
Bogg, A.L. (2005) 'Employment Relations Act 2004: Another False Dawn for Collectivism?' *Industrial Law Journal*, 34 (1): 72–82.
Boyer, R. (1987) 'Labour Flexibilities: Many Forms, Uncertain Effects'. *Labour and Society*, 12 (1): 107–29.
Boyer, R. (1988) *The Search for Labour Market Flexibility*. Oxford: Clarendon Press.
Brown, R.K. (1997) 'Flexibility and Security: Contradictions in the Contemporary Labour Market', in R.K. Brown (ed.), *The Changing Shape of Work*, 69–86. London: Macmillan.
Brown, W. (2004) 'The Future of Collectivism in the Regulation of Industrial Relations'. *Human Resources and Employment Review*, 2 (4): 196–201.
Brown, W., S. Deakin, M. Hudson, C. Pratten and P. Ryan (1999) *The Individualisation of Employment Contracts in Britain*. Employment Relations Research Series, No. 4. London: Department of Trade and Industry.
Bruhnes, B. (1989) 'Labour Market Flexibility in Enterprises: A Comparison of Firms in Four European Countries', in OECD, *Labour Market Flexibility. Trends in Enterprises*, 11–36. Paris: Organisation for Economic Cooperation and Development.
Bryson, A., and D. Wilkinson (2001) *Collective Bargaining and Workplace Performance: An Investigation Using the Workplace Employee Relations Survey 1998*. Employment Relations Research Series, No. 12. London: Department of Trade and Industry.
Burchell, B. (2002) 'The Prevalence and Redistribution of Job Insecurity and Work Intensification', in B. Burchell, D. Lapido and F. Wilkinson (eds), *Job Insecurity and Work Intensification*, 61–76. London: Routledge.
Burchell, B., S. Deakin and S. Honey (1999) 'The Employment Status of Workers in Non-standard Employment'. EMAR Research Series No. 6. London: Department of Trade and Industry.

Burchell, B., D. Lapido and F. Wilkinson (2002) *Job Insecurity and Work Intensification*. London: Routledge.

Burgess, J., and J. Connell (2004) 'International Aspects of Temporary Agency Employment. An Overview', in J. Burgess and J. Connell (eds), *International Perspectives on Temporary Agency Work*, 1–23. London: Routledge.

Burgess, S., C. Propper and D. Wilson (2001) *Explaining the Growth in the Number of Applications to Industrial Tribunals, 1972–1997*. Employment Relations Research Series, No. 10. London: Department of Trade and Industry.

Burkitt, N. (2001) *Workers' Rights and Wrongs: A New Approach to Employment Rights and Support for Employers*. London: Institute for Public Policy Research.

Burkitt, N. and R. Dunstan (2001) 'Enforce Workers' Rights'. *New Statesman* (22 January).

Burt, R. (1992) *Structural Holes: The Social Structure of Competition*. Cambridge, Mass.: Harvard University Press.

Bylund, B., A. Elmér, L. Viklund and T. Öhman (2004) *Anställningsskyddslagen. Med kommentar*. 9th ed. Stockholm: Prisma.

Cabinet Office (2002) *Better Regulation Task Force, Employment Regulation: Striking a Balance*. London: Cabinet Office. (www.brtf.gov.uk/pressreleases/2004/appoint.asp)

Cam, S., J. Purcell and S. Tailby (2003) 'Contingent Employment in the UK', in O. Bergström and D. Storrie (eds), *Contingent Employment in Europe and the United States*, 52–78. Cheltenham: Edward Elgar.

Cameron, D.R. (1984) 'Social Democracy, Corporatism, Labour Quiescence and the Representation of Economic Interest in Advanced Capitalist Society', in J.H. Goldthorpe (ed.), *Order and Conflict in Contemporary Capitalism. Studies in the Political Economy of Western European Nations*, 143–78. Oxford University Press.

Cappelli, P., L. Bassi, H. Katz, D. Knoke, P. Osterman and M. Useem (1997) *Change at Work*. New York: Oxford University Press.

Castles, F.G. (ed.) (1993) *Families of Nations. Patterns of Public Policy in Western Democracies*. Aldershot: Dartmouth.

Castles, F.G. (1998) *Comparative Public Policy Patterns of Post-war Transformation*. Cheltenham: Edward Elgar.

Castles, F.G. (2004) *The Future of the Welfare State. Crises Myths and Crises Realities*. Oxford University Press.

CBI (2005) *A Matter of Confidence: Restoring Faith in Employment Tribunals*. London: Confederation of British Industry.

Chandler, A.D. (1962) *Strategy and Structure*. Cambridge, Mass.: MIT Press.

Chandler, A.D. (1977) *The Visible Hand: Managerial Revolution in American Business*. Cambridge, Mass.: MIT Press.

Channon, D. (1973) *The Strategy and Structure of British Enterprise*. London: Macmillan.

Chapman, C. (2004) 'Employment Tribunal Reforms – An Integral Part of Workplace Dispute Resolution or an Economy Measure?' Industrial Law Society Spring Conference, 8 May. (www.industriallawsociety.org.uk/papers/chapmanpaper.html)

Chirumbolo, A., and J. Hellgren (2003) 'Individual and Organizational Consequences of Job Insecurity: A European Study'. *Economic and Industrial Democracy*, 24 (2): 217–40.

CIETT (2000) *Orchestrating the Evolution of Private Employment Agencies towards a Stronger Society*. Paris: International Confederation of Private Employment Agencies.

Citizens Advice (2001a) *Improving Employment Dispute Resolution: The CAB Service's Response*. London: National Association of Citizens' Advice Bureaux.

Citizens Advice (2001b) *Fairness and Enterprise: The CAB Service's Case for a Fair Employment Commission*. London: National Association of Citizens' Advice Bureaux.

Citizens Advice (2004a) *Employment Tribunals: The Intimidatory Use of Costs Threats by Employers' Legal Representatives*. March CAB Evidence. London: Citizens Advice Bureau.

Citizens Advice (2004b) *Geography of Advice: An Overview of the Challenges Facing the Community Legal Service*. Evidence Report (February). London: Citizens Advice Bureau.

Citizens Advice (2004c) *The Paperless Waiting Room*. April CAB Evidence. London: Citizens Advice Bureau.

Citizens Advice (2004d) *Empty Justice: The Non-payment of Employment Tribunal Awards*. September CAB Evidence. London: Citizens Advice Bureau.

Citizens Advice (2004e) *Somewhere to Turn: The Case for a Fair Employment Commission*. CAB Briefing October 2004. London: Citizens Advice Bureau.

Citizens Advice (2004f) *Citizens Advice Annual Report, 2003/04*. London: Citizens Advice Bureau.

Citron, J. (1989) *The Citizens Advice Bureaux, for the Community, by the Community*. London: Pluto Press.

Clarke, J., and J. Newman (1997) *Managerial State: Power, Politics and Ideology in the Remaking of Social Welfare*. London: Sage.

Cohany, S. (1998) 'Workers in Alternative Employment Arrangements: A Second Look'. *Monthly Labor Review*, 121 (11): 3–21.

Colling, T. (2004) 'No Claim, No Pain? The Privatization of Dispute Resolution in Britain'. *Economic and Industrial Democracy*, 25 (4): 555–79.

Consumers' Association (2000) *The Community Legal Service: Access for All?* London: Consumers' Association.

Crouch, C. (1993) *Industrial Relations and European State Traditions*. Oxford: Clarendon Press.

Cully, M., and S. Woodland (1999) 'Trade Union Membership and Recognition, 1997–1998'. *Labour Market Trends*, 106: 343–51.

Cully, M., S. Woodland, A. O'Reilly, and G. Dix (1999) *Britain at Work as Depicted by the 1998 Workplace Employee Relations Survey*. London: Routledge.

Dagens Industri.

Dagens Nyheter.

Davidson, J.O. (1990) 'The Road to Functional Flexibility: White Collar Work and Employment Relations in a Privatised Public Utility'. *Sociological Review*, 34 (4): 689–711.

De Grauwe, P., and F. Camerman (2002) *How Big Are the Big Multi-national Companies?* (www.econ.kuleuven.be/ew/academic/intecon/Degrauwe/PDG-papers/Recently_published_articles/How%20big%20are%20the%20big%20multinational%20companies.pdf)

De Witte, H., and K. Näswall (2003) ' "Objective" vs "Subjective" Job Insecurity: Consequences of Temporary Work for Job Satisfaction and Organizational

Commitment in Four European Countries'. *Economic and Industrial Democracy*, 24 (2): 149–88.

Deakin, S. (2002) 'The Evolution of the Employment Relationship'. Paper presented to France–ILO Symposium on the Future of Work, Employment and Social Protection. Lyon, France, 17–18 January.

Dickens, L., M. Jones, B. Weekes and M. Hart (1985) *Dismissed: A Study of Unfair Dismissal and the Industrial Tribunal System*. Oxford: Blackwell.

Directgov (2004) *New Temp Rules Now in Force*. (www.direct.gov.uk/Newsroom/ NewsArticle/fs/en?CONTENT_ID=4012120&chk=EK61Qz; accessed 04/11/18. page updated 25 February 2004.)

Dore, R. (1986) *Flexible Rigidities: Industrial Policy and Structural Adjustment in the Japanese Economy 1970–80*. London: Athlone.

Driver, S., and L. Martell (1998) *New Labour Politics after Thatcherism*. Malden, MA: Polity Press.

Driver, S., and L. Martell (2002) *Blair's Britain*. Cambridge: Polity Press.

DTI (2001a) *Routes to Resolution: Improving Dispute Resolution in Britain*. Consultation Document, July. London: Department of Trade and Industry.

DTI (2001b) *Regulatory Impact Assessment: Employment Bill 2001*. London: Department of Trade and Industry.

DTI (2001c) *Routes to Resolution: Improving Dispute Resolution in Britain, Government Response, November*. London: Department of Trade and Industry.

DTI (2002) *Findings from the 1998 Survey of Employment Tribunal Applications*. Employment Relations Research Series, No. 13. London: Department of Trade and Industry.

DTI (2004a) *Trade Union Membership 2003. Employment Market Analysis and Research*. London: Department of Trade and Industry and National Statistics.

DTI (2004b) *Findings from the Survey of Employment Tribunal Applications 2003*. Employment Relations Series, No. 33. London: Department of Trade and Industry.

DTI, REC and Equity (2003) *Guidance on the Conduct Regulations for Employment Agencies and Employment Businesses Regulations 2003*. Department of Trade and Industry in association with Recruitment and Employment Confederation and Equity.

Du Gay, P. (1996) *Consumption and Identity at Work*. London: Sage.

Dundon, T., and D. Rollinson (2004) *Employment Relations in Non-Union Firms*. London: Routledge.

Earnshaw, J., J. Goodman, R. Harrison and M. Marchington (1998) *Industrial Tribunals, Workplace Disciplinary Procedures, and Employment Practice*. Employment Relations Research Series, No. 2. London: Department of Trade and Industry.

Edwards, P., M. Hall, R. Hyman, P. Marginson, K. Sissin, J. Waddington and D. Winchester (1998) 'Great Britain: From Partial Collectivism to Neo-liberalism to Where?', in A. Ferner and R. Hyman (eds), *Changing Industrial Relations in Europe*, 1–54. 2nd ed. Oxford: Blackwell.

Edwards, P., M. Ram and J. Black (2003) *The Impact of Employment Legislation on Small Firms: A Case Study Analysis*. Employment Relations Research Series, No. 20. London: Department of Trade and Industry.

EIROnline (2002) 'Government and Social Partners Sign Pact for Italy' (July): (www.eiro.eurofound.ie/2002/07/feature/it0207104f.html)

EIROnline (2003) (23 May) (www.eiro.eurofound.ie/index.html)

Ekdahl, L. (2003) 'Mellan fackligt och politiskt dilemma. En bakgrund till Rehn-Meidnermodellen', in L. Erixon (ed.), *Den svenska modellens ekonomiska politik*. *Rehn-Meidnermodellens bakgrund, tillämpning och relevans i det 21:a århundradet*, 13–32. Stockholm: Atlas.

ELB (2004) 'Definition of "Employee" in Relation to Worker Supplied by Employment Business'. *Employment Law Bulletin* 20. (www.markeluk.com/ Employment%20Law%20Bulletin%20-%20October%202004.pdf);   accessed 29/11/04.

Elger, T., and P. Fairbrother (1992) 'Inflexible Flexibility: A Case Study of Modularisation', 89–106, in N. Gilbert, R. Burrows and A. Pollert (eds), *Fordism and Flexibility*. *Divisions and Change*. London: Macmillan.

Employment Tribunals (Constitution and Rules of Procedure) Regulations (2001).

Employment Tribunals Services (2003) and (2004). Annual Report and Accounts, 2002–2003, 2003–2004. London: Department of Trade and Industry.

Engstrand, Å.-K. (2003) *The Road Once Taken. Transformations of Labour Markets, Politics and Place Promotion in Two Swedish Cities, Karlskrona and Uddevalla 1930–2000*. Stockholm: National Institute for Working Life.

Engstrand, Å.-K. (2006) 'Talet om arbetets organisering i tid och rum. Historiska och internationella perspektiv på svensk debatt', in E. Sundin and E. Ekstedt (eds), *Den nya arbetsdelningen*, 125–56. Stockholm: National Institute for Working Life.

Erixon, L. (1994) 'En svensk ekonomisk politik. Rehn-Meidnermodellens teori, historia och aktualitet'. *Häften för kritiska studier*, 27: 67–103.

Erixon, L. (2001) 'A Swedish Economic Policy. The Rehn-Meidner Model's Theory, Application and Validity', in H. Milner and E. Wadensjö (eds), *Gösta Rehn, the Swedish Model and Labour Market Policies: International and National Perspectives*, 13–49. Aldershot: Ashgate.

Erixon, L. (2003) 'Den svenska modellens ekonomiska politik. En analys av Rehn-Meidner modellens tillämpning i Sverige', in L. Erixon (ed.), *Den svenska modellens ekonomiska politik*, 103–43. *Rehn-Meidnermodellens bakgrund, tillämpning och relevans i det 21:a århundradet*. Stockholm: Atlas.

Esping-Andersen, G. (1985) *Politics against Markets. The Social Democratic Road to Power*. Princeton, N.J.: Princeton University Press.

Esping-Andersen, G. (1990) *The Three Worlds of Welfare Capitalism*. Cambridge: Polity.

ETS (Employment Tribunals Services) (2003) *Annual Report and Accounts, 2002–2003*. London: Department of Trade and Industry.

ETS (2004) *Annual Report and Accounts, 2003–2004*. London: Department of Trade and Industry.

EU (2006) 'Why Flexicurity?' (www.eu2006.at.)

European Commission (1993) *White Paper on Growth, Competitiveness and Employment*. Luxembourg: Office for Official Publications of the European Communities.

European Commission (1997) *Partnership for a New Organisation of Work* (COM(97)128). Brussels: EU.

European Foundation (2003) 'March Employment Council Discusses Temporary Agency Work Proposal'. European Industrial Relations Observatory Online. Dublin: European Foundation for the Improvement of Living and Working

Conditions (www.eiro.eurofound.eu.int/about/2003/03/feature/eu0303203f.html). accessed 04/12/02.

European Foundation (2004) 'Temporary Work, Working Time and Equality Discussed at Council'. European Industrial Relations Observatory Online. Dublin: European Foundation for the Improvement of Living and Working Conditions (www.eiro.eurofound.eu.int/2004/10/feature/eu0410204f.html). accessed 04/12/02.

European Foundation (2005a) EMIRE. The European Employment and Industrial Relations Glossaries. Dublin: European Foundation for the Improvement of Living and Working Conditions (www.eurofound.eu.int/emire/GREECE/EMPLOYMENTAGENCY-GR.html).

European Foundation (2005b) *Industrial Relations Developments in Europe 2004*. Dublin: European Foundation for the Improvement of Living and Working Conditions.

European Parliament (2002) Working Document on the Proposal for a Directive of the European Parliament and the Council on Working Conditions for Temporary Workers (COM (2002) 149 - C5-0140/2002 - 2002/0072 (COD)). 14 May 2002. Committee on Employment and Social Affairs. Rapporteur: Ieke van den Burg.

Evans, A. (1973) *Flexibility in Working Life: Opportunities for Individual Choice*. Paris: Organisation for Economic Cooperation and Development.

Ewing, K. (2003) 'Labour Law and Industrial Relations', in P. Ackers and A. Wilkinson (eds), *Understanding Work and Employment: Industrial Relations in Transition*, 138–60. Oxford University Press.

Festinger, L. (1954) 'A Theory of Social Comparison Processes.' *Human Relations*, 7 (1): 117–40.

Festinger, L. (1957) *A Theory of Cognitive Dissonance*. Evanston, Ill.: Row, Peterson and Company.

Finanstidningen.

Fox, A. (1985) *History and Heritage*. London: Allen and Unwin.

Freeman, R. (2002) 'The Labour Market in the New Information Economy'. NBER Working Paper No. 9254 (October).

Froud, J., C. Haslam, S. Johal and K. Williams (2002) 'Cars after Financialisation: A Case Study in Financial Under-Performance, Constraints and Consequences'. *Competition and Change*, 6 (1): 13–42.

Froud, J., S. Johal, A. Leaver and K. Williams (2006) *Strategy and Financialisation: Narratives and Numbers*. London: Routledge.

Furåker, B. (2004) 'Mellan rörlighet och stabilitet. Om anställda och arbetsplatser i ett dynamiskt arbetsliv', in *Ett rörligt arbetsliv*, 7–20. Arbetslivsforum 2003. Stockholm: Swedish Council for Work Life and Social Research.

Furåker, B. (2005a) 'Anställningsform och inställning till rörlighet. En analys av data från tre svenska undersökningar', in D. Rauhut and B. Falkenhall (eds), *Arbetsrätt, rörlighet och tillväxt*, 63–91. Östersund: The Swedish Institute for Growth Policy Studies.

Furåker, B. (2005b) *Sociological Perspectives on Labour Markets*. Basingstoke: Palgrave Macmillan.

Furåker, B., and T. Berglund (2001) 'Atypical Employment in Relation to Work and Organizational Commitment', in B. Furåker (ed.), *Employment, Unemployment, Marginalization*, 49–71. Stockholm: Almqvist and Wiksell International/Göteborg University: Department of Sociology.

Furåker, B., and L. Johansson (1995) 'Arbetsmarknadsläget och anställdas inställning i arbetsmarknadsfrågor'. *Arbetsmarknad & Arbetsliv*, (2) 2: 133–48.

Furåker, B., and R. Lindqvist (2003) 'The Welfare State and Labour Market Policies', in T.P. Boje and B. Furåker (eds), *Post-industrial Labour Markets: North American and Scandinavian Profiles*, 77–95. London: Routledge.

Gall, G. (2000) 'What about the Workers? BPR, Trade Unions and the Emiseration of Labour', in D. Knights and H. Willmott (eds), *The Reengineering Revolution? Critical Studies of Corporate Change*, 134–53. London: Sage.

Gallie, D., and S. Paugam (2000) 'The Experience of Unemployment in Europe: The Debate', in D. Gallie and S. Paugam (eds), *Welfare Regimes and the Experience of Unemployment in Europe*, 1–22. Oxford University Press.

Gallie, D., M. White, Y. Cheng and M. Tomlinson (1998) *Restructuring the Employment Relationship*. Oxford University Press.

Genn, H. (1999) *Paths to Justice: What People Do and Think about Going to the Law*. Oxford and Portland, Oregon: Hart Publishing.

Godard, J. (2001) 'High Performance and the Transformation of Work? The Implications of Alternative Work Practices for the Experience and Outcomes of Work'. *Industrial and Labor Relations Review*, 54 (4): 776–805.

Goldthorpe, J.H., D. Lockwood, F. Bechhofer and J. Platt (1968) *The Affluent Worker. Industrial Attitudes and Behaviour*. Cambridge: Cambridge Studies in Sociology.

Goodman, J., M. Marchington, J. Berridge, E. Snape and G.J. Bamber (2003) 'Employment Relations in Britain', in G.J. Bamber and R.D. Lansbury (eds), *International and Comparative Employment Relations. A Study of Market Economies*, 34–62. London: Sage.

Göransson, H. (2004) *Arbetsrätten. En introduktion*. 3rd edition. Stockholm: Norstedts Juridik.

Gouliquer, L. (2000) 'Pandora's Box: The Paradox of Flexibility in Today's Workplace'. *Current Sociology*, 48 (1): 29–38.

Government Bill (2004/05:1).

Grönlund, A. (2004) *Flexibilitetens gränser: förändring och friktion i arbetsliv och familj*. Umeå: Borea.

Guadalupe, M. (2001) 'The Hidden Costs of Fixed Term Contracts: The Impact on Work Accidents'. Department of Economics and Centre for Economic Performance, London School of Economics (August).

Guardian (2000) 'Blair Leads the Fight to Scale Down Charter' (20 June), (browse.guardian.co.uk/ search?search=blair+leads+the+fight+to+scale+down+charter&N=3100&sort=relevance)

Guardian (2004) Special Report: European Integration: 'Blair Strikes Doubtful Note on European Constitutions – Britain Must Set Its Own Labour Laws, Says PM' (16 June) (www.guardian.co.uk/eu/story/0„1239820,00.html)

Guest, D. (2004) 'Flexible Employment Contracts, the Psychological Contract and Employee Outcomes: an Analysis and Review of the Evidence'. *International Journal of Management Review*, 5/6 (1): 1–19.

Gunge, S.P. (2000) 'Business Process Engineering and "The New Organization"', in D. Knights and H. Willmott (eds), *The Reengineering Revolution? Critical Studies of Corporate Change*, 114–33. London: Sage.

Gustafson, P. (2003) *Arbetslöshetsförsäkringen och de arbetslösa. Resultat från en attitydundersökning*. Research Report No. 28. Göteborg University, Department of Sociology.

Gustavsen, B. (1996) 'Changes in Work Organization and Public Support'. *Futures*, 28 (2): 139–52.

Håkansson, K. and T. Isidorsson (1999) 'Flexibla tider. Flexibilitetsstrategier inom detaljhandeln'. Department of Work Science, Göteborg University.

Håkansson, K., and T. Isidorsson (2003) 'Flexible Times: Dynamics and Consequences of Company Strategies for Flexibility', in D. Flemming and C. Thörnqvist (eds), *Nordic Management–Labour Relations and Internationalization – Converging and Diverging Tendencies*, 131–52. Copenhagen: Nordic Council of Ministers.

Håkansson, K., and T. Isidorsson (2004) 'Hyresarbetskraft. Användning av inhyrd arbetskraft på den svenska arbetsmarknaden'. *Arbetsmarknad & Arbetsliv*, 10 (3): 187–205.

Hall, P.A., and D. Soskice (2001) 'An Introduction to Varieties of Capitalism', in P.A. Hall and D. Soskice (eds), *Varieties of Capitalism. The Institutional Foundations of Comparative Advantage*, 1–70. Oxford University Press.

Hall, S. (2003) 'New Labour's Double-Shuffle'. *Soundings*, 24: 10–24.

Hammer, M. (1990) 'Reengineering Work: Don't Automate, Obliterate'. *Harvard Business Review*, 68 (4): 104–12.

Hammer, M., and J. Champy (1993) *Reengineering the Corporation: A Manifesto for Business Revolution*. New York: Harper.

Handy, C. (1989) *The Age of Unreason*. London: Hutchinson.

Hayek, F.A. (1960) *The Constitution of Liberty*. London: Routledge and Kegan Paul.

Hayek, F.A. (1984) *Unemployment and the Unions*. London: Institute of Economic Affairs.

Heckscher, C., and A. Donnellon (eds) (1994) *The Post-Bureaucratic Organisation. New Perspectives on Organisational Change*. London: Sage.

Hedborg, A., and R. Meidner (1984) *Folkhemsmodellen*. Stockholm: Rabén & Sjögren.

Hedborg, A., and R. Meidner (1986) *Ett friår mitt i livet*. Stockholm: Landsorganisationen.

Hedlund, G. (1993) 'Assumptions of Hierarchy and Heterarchy: An Application to the Multi-National Corporation', in S. Ghoshal and D. Westney (eds), *Organisation Theory and the Multinational Corporation*, 211–36. London: Macmillan.

Heffernan, R. (2001) *New Labour and Thatcherism. Political Change in Britain*. Basingstoke: Macmillan.

Hempel, C.G. (1965) *Fundamentals of Concept Formation in Empirical Science*. University of Chicago Press.

Hepple, B. (2003) 'Enforcement: The Law and Politics of Cooperation and Compliance', in B. Hepple (ed.), *Social and Labour Rights in a Global Context: International and Comparative Perspectives*, 238–57. Cambridge University Press.

Hepple, B., and G. Morris (2002) 'The Employment Act 2002 and the Crisis of Individual Employment Rights'. *Industrial Law Journal*, 31 (2): 245–69.

Hirst, P., and G. Thompson (1999) *Globalization in Question*. Cambridge: Polity.

Hirst, P., and G. Thompson (2000) 'Globalization in One Country: The Peculiarities of the British.' *Economy and Society*, 29 (3): 335–56.

Holmlund, B. (2003) 'Rehn-Meidners program i ljuset av modern nationalekonomisk forskning', in L. Erixon (ed.), *Den svenska modellens ekonomiska politik. Rehn-Meidnermodellens bakgrund, tillämpning och relevans i det 21:a århundradet*, 55–70. Stockholm: Atlas.

Holmlund, B., and D. Storrie (2002) 'Temporary Work in Turbulent Times: The Swedish Experience'. *The Economic Journal*, 112 (480): 245–69.

Hotopp, U. (2001) *Recruitment Agencies in the UK*. Employment Relations Directorate. Department of Trade and Industry, UK.

Houseman, S.N. (2001) 'Why Employers Use Flexible Staffing Arrangements: Evidence from an Establishment Survey.' *Industrial and Labor Relations Review*, 55 (1): 149–70.

Hudson, M. (2002a) 'Flexibility and the Reorganisation of Work', in B. Burchell, D. Lapido and F. Wilkinson (eds), *Job Insecurity and Work Intensification*, 39–60. London: Routledge.

Hudson, M. (2002b) 'Disappearing Pathways and the Struggle for a Fair Day's Pay', in B. Burchell, D. Lapido and F. Wilkinson (eds), *Job Insecurity and Work Intensification*, 77–91. London: Routledge.

Hult, C. (2004) *The Way We Conform to Paid Labour. Commitment to Employment and Organization from a Comparative Perspective*. Umeå: Department of Sociology, Umeå University.

Hutton, W. (2002) *The World We Are In*. London: Little, Brown.

Hyman, R. (1991) '*Plus ça change?* The Theory of Production and the Production of Theory', in A. Pollert (ed.), *Farewell to Flexibility?*, 259–83 Oxford: Blackwell.

Hyman, R. (1997) 'The Future of Employee Representation'. *British Journal of Industrial Relations*, 35 (3): 309–36.

IDS (2002) IDS Brief 705, 'Resolving Employment Disputes – Getting Your Head Round the Revolving Statistics'. London: Income Data Services.

IDS (2004) *Statutory Disciplinary and Grievance Procedures*. Employment Law Supplement. London: Income Data Services.

IRLB (2003) 'Agency Worker Was an Employee'. *Industrial Relations Law Bulletin* (May): 8–12.

Isaksson, K., G. Aronsson, K. Bellaagh and S. Göransson (2001) *Att ofta byta arbetsplats: en jämförelse mellan uthyrda och korttidsanställda*. Stockholm: National Institute for Working Life.

Isidorsson, T. (2001) *Striden om tiden. Arbetstidens utveckling i Sverige under 100 år i ett internationellt perspektiv*. Department of History, Göteborg University.

Jahoda, M., P.F. Lazarsfeld and H. Zeisel (1971 [1933]) *Marienthal: The Sociography of an Unemployed Community*. Chicago: Aldine Atherton.

Joint Committee on Human Rights (2002a) Twelfth Report. United Kingdom Parliament.

Joint Committee on Human Rights (2002b) Eighteenth Report. United Kingdom Parliament.

Jonsson, I. (2004) *Deltidsarbete inom svensk detaljhandel. En genuskritisk studie av arbetstidsmönster*. Uppsala: Uppsala University.

Junestav, M. (2004) *Arbetslinjer i svensk socialpolitisk debatt och lagstiftning 1930– 2001*. Uppsala: Uppsala University.

Kahn-Freund, O. (1977) *Labour and the Law*. 2nd ed. London: Stevens.

Kalleberg, A.L. (2000) 'Nonstandard Employment Relations: Part-time, Temporary and Contract Work.' *Annual Review of Sociology*, 26: 341–65.

Kalleberg, A.L. (2001) 'Organizing Flexibility: The Flexible Firm in a New Century.' *British Journal of Industrial Relations*, 39 (4): 479–504.

Kalleberg, A.L., J. Reynolds and P.V. Marsden (2003) 'Externalizing Employment: Flexible Staffing Arrangements in US Organizations'. *Social Science Research*, 32 (4): 525–52.

Karlsson, J.Ch., and B. Eriksson (2000) *Flexibla arbetsplatser och arbetsvillkor*. Lund: Arkiv.

Katz, D., and R.L. Kahn (1978) *The Social Psychology of Organizations*. New York: John Wiley and Sons.

Kauhanen, M. (2001) *Temporary Agency Work in Finland*. Helsinki: Labour Institute for Economic Research.

Kelemen, M., P. Forrester and J. Hassard (2000) 'BPR and TQM: Divergence or Convergence?', in D. Knights and H. Willmott (eds), *The Reengineering Revolution? Critical Studies of Corporate Change*, 154–73. London: Sage.

Keller, B., and H. Seifert (2000) 'Flexicurity – das Konzept für mehr soziale Sicherheit flexibler Beschäftigung'. *WSI Mitteilungen*, 53: 291–300.

Kirkpatrick, I., S. Ackroyd and R. Walker (2005) *The New Managerialism and the Public Service Professions*. Basingstoke: Palgrave Macmillan.

Kjellberg, A. (1998) 'Sweden: Restoring the Model?', in A. Ferner and R. Hyman (eds), *Changing Industrial Relations in Europe*, 74–117. 2nd ed. Oxford: Blackwell.

Kjellberg, A. (2002) 'Ett nytt fackligt landskap – i Sverige och utomlands'. *Arkiv*, 86–87: 44–96.

Klammer, U., and K. Tillmann (2001) 'Flexibilität und soziale Sicherung – eine vielschichtige Herausforderung für politische Gestaltung', in U. Klammer and K. Tillmann (eds), *Flexicurity: Soziale Sicherung und Flexibilisierung der Arbeits- und Lebensverhältnisse*, 1–23. Düsseldorf: Wirtschafts- und Sozialwissenschaftliches Institut.

Kline, R.B. (2004) *Principles and Practice of Structural Equation Modelling*. New York: The Guilford Press.

Knight, F. (1921) *Risk, Uncertainty and Profit*. Boston: Houghton, Mifflin.

Knights, D., and H. Willmott (2000) 'The Reengineering Revolution? An Introduction', in D. Knights and H. Willmott (eds), *The Reengineering Revolution? Critical Studies of Corporate Change*, 1–25. London: Sage.

Koene, B., J. Paauwe and J. Groenewegen (2004) 'Understanding the Development of Temporary Agency Work in Europe'. *Human Resource Mangement Journal*, 14 (3): 53–73.

Korpi, W. (1983) *The Democratic Class Struggle*. London: Routledge & Kegan Paul.

LAG (2001) *Briefing: Changes to Employment Tribunal Costs Rules*. London: Legal Action Group.

Lairg, Lord Irvine of (1996) 'The Legal System and Law Reform under Labour', in D. Bean (ed.), *Law Reform for All*, 4–29. London: Blackstone.

Lane, C. (1995) *Industry and Society in Europe. Stability and Change in Britain, Germany and France*. Aldershot: Edward Elgar.

Lapido, D., and F. Wilkinson (2002) 'More Pressure, Less Protection', in B. Burchell, D. Lapido and F. Wilkinson (eds), *Job Insecurity and Work Intensification*, 8–38. London: Routledge.

Law Society (2002) *Access Denied*. London: The Law Society.

Lazonick, W. (2005) 'Corporate Restructuring', in S. Ackroyd, R. Batt, P. Thompson and P. Tolbert (eds), *The Oxford Handbook of Work and Organisation*, 577–601. Oxford University Press.

Lazonick, W., and M. O'Sullivan (2000) 'Maximizing Shareholder Value: A New Ideology for Corporate Governance'. *Economy and Society*, 29 (1): 13–35.

Leggatt, Sir Andrew (2001) Report of the Review of Tribunals by Sir Andrew Leggatt (www.tribunals-review.org.uk/leggatthtm/leg-00.htm)

Lehmbruch, G. (1984) 'Concertation and the Structure of Corporatist Networks', in J.H. Goldthorpe (ed.), *Order and Conflict in Contemporary Capitalism. Studies in the Political Economy of Western European Nations*, 60–80. Oxford University Press.

Lincoln, J.R., and A.L. Kalleberg (1990) *Culture, Control, and Commitment. A Study of Work Organization and Work Attitudes in the United States and Japan.* Cambridge University Press.

Lister, R. (2001) 'Toward a Citizens' Welfare State. The 3+3 'R's of Welfare Reform'. *Theory, Culture & Society*, 18 (2–3): 91–111.

LO (1951) *Fackföreningsrörelsen och den fulla sysselsättningen.* Stockholm: Landsorganisationen.

Long, J.S. (1997) *Regression Models for Categorical and Limited Dependent Variables.* London: Sage.

Lord Chancellor's Department (1998) 'White Paper, Modernising Justice: the Government's Plans for Reforming Legal Services and the Courts', Cm 4155 (www.open.gov.uk/lcd).

Lord McCarthy (2002) House of Lords Debates (26.2.02). Hansard.

Lord Wedderburn (2002) House of Lords Debates (11.6.02). Hansard.

LO-tidningen.

Loveridge, R., and F. Mueller (1997) 'Institutional, Sectoral and Corporate Dynamics in the Creation of Global Supply Chains', in R. Whitley and P. Kristensen (eds), *Governance at Work*, 139–57. Oxford University Press.

LSC (2002) *Legal Services Commission Annual Report, 2001–2002.* London: The Stationery Office.

Lunning, L., and G. Toijer (2002) *Anställningsskydd.* 8th ed. Stockholm: Norstedts.

Lysgaard, S. (1985 [1961]) *Arbeiderkollektivet.* Oslo: Universitetsforlaget.

Malone, T., J. Yates and R. Benjamin (1987) 'The Logic of Electronic Markets'. *Harvard Business Review*, 67 (3): 166–71.

Mandelbaum, M. (1978) *Flexibility in Decision Making. An Exploration and Unification.* Toronto: Department of Industrial Engineering, University of Toronto.

Mankelow, R. (2002) 'The Organisational Costs of Job Insecurity and Work Intensification' in B. Burchell, D. Lapido and F. Wilkinson (eds), *Job Insecurity and Work Intensification*, 137–53. London: Routledge.

Marsden, D.W. (1999) *A Theory of Employment Systems: Micro-Foundations of Societal Diversity.* Oxford University Press.

McCarthy, W. (1992) 'The Rise and Fall of Collective Laissez Faire', in W. McCarthy (ed.), *Legal Intervention in Industrial Relations, Gains and Losses*, 1–70. Oxford: Blackwell.

McIlroy, J. (1995) *Trade Unions in Britain Today.* 2nd ed. Manchester University Press.

McIlroy, J. (1998) 'The Enduring Alliance? Trade Unions and the Making of New Labour, 1994–1997'. *British Journal of Industrial Relations*, 36 (4): 537–64.

McIlroy, R., P. Marginson and I. Regalia (2004) 'Regulating External and Internal Forms of Flexibility at Local Level: Five European Regions Compared'. *International Journal of Human Resource Management*, 15 (2): 295–313.

McKay, S. (2001) 'Shifting the Focus from Tribunals to the Workplace'. *Industrial Law Journal*, 30 (3): 331–3.

McOrmond, T. (2004) 'Changes in Working Trends Over the Past Decade.' *Labour Market Trends* (January), 25–35.

Meager, N., C. Tyers, S. Perryman, J. Rick and R. Willison (2002) *Awareness, Knowledge and Exercise of Individual Employment Rights*. Employment Relations Research Series, No. 15. London: Department of Trade and Industry.

Meidner, R. (2003) 'Några tankar vid ett seminarium', in L. Erixon (ed.), *Den svenska modellens ekonomiska politik. Rehn-Meidnermodellens bakgrund, tillämpning och relevans i det 21:a århundradet*, 218–20. Stockholm: Atlas.

Menard, S. (1995) *Applied Logistic Regression Analysis*. Thousand Oaks: Sage.

Merton, R.K. (1957) *Social Theory and Social Structure*. Glencoe, Ill.: The Free Press.

Milgrom, P., and J. Roberts (1992) *Economics, Organisation and Management*. Englewood Cliffs, N.J.: Prentice Hall.

Miljöpartiet (1999) 'Friår. Ett år ledigt minskar arbetslösheten.' Unpublished memo.

Ministry of Finance (2006) 'Mål för den ekonomiska politiken'. 18 April (www.regeringen.se/sb/d/1881/a/19937); accessed 06/05/08.

Mordsley, B. (1995) 'Defining the Employment Status of Agency Workers'. *People Management*, 1 (24): 41.

Morgan, G. (2005) 'Understanding Multi-National Corporations', in S. Ackroyd, R. Batt, P. Thompson and P. Tolbert (eds), *The Oxford Handbook of Work and Organisation*, 554–76. Oxford University Press.

Mowday, R.T., L.W. Porter and R.M. Steers (1982) *Employee-Organization Linkages. The Psychology of Commitment, Absenteeism, and Turnover*. New York: Academic Press.

National Statistics (2003) Internet Access, Individuals and Households, December. (www.statistics.gov.uk/pdfdir/intc1203.pdf)

Neathey, F., and J. Arrowsmith (2001) *Implementation of the Working Time Regulations*. Employment Relations Research Series, No. 11. London: Department of Trade and Industry.

Nesheim, T. (2003) 'Short-Term Hires and Leasing of Personnel in Norwegian Firms: Promoting Numerical Flexibility and Stability'. *Scandinavian Journal of Management*, 19 (3): 309–31.

Nesheim, T. (2004) '20 år med Atkinson-modellen: Åtte teser om "Den flexible bedrift" '. *Sosiologisk tidsskrift*, 12: 3–24.

Neugart, M., and D. Storrie (2006) 'The Emergence of Temporary Work Agencies'. *Oxford Economic Papers*, 58 (1): 137–56.

Nolan, J. (2002) 'The Intensification of Everyday Life', in B. Burchell, D. Lapido and F. Wilkinson (eds), *Job Insecurity and Work Intensification*, 112–36. London: Routledge.

Norma (1996) *Normative Development within the Social Dimension*. Faculty of Law, University of Lund.

Nyhetsbyrån Direkt.

OECD (1970) *Flexibility of Retirement Age*. Paris: Organisation for Economic Cooperation and Development.

OECD (1986) *Flexibility in the Labour Market. The Current Debate*. Paris: Organisation for Economic Cooperation and Development.

OECD (1994) *Jobs Strategy*. Paris: Organisation for Economic Cooperation and Development.

OECD (1999) *Employment Outlook*. Paris: Organisation for Economic Cooperation and Development.

OECD (2004a) *Benefits and Wages*. Paris: Organisation for Economic Cooperation and Development.

OECD (2004b) *Employment Outlook*. Paris: Organisation for Economic Cooperation and Development.

O'Sullivan, M. (2000) *Contests for Corporate Control: Corporate Governance and Economic Performance in the United States and Germany*. Oxford University Press.

Pahl, R.E., and J. Winkler (1974) 'The Coming of Corporatism'. *New Society*, 10: 72–6.

Paoli, P., and D. Merllié (2001) *Third European Survey on Working Conditions and Second European Survey on Working Conditions*. Luxembourg: Office for Official Publications of the European Commission.

Parnes, H.S. (1954) *Research on Labor Mobility. An Appraisal of Research Findings in the United States*. New York: Social Science Research Council.

Parnes, H.S. (1968) 'Markets and Mobility', in D.L. Sills (ed.), *International Encyclopedia of the Social Sciences 8*, 481–87. New York: Macmillan and Free Press.

Peck, J.A., and N. Teodore (2002) 'Temped Out? Industry Rhetoric, Labor Regulation and Economic Restructuring in the Temporary Staffing Business'. *Economic and Industrial Democracy*, 23 (2): 143–75.

Peck, J., and A. Tickell (1994) 'Searching for a New Institutional Fix: the After Fordist Crisis' in A. Amin (ed.), *Post Fordism: A Reader*, 280–315. Oxford: Blackwell.

Petrongolo, B., and C. Pissarides (2001) 'Looking Into the Black Box: A Survey of the Matching Function.' *Journal of Economic Literature*, 39 (2): 390–431.

Pettersson, M. (1981) *Deltidsarbetet i Sverige. Del 1. Deltidssökningens orsaker, deltidsanställdas levnadsförhållanden*. Stockholm: Arbetslivscentrum.

Pettigrew, A.M., and E.M. Fenton (eds) (2000) *The Innovating Organisation*. London: Sage.

Pettigrew, A.M., R. Whittington, L. Melin, C. Sanchez-Runde, F. van den Bosch, W. Riugrok and T. Numagami (eds) (2003) *Innovative Forms of Organizing: International Perspectives*. London: Sage.

Piore, M.J., and C.F. Sabel (1984) *The Second Industrial Divide. Possibilities for Prosperity*. New York: Basic Books.

Pleasence, P., A. Buck, N. Balmer, A. O'Grady, H. Genn and M. Smith (2004) *Causes of Action: Civil Law and Social Justice*. Legal Services Commission. London: TSO.

Pochet, P. (2005) 'The Open Method of Co-ordination and the Construction of Social Europe: A Historical Perspective', in J. Zeitlin and P. Pochet (eds) (with L. Magnusson), *The Open Method of Co-ordination in Action. The European Employment and Social Inclusion Strategies*, 1–53. Brussels: PIE-Peter Lang.

Pollert, A. (1988) 'The "Flexible Firm": Fixation or Fact?' *Work, Employment & Society*, 2 (3): 281–316.

Pollert, A. (1991) 'Introduction', in A. Pollert (ed.), *Farewell to Flexibility?*, xvii–xxiv. Oxford: Blackwell.

Pollert, A. (ed.) (1991) *Farewell to Flexibility?* Oxford: Blackwell.

Powell, G.N., and L.A. Mainiero (1999) 'Managerial Decision Making Regarding Alternative Work Arrangements'. *Journal of Occupational and Organizational Psychology*, 72 (1): 41–56.

Prechel, H. (1997) 'Corporate Form and the State: Business Policy and Change from the Multi-Divisional to the Multilayered Subsidiary Form'. *Sociological Inquiry*, 67 (2): 151–74.

Purcell, K., and J. Purcell (1998) 'In-sourcing, Outsourcing, and the Growth of Contingent Labour as Evidence of Flexible Employment Strategies'. *European Journal of Work and Organizational Psychology*, 7 (1): 39–59.

Pyke, F., and W. Sengenberger (1992) *Industrial Districts and Local Economic Regeneration*. Geneva: International Labour Organisation.

Ramsay, H., D. Scholarios and B. Harley (2000) 'Employees and High-Performance Work Systems: Testing inside the Black Box'. *British Journal of Industrial Relations*, 38 (4): 501–31.

Regini, M. (2003) 'Tripartite Concertation and Varieties of Capitalism'. *European Journal of Industrial Relations*, 9 (3): 251–63.

Rehn, G. (1944) '3 månaders semester som medel mot arbetslöshet. Del I och II.' *Fackföreningsrörelsen*, 24: 110–16, 126–32.

Rehn, G. (1975) 'Flextid och flexliv.' *Ekonomisk Debatt*, 1: 72–88.

Rehn, G. (1985 [1974]) *På väg mot valfrihetens samhälle*. Stockholm: Delfa.

Richard, J. (1989) *50 Years of the CAB*. London: Citizens Advice Bureaux.

Rubery, J., and D. Grimshaw (2003) *The Organization of Employment. An International Perspective*. Basingstoke: Palgrave.

Russell, C., and D. Eyers (2002) *Clutching at Straws, Rights at Work*. Briefing Paper No. 53. West Midlands Employment and Low Pay Unit.

Sabel, C.F., and J. Zeitlin (1997) *World of Possibilities. Flexibility and Mass Production in Western Industrialization*. Cambridge University Press.

SAF (1992) *Flexibilitet i företag*. Stockholm: Svenska arbetsgivareföreningen.

SAF (1996) *Arbete utan fast anställning: Om de förändrade relationerna på arbetsmarknaden*. Stockholm: Svenska arbetsgivareföreningen.

Saf-tidningen.

Sandkull, B., and J. Johansson (2000) *Från Taylor till Toyota: betraktelser av den industriella produktionens organisation och ekonomi*. Lund: Studentlitteratur.

Sarkar, M., B. Butler and C. Steinfeld (1995) 'Intermediaries and Cybermediaries: A Continuing Role for Mediating Players in the Electronic Marketplace'. *Journal of Computer-Mediated Communication, Special Issue on Electronic Commerce*, 1 (3).

Sayer, A., and R. Walker (1992) *The New Social Economy. Reworking the Division of Labour*. Cambridge: Blackwell.

Schmid, G., and D. Storrie (2001) 'Employment Relationships in the New Economy', in L.-H. Röller and C. Wey (eds), *Die Soziale Marktwirtschaft in der neuen Weltwirtschaft*, 57–89. Berlin: WZB.

Schmidt, M.G. (1982) 'Does Corporatism Matter? Economic Crisis, Politics and the Rate of Unemployment in Capitalist Democracies in the 1970s', in G. Lehmbruch and P. Schmitter (eds), *Patterns of Corporatist Policy-Making*, 237–58. London: Sage.

Schmitter, P.C., and G. Lehmbruch (eds) (1979) *Trends toward Corporatist Intermediation*. London: Sage.

Seifert, H., and A. Tangian (2006) *Globalization and Deregulation: Does Flexicurity Protect Atypically Employed?* Düsseldorf: Wirtschafts- und Sozialwissenschaftliches Institut.

Select Committee on Constitutional Affairs (2004) *Constitutional Affairs Fourth Report*. United Kingdom Parliament, House of Commons, July, (www.

parliament.the-stationery-office.co.uk/pa/cm200304/cmselect/cmconst/391/
39106.htm)
Sennett, R. (1999) *Corrosion of Character: The Personal Consequences of Work in the New Capitalism.* New York: Norton.
Sethi, A.K., and S.P. Sethi (1990) 'Flexibility in Manufacturing: A Survey'. *The International Journal of Flexible Manufacturing Systems,* 3(2): 289–328.
SFS (1976) *Lag om medbestämmande i arbetslivet.* No. 580.
SFS (1982) *Lag om anställningsskydd.* No. 80.
Shutt, J., and R. Whittington (1987) 'Fragmentation Strategies and the Rise of Small Units'. *Regional Studies,* 21 (1): 13–23.
Sigeman, T. (2001) *Arbetsrätten – en översikt av svensk rätt med europarätt.* Stockholm: Norstedt.
Sklair, L. (2001) *The Transnational Capitalist Class.* Oxford: Blackwell.
Smith, C. (2005) 'Beyond Convergence and Divergence: Explaining Variations in Organisational Practices and Forms', in S. Ackroyd, R. Batt, P. Thompson and P. Tolbert (eds), *The Oxford Handbook of Work and Organisation,* 602–25. Oxford University Press.
Smith, C., and P. Meiksins (1995) 'System, Society and Dominance Effects in Cross National Organisational Analysis'. *Work, Employment & Society,* 9 (2): 241–67.
Smith, M.R. (1992) *Power, Norms, and Inflation. A Skeptical Treatment.* New York: Aldine de Gruyter.
Smith, P., and G. Morton (2001) 'New Labour's Reform of Britain's Employment Law: The Devil Is Not Only in the Detail But in the Values and Policy Too'. *British Journal of Industrial Relations,* 30 (1): 119–38.
Smith, V. (1997) 'New Forms of Work Organization'. *Annual Review of Sociology,* 23: 315–39.
Söderström, H. Tson (ed.) (1985) *Vägen till ett stabilare Sverige.* Stockholm: SNS.
Soidre, T. (2001) 'Arbetslöshetsrisk och inställning till a-kassans regler'. *Arbetsmarknad & Arbetsliv,* 7 (3): 255–69.
Soidre, T. (2004) 'Unemployment Risks and Demands on Labour-Market Flexibility: an Analysis of Attitudinal Patterns in Sweden'. *International Journal of Social Welfare,* 13 (1): 124–33.
SOU (1968) *Allmän arbetstidslag.* No. 66.
SOU (1975) *Förkortad arbetstid för småbarnsföräldrar.* No. 62.
SOU (1976) *Deltidsanställdas villkor.* No. 6.
SOU (1979) *Arbetstiderna inför 80-talet.* No. 48.
SOU (1992) *Privatförmedling och uthyrning av arbetskraft.* No. 116.
SOU (1996) *Arbetstid – längd, förläggning och inflytande.* No. 145.
SOU (1997) *Personaluthyrning.* No. 58.
Spence, M. (1973) 'Job Market Signalling'. *Quarterly Journal of Economics,* 87 (2): 355–74.
Standing, G. (1988) *Unemployment and Labour Market Flexibility: Sweden.* Geneva: International Labour Organisation.
Standing, G. (1999) *Global Labour Flexibility: Seeking Distributive Justice.* New York: St. Martin's Press.
Standing, G. (2002) *Beyond the New Paternalism. Basic Security as Equality.* London: Verso.
Storrie, D. (2002) *Temporary Agency Work in the European Union.* Dublin: European Foundation for the Improvement of Living and Working Conditions.

Storrie, D. (2003a) 'The Regulation and Growth of Contingent Employment in Sweden', in O. Bergström and D. Storrie (eds), *Contingent Employment in Europe and the United States*, 79–106. Cheltenham: Edward Elgar.

Storrie, D. (2003b) 'Conclusions: Contingent Employment in Europe and the Flexibility Security Trade-off', in O. Bergström and D. Storrie (eds), *Contingent Employment in Europe and the United States*, 224–48. Cheltenham: Edward Elgar.

Svenska Dagbladet.

Swenson, P.A. (2002) *Capitalists against Markets. The Making of Labor Markets and Welfare States in the United States and Sweden.* Oxford University Press.

Tam, M. (1997) *Part-Time Employment: A Bridge or a Trap?* Aldershot: Avebury.

Taylor, F.W. (1911) *The Principles of Scientific Management.* London: Harper & Row.

Taylor, F.W. (1961) 'The Principles of Scientific Management', in *Scientific Management, Comprising 'Shop Management', 'The Principles of Scientific Management' and 'Testimony Before the House Special Committee.'* London: Harper & Row.

Terry, M. (2003) 'Employee Representation', in P. Edwards (ed.), *Industrial Relations, Theory and Practice*, 257–84. 2nd ed. Oxford: Blackwell.

Tett, R.P., and J.P. Meyer (1993) 'Job Satisfaction, Organizational Commitment, Turnover Intention, and Turnover: Path Analyses Based on Meta-Analytic Findings'. *Personnel Psychology*, 46 (2): 259–93.

Thelen, K. (2001) 'Varieties of Labour Politics in the Developed Democracies', in A. P. Hall and D. Soskice (eds), *Varieties of Capitalism. The Institutional Foundations of Comparative Advantage*, 71–103. Oxford University Press.

Thompson, G. (2004) *Between Hierarchies and Markets: The Logic and Limits of Network Forms of Organization.* Oxford University Press.

Thompson, P., and D. McHugh (2002) *Work Organisations.* Basingstoke: Palgrave.

Titmuss, R.M. (1974) *Social Policy.* London: Allen and Unwin.

Treu, T. (1992) 'Labour Flexibility in Europe.' *International Labour Review*, 131 (4/5): 497–512.

TT Nyhetsbanken.

TUC (2001) *TUC Response to Government Consultation, Routes to Resolution: Improving Dispute Resolution in Britain.* London: Trades Union Congress.

TUC (2002) *Focus on Employment Tribunals. Trade Union Trends Survey 04/02.* London: Trades Union Congress.

TUC (2005) 'Below the Minimum: Agency Workers and the Minimum Wage'. Trades Union Congress EERD/04/02/2005.

UNICE (2000) Press release Brussels, 3 May.

Van Apeldoorn, B. (2000) 'Transnational Class Agency and European Governance: The Case of the European Round Table of Industrialists'. *New Political Economy*, 5 (2): 157–81.

Van den Berg, A., B. Furåker and L. Johansson (1997) *Labour Market Regimes and Patterns of Flexibility. A Sweden-Canada Comparison.* Lund: Arkiv.

Van Oorschot, W. (2004) 'Balancing Work and Welfare: Activation and Flexicurity Policies in The Netherlands, 1980–2000'. *International Journal of Social Welfare*, 13 (1): 15–27.

Veckans Affärer.

Visser, J. (1999) 'Two Cheers for Corporatism, One for the Market'. *British Journal of Industrial Relations*, 36 (2): 262–92.

Visser, J. (2004) 'Patterns and Variations in European Industrial Relations', in *Industrial Relations in Europe 2004*, 11–57. Brussels: European Commission.

Waddington, J. (2005) 'Trade Unions and the Defence of the European Social Model'. *Industrial Relations Journal*, 36 (6): 518–40.

Wadensjö, E. (1979) 'Arbetsmarknadspolitiken. Från rörlighetsstimulans till företagsstöd'. *Ekonomisk Debatt*, 7: 103–9.

Walter, L. (2005) *Som hand i handske. En studie av matchning i ett personaluthyrningsföretag.* Göteborg: BAS förlag.

Wedderburn, Lord (1989) 'Freedom of Association and Philosophies of Labour Law'. *Industrial Law Journal*, 18 (1): 1–38.

Weinkopf, C. (2005) 'The Role of Temporary Agency Work in the German Employment Model'. Paper presented to the 26th Conference of the 'International Working Party On Labour Market Segmentation', 8–10 September, Berlin, Germany.

West Midlands Low Pay Unit (2001) *Kept in the Dark? Individual Awareness of Employment Rights in the West Midlands*. Briefing Paper 51.

Whiteside, N. (2000) 'From Full Employment to Flexibility: Britain and France in Comparison, 1960–2000', in B. Stråth (ed.), *After Full Employment. European Discourses on Work and Flexibility*, 107–33. Brussels: Peter Lang.

Whittington, R., and M. Mayer (2002) *The European Corporation: Strategy, Structure and Social Science*. Oxford University Press.

Wichert, I. (2002) 'Job Insecurity and Work Intensification: the Effects on Health and Well-Being', in B. Burchell, D. Lapido and F. Wilkinson (eds), *Job Insecurity and Work Intensification*, 92–111. London: Routledge.

Wilthagen, T., and R. Rogowski (2000) 'The Legal Regulation of Transitional Labour Markets', in G. Schmid and B. Gazier (eds), *The Dynamics of Full Employment. Social Integration through Transitional Labour Markets*, 233–73. Cheltenham: Edward Elgar.

Wilthagen, T., and F. Tros (2004) 'The Concept of "Flexicurity": A New Approach to Regulating Employment and Labour Markets.' *Transfer*, 10 (2): 166–86.

Winlund, E., and L. Sturesson (forthcoming) *Flexibilitet i fackpressen*. Stockholm: National Institute for Working Life.

Yeandle, S., J. Philips, F. Scheibl, A. Wigfield and S. Wise (2003) *Line Managers and Family-Friendly Employment: Roles and Perspectives*. London: Policy.

Zey, M., and T. Swenson (1999) 'The Transformation of the Dominant Corporate Form from Multidivisional to the Multisubsidiary'. *Sociological Quarterly*, 40 (2): 241–67.

Index